LAS VEGAS
ACCESS®

Orientation — 1

Downtown — 12

The Strip — 28

West Las Vegas — 58

East Las Vegas — 74

Gambling — 88
- Baccarat
- Blackjack
- Craps
- Keno
- The Money Wheel
- Roulette
- Slots
- Sports Betting
- Video Poker

Excursions — 108
- Hoover Dam
- Lake Mead
- Valley of Fire
- Death Valley
- The Grand Canyon
- Zion National Park

History — 127

Index — 130

W9-DCO-300

Orientation

Whether you first glimpse Las Vegas from an airplane window at night or approach it via highway after a dusty drive through the desert, it's a surreal panorama of flashing lights, bright neon, and exaggerated architecture—a unique shrine to the phantasmagoric extremes of the American Way.

Las Vegas represents different things to different people. To some, it's entirely about gambling: the hypnotic lure of the video-poker screen and the spinning of the roulette wheels, the hush and then the screams heard at the crap table, the ever-present clanging of the ever-present slots, the half moon of hopefuls at the blackjack table, all coexisting in a perpetual twilight zone where there is no day or night, only cards, dice, and, hopefully, three cherries. Put in a quarter. . . . Hey, you never know; this may be your lucky day.

To others, Las Vegas is a playground, a place to indulge at the $4.99 buffets, bask in the sun, play golf, or hang out at the lounges.

There are those to whom Las Vegas is a place called home. Cheaper than San Francisco, warmer than Minneapolis, it's the fastest-growing city in the country. Retirees and young families alike—835,000 of them at last count—have bought homes in this new frontier, this burgeoning desert neighborhood where an old-timer is someone who's lived here for 10 years.

Las Vegas began as an Old West–whistle-stop and might have remained one if not for two significant events: the construction of **Hoover Dam** and the legalization of gambling. The Boulder Canyon Project Act of 1928 put approximately 3,500 people to work for five years, nearly doubling the population of the town. In 1931, Nevada bucked the Great Depression by legalizing gambling and setting its sights on tourists. The payoff has proved bigger than any lucky gambler's jackpot; in 1994, 23.5 million visitors filled 85,000 hotel rooms and generated $14.7 billion, including gaming revenues.

Most people begin their visit to Las Vegas on the **Strip.** Originally **US Highway 91** to Los Angeles, **Las Vegas Boulevard** began its evolution into the Strip in 1941, when the builders of **El Rancho Vegas**— Las Vegas's first resort hotel—sought to avoid city taxes by moving to unincorporated land on the outskirts of town, in this case a large piece of low-cost highway property. **El Rancho** was soon joined by the **Last Frontier,** and the four-mile stretch of freeway began filling in. Next came the **Flamingo,** the **Thunderbird,** the **Desert Inn,** the **Sahara,** the **Sands,** the **Dunes,** and by 1955, the **Riviera,** a nine-story high rise that put to rest any notion that this city would be content to retain a low-profile, Palm Springs–style landscape.

In the past 10 years, the Strip has evolved into the ultimate pedestrian thoroughfare, its sidewalks filled with gawking tourists and hawking hucksters passing out coupons and pamphlets advertising X-rated amusements. The resorts that used to sit back from the highway have either extended their casinos to the sidewalk or—in the case of **Caesars Palace**—shuttle guests in on moving sidewalks.

In each hotel's quest to outdo the next, **Caesars Palace** began beckoning pedestrians with a "temple" in which a holographic emperor welcomes friends, Romans, and assorted countrymen to his realm. **The Mirage** added its landmark volcano to the horizon in late 1989. Possibly the most-photographed sight in the city, the volcano belches smoke and natural-gas flames every 15 minutes from 5:30PM to midnight. In 1994, **Bally's** jumped into the fray by turning its front parking lot into a garden replete with cascading waterways and a huge "floating" orb that's the source of a nighttime laser-and-light show. And then **Treasure Island** attempted to outgun them all with an armada of full-scale pirate ships that blast cannon fire every 1.5 hours from 3:30PM to 10:00PM in a battle staged for the amusement of passersby.

Fremont Street (also known as **"Glitter Gulch"**) offers a carnival midway environment in downtown Las Vegas: Sidewalk solicitors in goofy hats pepper pedestrians with "can't lose" promotions as they pass under the familiar wave of "Vegas Vic," the **Pioneer Hotel**'s famous cowboy mascot. Some of the glamour of Fremont Street has faded since the neon first started glowing here in the mid-1940s. Local residents have taken their business to suburban casinos that sprang up closer to their own neighborhoods, while tourists head to the megaresorts on the Strip. Downtown resort owners are fighting back with the Fremont Street Experience: Starting 1 December 1995, Fremont Street will be covered by a $60-million canopy under which a light show similar to Disneyland's will take place nightly.

But there is more to Vegas than casinos and gift shops. Those with a car might want to explore **East Las Vegas,** the city's older residential area, and home to attractions such as **The Liberace Museum,** which houses the opulent jewelry, costumes, and pianos collected by the late King of Glitz, and the **Mormon Temple,** the palatial landmark on **Sunrise Mountain** that serves as an ever-present reminder of the area's large population of members of the Church of Jesus Christ of Latter-day Saints. **West Las Vegas** is home to the **Las Vegas Art Museum** and the **Nevada State Museum and Historical Society,** as well as

How To Read This Guide

LAS VEGAS ACCESS® is arranged by neighborhood so you can see at a glance where you are and what is around you. The numbers next to the entries in the following chapters correspond to the numbers on the maps. The text is color-coded according to the kind of place described:

Restaurants/Clubs: Red   Hotels: Blue
Shops/🍴 Outdoors: Green   Sights/Culture: Black

Rating the Restaurants and Hotels

The restaurant star ratings take into account the quality, service, atmosphere, and uniqueness of the restaurant. An expensive restaurant doesn't necessarily ensure an enjoyable evening; however, a small, relatively unknown spot could have good food, professional service, and a lovely atmosphere. Therefore, on a purely subjective basis, stars are used to judge the overall dining value (see the star ratings at right). Keep in mind that chefs and owners often change, which sometimes drastically affects the quality of a restaurant. The ratings in this guidebook are based on information available at press time.

The price ratings, as categorized below, apply to restaurants and hotels. These figures describe general price-range relationships among other restaurants and hotels in the area. The restaurant price ratings are based on the average cost of an entrée for one person, excluding tax and tip. Hotel price ratings reflect the base price of a standard room for two people for one night during the peak season.

Restaurants

★	Good	
★★	Very Good	
★★★	Excellent	
★★★★	Extraordinary Experience	
$	The Price Is Right	(less than $13)
$$	Reasonable	($13-$20)
$$$	Expensive	($20-$25)
$$$$	Big Bucks	($25 and up)

Hotels

$	The Price Is Right	(less than $30)
$$	Reasonable	($30-$50)
$$$	Expensive	($50-$80)
$$$$	Big Bucks	($80 and up)

Map Key

▲ Mountain

40 Interstate Hwy.
95 US Hwy.
89 State Hwy.

1 Entry Number

Freeway] ▪▪▪ [Tunnel

• City/Town

Highway

Road

Unpaved Road

■ Point of Interest

Trail/Pedestrian Path

some of the most popular casinos in town. Also on the westside are newer residential developments, particularly as you approach **Red Rock Canyon**, a hundred-square-mile recreation area of sweeping, rugged red sandstone formations a mere 15 miles from the concrete canyons of the Strip. On the way to the engineering marvel of Hoover Dam, stop in the suburban community of **Henderson** for a visit to the **Ethel M. Chocolate Factory**, which produces—and gives free samples of—sweet treats. Or head northwest for the higher altitudes of **Mount Charleston**, proof that people who claim to have gone skiing in Las Vegas—or at least an hour away from it—weren't kidding. Or travel 35 miles northeast on I-15 to the **Valley of Fire**, Nevada's oldest state park, where eons of erosion have carved out geological artworks in a haven of desert flora and wildlife.

So look around. Whatever you're in search of—good or bad, reality or fantasy—you'll probably find it here. Las Vegas may not yet have found a way to beguile everyone, but it hasn't stopped trying.

The Main Events

Not just a neon-lined lair for guzzling and gambling, Las Vegas proves there's more to life than green-felt tabletops. For the sports-minded, there are rodeos, golf tournaments, football championship games, and world-class boxing matches. For businesspeople, the city hosts numerous conventions, some of which—the International Food Service Executives Association (IFSEA) Chocolate Fest and the Computer Distribution Expo (COMDEX), for example—are open to the public. If you're feeling philanthropic, Las Vegas is also a major venue for charity benefits, attracting (and often spearheaded by) the rich and famous who call the city home. For culture seekers, there are dance performances in winter and classical music series in summer. So though visions of royal flushes dance in your head, take a break and sample the other Las Vegas.

January
Consumer Electronics Show
Nevada Dance Theater Gala

February
City of Hope Dinner
Las Vegas International Marathon and Half-Marathon

March
Big West Basketball Tournament
Academy Award party at Spago

April
LPGA Tournament
IFSEA Chocolate Fest
Share Our Strength's Taste of the Nation
UNLV Foundation Dinner

May
Helldorado Days
UNLVino Wine Tasting Event

City Department of Recreation Rib Burn Off
World Series of Poker

June
Several summer concert series in the park (check local newspaper listings)

July
Nevada Symphony Summer Pops concerts

August
Nevada Symphony Summer Pops concerts

September
Las Vegas International Mariachi Festival

October
Boulder City Art Fair
Holiday Market, Nevada Dance Theatre
Nevada Opera Theatre Gala
Columbus Day Parade
Oktoberfest celebrations
Greek Food Festival
Lobster Fair
Las Vegas PGA Invitational
North Las Vegas Hot Air Balloon Races

November
COMDEX
PBS Wine Festival

December
Mount Charleston Lodge Tree Trimming
Nevada Dance Theatre's *Nutcracker* performances
Bally's Sterling Club holiday dinner
National Finals Rodeo
Las Vegas Bowl (football)
Holiday Prep Classic Basketball Tournament

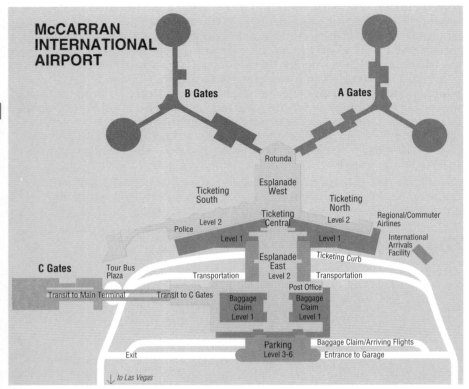

McCARRAN INTERNATIONAL AIRPORT

B Gates

A Gates

Rotunda

Esplanade West

Ticketing South

Ticketing Central

Ticketing North

Regional/Commuter Airlines

Police

Level 2

Level 2

Level 1

Level 1

International Arrivals Facility

C Gates

Tour Bus Plaza

Esplanade East

Ticketing Curb

Level 2

Transportation

Transportation

Post Office

Transit to Main Terminal

Transit to C Gates

Baggage Claim Level 1

Baggage Claim Level 1

Exit

Parking Level 3-6

Baggage Claim/Arriving Flights

Entrance to Garage

↓ to Las Vegas

Area code 702 unless otherwise noted.

Getting to Las Vegas

Airport

McCarran International Airport (LAS)

Nearly 43 percent of all Las Vegas visitors and 65 percent of its convention delegates arrive via **McCarran,** the 16th busiest airport in the nation. Approximately 24 million passengers passed through its gates in 1993, for an average of 645 flights a day or 235,425 per year.

The airport sits on 2,820 acres off **Tropicana Avenue,** about a mile east of the Strip. There are 79 gates in three terminals: 48 in the main terminal; 23 in concourse C, which is serviced by a monorail; and eight in the **Charter/International Terminal,** a separate facility just north of the main terminal that handles international flights and houses all international processing operations. Ticketing, baggage claim, and transportation are found in the main terminal.

Modern and user-friendly, **McCarran** owes its size and efficiency to the local convention industry. City officials realized in the late 1950s that conventions could diversify the economy beyond gambling and made the airport a top consideration. The festive design is more like that of a shopping mall, and it boasts a wide variety of food and cocktail outlets, and specialty shops—even slot machines for that first and last taste of Vegas.

Ten commercial airlines, 10 commuter airlines, and more than 20 charters service **McCarran.**

Airport Services

Airport Emergencies.................................261.5201
Business Service Center...........................261.5650
Currency Exchange 261.5650
Customs...388.6480
Ground Transportation.............................261.5743,
....261.5434, 261.5094
Immigration 388.6024
Information 261.5743, 261.5434, 261.5094
Lost and Found 261.5134
(or check with individual airlines)
Parking...261.5121
Police...261.5377
Traveler's Aid...........261.5743, 261.5434, 261.5094

The least crowded, and therefore least expensive, time to visit Las Vegas is between Thanksgiving and Christmas. The most hectic periods are on Super Bowl weekend and during the three largest conventions: Consumer Electronics Show (second week of January), Construction Manufacturers Association (third week of March), and COMDEX—the Computer Distribution Expo—(third week of November).

Airlines

American	800/433.7300
America West	798.1715, 800/235.9292
Continental	383.8291, 800/231.0856
Delta	800/221.1212
Northwest	800/225.2525
Reno Air	800/736.6247
Southwest	800/435.9792
TWA	385.1000, 800/221.2000
United	800/241.6522
USAir	800/428.4322

Getting to and from the Airport

By Bus The **Citizens Area Transit** or **CAT** (228.7433) operates buses to and from the airport departure terminal every half hour from 6AM to 1AM daily. For service to the **Downtown Transportation Center,** take the *109* ($1); to the Strip take the *302* ($1.50). Exact fare in bills or coins is required.

By Car The airport's main exit leads to **Swenson Avenue** traveling north, and the first main cross street with a traffic light is **Tropicana Boulevard.** A left turn on Tropicana brings you to the **San Remo, Tropicana, MGM Grand,** and **Excalibur** hotels. If you continue on Tropicana, you'll reach Las Vegas Boulevard South (the Strip), which is at most 15 minutes from the airport. A left turn leads to the **Luxor** and **Hacienda,** while a right turn passes most of the major hotels. For downtown, continue on the Strip about four to five miles. To return to the airport, take **Paradise Road** south. There are both long and short-term parking lots at the airport.

Rental Cars The following rental car agencies have counters at the airport, which are typically open from 5AM to 2AM. **Allstate**'s counter is open 24 hours a day.

Allstate	736.6147, 800/634.6186
Avis	261.5595, 800/331.1212
Hertz	736.4900, 800/654.3131

Several others are clustered along Paradise Road near the entrance to **McCarran** and offer shuttle service to the airport. Of these, only **Budget** is open 24 hours a day.

Alamo	597.0051, 800/327.9633
Budget	736.1212, 800/527.0700
Thrifty	736.4706, 800/367.2277

By Limo Frequent visitors to Las Vegas often rely on **Bell Trans** (736.4428, 739.7990) limousines and buses to get from **McCarran** to their hotel. The savings can be significant compared to a taxi: **Bell** charges $3.50 from the airport to any Strip hotel and $4.75 to downtown hotels. The trade-off is that it's usually a long ride. You share the trip with other passengers and may stop at four or five other hotels to drop them off before arriving at yours. The **Bell** booth is located inside the airport near the rental car booths.

By Taxi There is a taxi stand at the airport. It's approximately a 15-minute cab ride to downtown for about $16.

Bus Station (Long-Distance)

The **Greyhound Station** (200 S Main St, at Union Plaza, 800/231.2222) is open from 5AM each morning until 1AM the following morning. Taxis are available in front of the station.

Train Station (Long-Distance)

Amtrak (386.6896, 800/872.7245) has a station in the **Plaza Hotel** (1 Main St, at Fremont St). The station is open from 6AM to 7:30PM. A number of eastbound and westbound trains make stops in Las Vegas. Taxis are available at the front of the hotel.

Getting Around Las Vegas

It's not difficult to move around Las Vegas. The Strip is only five miles long. So walking, bicycling, public transportation, and—if you're extremely independent and have lots of time on your hands—driving are all viable options.

Bicycles Though you certainly could get from place to place by bicycle if you're staying on the Strip or downtown, most serious bicyclists prefer trips up to Mount Charleston or through the Red Rock recreation areas. There are a number of bicycle-rental outlets, including **McGhies Ski Chalet** (4503 W Sahara Ave, at Arville Rd, 252.8077; and 3310 E Flamingo Rd, at Pecos Rd, 433.1120); and **Bikes USA** (1539 N Eastern Ave, at Owens Ave, 642.2453).

Buses Las Vegas has an excellent bus system serving virtually every destination downtown and on the Strip. The **Citizens Area Transit Authority** (**CAT;** 228.7433) maintains a fleet of 128 buses that carry 40 passengers each, covering 21 routes.

Bus schedules are available at the **Downtown Transportation Center** (Stewart Ave and Casino Center Blvd), the connecting point for most routes. Buses run daily from 5:30AM to 1:30AM on municipal routes and 24 hours a day on the Strip. One-way fare for adults is one dollar ($1.50 on the Strip); people 65 and older, children 5 to 17, and the disabled pay 50¢. Younger children ride free. Same-day transfers from other routes are free.

Cruises Lake Mead Cruises (293.6180) offers boat trips to Hoover Dam on the *Desert Princess* from the **Lake Mead Marina.** There are two cruises a day, plus dinner cruises on Friday, Saturday, and Sunday.

Driving It's not necessary to rent a car if you're staying downtown or on the Strip. Most everything you'll need or want to see is within walking distance of each other in these areas. However, if you're staying in East or West Las Vegas, you'll need a car. Also, if you plan to take advantage of Vegas's proximity to **Grand Canyon** or Hoover Dam, you may prefer renting a car to taking a group tour.

If you do plan to drive down the Las Vegas Strip, avoid weekend evenings, when the traffic slows to a crawl. The Strip lures not only tourists but teenagers who want to impress you with the volume of their stereos (at least until their 9PM curfew, imposed nightly on the Strip). If you're trying to get to a show on time at the other end of the Strip, use **Koval Lane** or **Paradise Road** to the east and **Industrial Road** to the west.

Parking Street parking is nonexistent on the Strip and is very difficult to find downtown. There are public and private parking lots, and major hotels offer a choice between valet and self-parking. Valet parking is free, but can mean a long wait for your car. Self-parking is sometimes easier, depending on the layout of the hotel and how recently the garage was built. The **Caesars Palace** and **Mirage** garages, for instance, are well designed and easy to navigate (although you may have trouble finding a space). At **Bally's,** parking is more problematic because the exit funnels traffic right onto the Strip or onto Flamingo Road. Downtown, **Fitzgeralds'** garage is downright thrilling, with turns tight enough to remind you of a roller coaster.

Taxis Las Vegas is not the cheapest city in which to catch a cab across town. Because most tourists stay in the concentrated region of the Strip, which is close to the airport, it costs $2.20 to step into a cab and 30¢ for each one-fifth of a mile. Waiting time is 30¢ per minute (these rates were established by the Nevada Taxicab Authority). Clark County tacks on a $1.20 fee for each trip from **McCarran.**

On the positive side, Las Vegas *is* one of the *easiest* towns in which to catch a cab. There's no need to call or even hail one down; they line up outside the hotels and wait. Plan ahead before leaving your destination —if it's not within a hotel—you'll need to call for a dispatch. Clark County has 603 registered cabs licensed to 13 companies. The major cab companies are:

Checker Cab 873.2000
Desert Cab...............................376.2687, 376.2688
Western Cab..736.8000
Whittlesea Blue Cab 384.6111
Yellow Cab 873.2000

Tours There are more than 50 tour operators based in Las Vegas. The most popular is the trip to the Grand Canyon by plane or helicopter. **Scenic Airlines** (241 E Reno Ave, between Tropicana Ave and Koval La, 739.1900) offers flights every hour on the half hour during daylight, seven days a week. **Canyon Copters** (6005 Las Vegas Blvd S, 1.5 blocks south of Russell Rd, 895.9757) offers flights landing on the **Hualapai Indian Reservation. Desert Action Tours** (2812 S Highland Dr, between Sahara Ave and Spring Mountain Rd, 796.9355) provides Jeep tours of the Grand Canyon, Red Rock Canyon, Valley of Fire, and Mount Charleston. **Guaranteed Tours** (3734 Las Vegas Blvd, between E Harmon Ave and E Tropicana Ave, 369.1000) offers trips to Hoover Dam, **Laughlin,** cruises on **Lake Mead,** river rafting, plus Grand Canyon flights.

Trains There are no convenient trains for travel to nearby excursions in Nevada or to the Grand Canyon.

Walking Walking tours of Las Vegas are not recommended, especially in summer when the temperatures soar over 100 degrees. The main section of the Strip, from the **Las Vegas Hilton** south to the **Hacienda,** is an interesting walk, but though it appears to be a short distance, it is actually several miles. Allow two or more hours, especially if you want to stop at some of the hotels along the way.

FYI

Accessibility for the Disabled County law mandates that all restaurants and hotels be accessible to and provide facilities for disabled persons.

Accommodations Despite the fact that there are 85,000 hotel rooms in Las Vegas, reservations are always necessary. Especially busy times include long weekends (Fourth of July, Labor Day, and President's Day), holidays, and anytime there's a major convention in town, which is practically all the time. There are no bed-and-breakfast accommodations but there are vacation time-share facilities. For time-share information, contact **Hilton Grand Vacations** (3575 Las Vegas Blvd S, between Flamingo and Audrey Rds, Las Vegas, NV 89109, 251.4482); **Jockey Club Resort Properties** (3700 Las Vegas Blvd S, at Flamingo Rd, Las Vegas, NV 89109, 739.8686); **Olympian Palms Resort Club** (3875 Cambridge St, between Flamingo Rd and Twain Ave, Las Vegas, NV 89119, 737.8388); or **Polo Towers,** 3745 Las Vegas Blvd S, between Flamingo Rd and Tropicana Ave, Las Vegas, NV 89109, 261.1000).

Climate It seems as if Las Vegas has only two seasons: a long, hot summer and a mild winter. But don't make the same mistake as many a misinformed visitor from back East seen shivering in shorts and a T-shirt on a February evening. This is a desert town, and temperatures drop 20 degrees or more when the sun goes down.

Each year, the city enjoys an average of 310 sunny days and four inches of rain (Mother Nature can be unpredictable: 1992 had more than twice the normal amount of precipitation). Locals joke that most of those four inches come in as many days.

	Average Temperatures (°F)	
Season	**Lows**	**Highs**
Winter	33 – 39	57 – 63
Spring	44 – 60	69 – 88
Summer	69 – 74	100 – 106
Fall	43 – 66	67 – 95

Dress As Las Vegas evolved into a family and middle-class vacation destination, its dress code virtually disappeared. Dinner jackets and evening gowns are no longer necessary, although you still see people wearing them, depending on the season and occasion. T-shirts and shorts are common in the summer, even in showrooms and full-service restaurants, with the exception of gourmet dining rooms in hotels. Convention attire is a different matter, tending to be dressier.

Drinking The drinking age is 21. Most casinos serve cocktails 24 hours a day. Bars are open from mid-morning until the wee hours. Nevada has the second-highest alcohol-consumption rate in the country and was one of the last states to ban open containers in vehicles. Pedestrians are still allowed to carry open containers from casino to casino on Fremont Street and the Strip.

Gambling You must be 21 years or older to gamble in a Nevada casino, although no one checks IDs at the door. Underage gamblers beware: Should you win, the casinos are not obligated to pay you your winnings.

Money The major banks in Las Vegas are PriMerit, US Bank of Nevada, and Bank of America (formerly Valley Bank). Most hotels and casinos are joined to an ATM network called "Casino Cash," which accepts the following cards and networks: Cirrus, Discover, The Exchange, Instant Teller, Plus, Pulse, and Star.

Personal Safety Las Vegas tourist zones are probably safer than the streets of New York or Los Angeles, since police concentration is heavy and each casino maintains its own private security force. Take the usual common sense precautions against pickpockets and purse snatchers. If you run into trouble, look for the Metro police bicycle patrol; these officers wear bright yellow shirts and black shorts and use bikes to skirt gridlocked traffic.

Postal Service Many hotels can handle basic postal needs, including stamps, UPS, and Federal Express. The post office nearest the Strip is located on Sunset Road across the street from the south end of **McCarran International Airport.** The **Forum Shops at Caesars'** information desk offers postal service as well, at no extra charge.

Prostitution Since prostitution is illegal within Las Vegas and Clark County, it is unregulated. Prostitutes in the state's legal brothels are tested regularly for sexually transmitted diseases, including AIDS.

Publications The city's two daily newspapers work under a joint operating agreement, sharing business operations but maintaining separate editorial staffs. The *Las Vegas Review-Journal* is the morning newspaper and has a circulation of about 130,000 readers. The *Las Vegas Sun,* which comes out in the evening, has a circulation of about 35,000. In addition, the *New York Times, Los Angeles Times, Wall Street Journal,* and *USA Today* are sold on street racks and in hotel newsstands. Several weekly publications, such as *The Israelite, Showbiz,* and *Vegas Visitor,* offer restaurant and show information and are available free of charge in hotel rooms and lobbies.

Radio Stations

KDWN (Talk Radio/Big Band/Sports)	720AM
KORK (Nostalgia)	920AM
KNNU (News)	970AM
KENO (Oldies)	1460AM
KCEP (Urban/Community)	88.1FM
KNPR (National Public Radio)	89.5FM
KUNV (University of Nevada, Las Vegas)	91.5FM
KOMP (Album Rock)	92.3FM
KWNR (Country)	95.5FM
KKLZ (Classic Rock)	96.3FM
KLUC (Contemporary)	98.5FM
KFMS (Country)	101.9FM
KEDG (Alternative Rock)	103.5FM
KRRI (Oldies)	105.5FM

Restaurants For the most part, except where indicated otherwise, reservations are requested but not required. However, it is always wise to call ahead. The only constant in Las Vegas is change. Hours open or meals served may have been added or deleted. Reservations are a particularly good idea on weekends and holidays, when tables are at a premium, especially in the more expensive hotel dining rooms. Also in these establishments, you may find jackets and ties are the norm, but they are rarely required.

Shopping Though there are no specific shopping areas in Las Vegas, the city has an abundance of shopping centers and malls. Choose from **The Boulevard Mall, Fashion Show Mall, Forum Shops at Caesars,** and **The Meadows Mall.** For more details, check the index for individual listings.

Smoking Of all 50 states, Nevada has the highest percentage of people who smoke. Even so, smoking is prohibited by state law in most elevators and public buildings. Most hotel showrooms have banned smoking, and the **Silver City Casino** prohibits it entirely. Passengers in taxicabs may smoke.

Street Plan Las Vegas is divided into east and west by Las Vegas Boulevard, otherwise known as the Strip. The north-south drag is home to most of the big hotel-casinos. It's intersected by five major east-west arterial streets, three of which carry the names of famous resorts: **Sahara, Flamingo,** and **Tropicana.** North of the Strip is downtown, home of famous Fremont Street (also known as "Glitter Gulch"). Two expressways form a rough "T" shape through the city: Interstate 15 runs basically parallel to the Strip, while Interstate 95 bisects it near downtown and heads east and west.

Taxes Clark County has a 7 percent sales tax (food items are exempt). Hotel guests pay an 8 percent room tax, and showgoers pay a 10 percent entertainment tax on every ticket. (The trick to the latter is discerning whether the tax is built into the advertised price or added on later. Read the fine print and ask when you make reservations or buy your ticket.)

Tickets It used to be that you could not get tickets in advance for any show in Las Vegas. You could only make a reservation on the day of the show, and even that would not guarantee you a particular location in the theater or club. Seating was, and still is, in some venues, at the discretion of the maître d'. The management's plan was to save the best seats up until the last minute for any high rollers or other VIPs who might require them. Today there are still some shows on the reservation (i.e., no tickets) system. Or there are some that will give you a ticket, but the ticket won't specify a seat. However, more and more theaters are switching over to a traditional ticket system. It is best to call the hotel or box office directly to find out the policy for the show you want to see. There are also recorded announcements on local events provided by **Centel** (385.4444) and **Ticketmaster** (893.3033, sales number 474.4000).

Time Zones Las Vegas is on the eastern edge of the Pacific Standard Time Zone. The zone changes to Mountain Standard Time on the Arizona side of Hoover Dam.

Tipping The hotel-casino industry seems half driven by "tokes," as gaming people traditionally refer to their tips. There are no concrete guidelines for tipping, but the following standards are generally accepted.

Bellhops: Two to five dollars, depending on whether you need service or advice.

Bingo/Keno runners: Not necessary for a single game (unless you win and feel like sharing the credit); a dollar from time to time if playing for an extended period.

Cocktail waitresses: Drinks are free if you are playing table games such as blackjack, so a dollar tip per round is still a bargain (if you hang on at the table long enough for her to return).

Dealers: Casino policies vary; most pool the tips left at the table. If your dealer acts like a robot, don't feel obligated to tip. If he or she gives good advice (within the limits of the rules), it's courteous to acknowledge the help. Many dealers enjoy having you place a side bet for them; if you win, they do, too. These can range from a dollar to half of your bet.

Restaurants/Room service: The standard 15 to 20 percent rule of thumb applies.

Showroom maître d' and staff: Most major showrooms have converted to reserved-seat ticketing systems, where no maître d' tipping is required. For rooms that still accept reservations, the unwritten code for improving seating is still in effect: Pass $5 to $10 to the maître d' and a better table usually becomes available.

If your ticket was purchased in advance, see if it says gratuity is included. If so, you are not obligated to tip. If not, tip according to the amount and quality of cocktail service provided; $2 to $10, depending on the size of your group and the service rendered.

Taxi drivers: One to two dollars for a direct route, more if the driver was courteous and helpful.

Valet parking: One dollar is standard; two dollars is proper if the service was impressively quick.

Visitors' Information Centers There are two visitors' information centers in Las Vegas that you can call, write, or visit. For a tourist guide to hotels, entertainment, and general information, send a self-addressed, stamped envelope with 52¢ postage to the **Las Vegas Area Chamber of Commerce** (711 E Desert Inn Rd, between Paradise Rd and Joe W. Brown Dr, Las Vegas, NV 89109, 735.1616). Or you can contact the **Las Vegas Convention and Visitors Authority** (Visitor Information Center/Brochure Room, 3150 Paradise Rd, between Desert Inn Rd and the Las Vegas Hilton, Las Vegas, NV 89109, 892.0711).

Phone Book
Emergencies

Ambulance/Fire/Police	911
AAA Emergency Road Service	800/222.4357
Auto Impound	382.9261, 649.5711
Auto Theft	229.3586
Dental Emergency	735.8189
Hospitals	
Boulder City Hospital	293.4111
Desert Springs Hospital	733.8800
Lake Mead Hospital Medical Center	649.7711
St. Rose Dominican Hospital	564.2622
Sunrise Hospital and Medical Center	731.8000
University Medical Center	383.2000
Valley Hospital	388.4000
Pharmacies	
Century Pharmacy	364.0880
White Cross Drugs (24 hours)	382.1733
Poison Control	732.4989
Police (nonemergency)	795.3111

Visitors' Information

American Youth Hostels	382.8119
Amtrak	386.6896
Better Business Bureau	735.6900, 731.9877
Bell Trans (airport shuttle)	736.4428, 739.7990
Citizens Area Transit (bus)	228.7433
Convention and Visitors Authority	892.0711
Greyhound Bus	800/231.2222
Disabled Visitors' Information	892.0711
Las Vegas Strip Trolley	382.1404
Road Conditions	486.3116
Telegraphs:	
American Telegram	800/343.7363
Western Union	737.7111, 800/325.6000
Time and Temperature	118
US Customs	388.6480
US Passport Office	451.3597
Weather	734.2010

Bests

Max Rubin
Professional Gambler/Author of *Comp City*

Rudest pit bosses: No contest here. They're at the **Barbary Coast.** Go in and play blackjack. They break out in a cold sweat when anyone buys in for more than a hundred bucks. If you double your money, they'll change the cards. If you win $500, they'll change dealers. If you win more than $1,000, they'll change their shorts.

Best cocktail waitresses: The **Rio.** They're cute, they're young, they're friendly, and they're not wearing any clothes.

Best Mexican food: El Sombrero on Main Street. Forget ambience here. It's a seedy little dive that Las Vegas's elite packs every noon. For pure pork ambrosia (if you've got a cast-iron gut), try the *chile verde* with corn tortillas—so good it's ridiculous. When they serve this greasy goop in a plain soup bowl, it looks like weeks-old glop, but the memory and the heartburn can stay with you for life.

Best appetizer: The neck bones at the **Venetian.** Long regarded as the top Italian restaurant in town, their best-kept secret is the jumbo bowl of neck bones served nightly. It comes with Italian bread and sweet peppers. Wear a bib, use your fingers, and try not to sit next to any wedding parties. Washed down with a bottle of chianti, it's a slop-o-rama matched only by the dead crab fest on Fisherman's Wharf in San Francisco and it's twice as good.

Best parking place: I hate to tell you this. It's like turning on the public to my best fishing spot, but here it is: Turn into **Harrah's** on the north side of the **Strip** and drive toward the rear. There's a small entrance to a garage that holds about a hundred cars. Employees can't park there, and if you're going to **The Mirage, Treasure Island, Sands, Harrah's, Flamingo,** or the ever-popular **Denny's** it's quicker than any other spot in town and you don't have to tip some snotty valet-parking attendant.

Best desert architecture: For sports nuts, nothing in Vegas comes close to **Cashman Field.** A Triple-A baseball complex, it's a fan's park finished with Southwest hues absolutely in tune with the surrounding mountains, which are visible from every seat in the house. The games are okay and the food is lousy and costs too much, but the stadium is a well-kept, state-of-the-art batter's dream, with short walls adorned with dreadful 20-foot-high local advertising. Take the family here for a different look at Vegas nightlife.

Best snake hunting locale: It's not the most common pastime, but you're guaranteed to catch something if you take Highway 95 east and turn toward Searchlight and follow any off-road from March through October. Caution: Most of the snakes you'll see can kill you. Don't pick them up until you've run over them first. Sautéed rattlesnake makes an especially tasty and controversial appetizer. With any luck you might even be able to host a road-kill cocktail party.

Best place to see ugly people: Stand on the corner of **Fremont** and **Casino Center Boulevard** any time between 8AM and midnight. You won't believe the down-and-out dregs that'll pass you by.

Most dangerous meal: Order the chili at **Binion's Horseshoe** after midnight, tell the waitress to float it with a lobster tail (the Amarillo surf 'n' turf), and wash it down with a quadruple Wild Turkey. It'll cost you about $12.

Cheapest thrill: The free tub o' popcorn at **Slots A Fun,** next to **Circus Circus.** All you gotta do is show up. It's not that nutritional, but if you're busted, it'll get you home with a full belly. Try not to make skin contact with any of the fleas who are also lined up waiting for the free eats.

Best shopping: The **Forum Shops at Caesars.** If you've got $20 or $1,000,000, there's someone there who'll take it from you with a smile.

Best place to buy the house a round: The **Sahara Casbar Theater** after midnight. Nobody's ever there.

Stanford Wong
Writer/Publisher, Pi Yee Press

Caesars Palace is one of the most spectacular buildings in the world. Do not miss the view from **Las Vegas Boulevard** at night.

The Mirage routinely accepts very large bets. If you want to gamble with thousands of dollars per hand or if you want to watch other people doing it, **The Mirage** is the place.

Binion's Horseshoe has the most authentic old-time atmosphere.

The cocktail waitresses at the **Rio** casino have the sexiest costumes.

Harrah's and the **Frontier** are two of the friendliest casinos in Las Vegas.

The **Wet 'n Wild** water park is *the* place for kids. I sometimes drive to Las Vegas with a carload of teenagers who go for the sole purpose of spending the whole day at **Wet 'n Wild.**

In-N-Out Burger, the legendary Southern California chain, has recently opened a few outlets in Las Vegas. The double-doubles are the best cheeseburgers I have ever tasted. What makes **In-N-Out's** burgers special? They don't freeze the beef.

Gambler's Book Club bookstore has thousands of titles, and all of them are on gambling!

The cost of a hotel room in Las Vegas is determined by who's paying for it. The casino rate for preferred customers is the least expensive, although regular guests in the short off-season may get similar discounts. Packages sponsored by wholesalers, airlines, and the hotel itself offer rooms at a slightly higher rate. Then comes the corporate discount, 10 to 15 percent lower than the standard room rate. Convention rates are typically the highest.

Downtown

Low rollers, grannies with shopping bags, and sweat-suited suburbanites parade through the central core of neon Las Vegas amid icons of kitsch, including the world's largest gold nugget (a 60-pound gem under glass); the biggest slot machine on the planet; and "Vegas Vic," a 50-foot-tall neon cowboy who stands guard over the area's 24-hour display of unapologetic tackiness. Compared with the clean and classy Strip (the stretch of Las Vegas Boulevard south of Sahara Avenue), honky-tonk downtown may be found wanting. But what the city's core lacks in tastefulness, it makes up for in price. You'll find some of the most unbelievable lodging and dining bargains in a town where casino-subsidized prices already leave visitors incredulous.

Beyond the neon nucleus, however, central Las Vegas reverts to its origins—a slightly decrepit, turn-of-the-century commercial town that, like scores of other decaying cities throughout the western US, was founded by a railroad company. When the train carrying its cargo of pigs rumbles through on a sweltering summer night, their aroma wafting all the way to the Strip, you can imagine the town as it was before the downtown gulch had any glitter at all.

Las Vegas was little more than a dusty watering hole from the time the train tracks arrived in 1904, and the town was laid out a year later, until the early 1930s, when it began to perceive—and pursue—its destiny. During that period, the only real excitement took place in the brothels and bars of downtown's red-light district, known as Block 16. In 1931, at the height of the Great Depression, 5,000 construction workers arrived to build **Boulder** (now **Hoover**) **Dam**; 5,000 more were turned away. They all disembarked at the Las Vegas depot, and after construction of the dam, many stayed on, doubling the population almost overnight. At the same time, gambling was legalized throughout Nevada, and the casinos that opened on **Fremont Street** enticed with roulette, alcohol, and air-conditioning. The tourists arrived right on schedule—and not only to view the dam and the new Lake Mead filling up behind it. Now that downtown Las Vegas offered saloons, bordellos, and gaming, they were hungry to get a taste of the last slice of the wild West.

World War II doubled the town's population once again, and the massive influx of servicemen and women precipitated the closing of Block 16; the War Department, prompted by the complaints of wives, didn't want to condone the sale of sex. But the Fremont Street casinos flourished from the military payroll. In the post-war boom, a rash of sleek luxury resorts began to spring up out in the desert on the newly established Las Vegas Strip. But downtown's frontier atmosphere held fast well into the 1950s. "Vegas Vic" first graced the facade of the **Pioneer Club** in 1950; **Binion's**

Horseshoe Hotel and Casino opened in 1951; and even the **Golden Nugget**, a fancy downtown casino, clung steadfastly to its saloon ambience.

The first intimation that downtown was on the upswing came in 1956, with the construction of the 15-story **Fremont Hotel**, yet it was another decade until the area fully emerged into the modern era. Between 1965 and 1971, four tall and tony hotel-casinos were added to the Fremont Street skyline, ushering downtown Las Vegas out of its historical reverie and into the last quarter of the 20th century.

Today, downtown is a mélange of odd alliances. Remnants of the early days are jarringly juxtaposed with contemporary images. Low-roller penny poker, quarter craps, and $15 a night hotels vie with resorts packed with high-end suites with a view and gourmet restaurants for space as well as customers.

Downtown's principal competition, of course, comes from the Strip. Local merchants in downtown have come up with all manner of marketing schemes, from flooding the streets to achieve a Venetian-canal effect to installing a one-hundred-foot-high awning over **Glitter Gulch** (the four blocks of Fremont Street between **Main** and **Fourth Streets**, also known as **Casino Center**). Fremont Street is closed to vehicular traffic from Main Street to **Las Vegas Boulevard**—though access to all businesses remains open—for the construction of a one-of-a-kind pedestrian mall, the **Fremont Street Experience**. At press time, it was slated to open 1 December 1995. Land-scaping and patterned paving will soften the urban streetscape, and winding paths will encourage visitors to stroll in this unique outdoor venue; overhead will loom a frame, approaching 100 feet high at its apex and 1,500 feet long. Set into the inner surface of the frame will be nearly 1.4 million lights that will come to life nightly in a multisensory show.

In the meantime, downtown hangs on to its identity as the robust, bargain basement of the city, a role that works entirely to the advantage of millions of visitors.

1 Jackie Gaughan's Plaza Hotel-Casino $$
With one side facing the neon playground of Glitter Gulch and the other overlooking the railroad tracks, this structure embodies downtown's dichotomy. The hotel straddles the original boundary between the railroad and the town; the **Amtrak** station adjoins the casino. A large mural graces the hallway connecting the two buildings; it depicts an illustrated map of the iron horse route linking the West Coast and eastern Utah, along with a rendering of a futuristic bullet train, proposed to zip from Los Angeles to Las Vegas in little more than an hour.

The south tower addition brings the room total to more than one thousand, making this downtown's second-largest hotel (the **Golden Nugget** takes top honors with more than 1,900 rooms and suites). Accommodations are routine and are usually available, even when the city is crowded. Amenities include swimming and tennis, and a two-block car lot that's especially convenient if you prefer ground-level parking to dizzying high-rise structures. ♦ 1 Main St (at Fremont St). 386.2110, 800/634.6575; fax 382.8281

Within Jackie Gaughan's Plaza Hotel-Casino:

Plaza Casino The first race and sports book (a room set aside for betting on races and sports) in a Las Vegas casino opened here in 1975. The casino also has slots and video poker aplenty, with more than 1,500 machines. Typical of downtown, there are low blackjack minimums, and you can test your luck against craps, roulette, and keno. A bank of penny reel slots is located by the south doors. ♦ Daily 24 hours. 386.2110

Center Stage Restaurant ★★$$ You would think this dining room's tinted-glass dome, tuxedoed and white-gloved wait staff, and comfortable private booths could not be upstaged, but they are, by one of the classic views of the city. Ask for a front-window seat so you can face the gleaming gullet of Glitter Gulch from a second-story vantage. One of these tables is perhaps the best place in town to wine, dine, and talk a partner into doing something a little out of the ordinary—like getting married in the wedding chapel next door to the bar. The fare is typical beef and potatoes, but at an extremely reasonable price, considering the scenery. Be sure to stroll through the mezzanine and descend the curving, mirrored escalators—it's one of Las Vegas's best psychedelic experiences. ♦ Steak house ♦ Daily dinner. Reservations recommended. 386.2512

Plaza Coffee Shop ★$ The bacon or steak and eggs platters served here are two of the town's most beloved bargain breakfasts. The atmosphere is informal, but you'll always find hearty meals at very good prices. ♦ American ♦ Daily 24 hours. 386.2110

Omaha Lounge This bar rocks around the clock, mostly with live country lounge acts. Though it's hit-or-miss on performance quality, the price is right. There is no cover charge or drink minimum, and it's always a lively show. The stage overlooks the casino's central gambling area. Seating is particularly prized on weekends. ♦ Free. Daily 24 hours. 386.2110

2 Victory Hotel $ The oldest hotel in Las Vegas, this whitewashed, Mission-style structure (pictured above) hasn't changed much since it was built in 1910. The 32 rooms are basically the same, too, but they're inexpensive and, since they surround a little courtyard, blessedly quiet. A second-story balcony overlooking the railroad yard provides early afternoon shade on the veranda. There is no restaurant or casino. ♦ 307 S Main St (at Bridger Ave). 384.0260

3 Golden Gate $ The earliest occupant of this site was Las Vegas's first modern hotel, the **Nevada,** the picture of progress with running water and wooden walls (previously, public lodging places were made of canvas). In the lobby is a black-and-white photograph of the historic building, which was replaced in the pivotal year of 1931 (when gambling was legalized in the state) by the **Sal Sagev Hotel** (Las Vegas spelled backwards). In the mid-1950s, a group of investors from San Francisco bought the property, gave it its present name, and began making the shrimp cocktails for which the hotel's **San Francisco**

Bar is renowned. The 106 rooms have been renovated and restored to their early–20th-century style. ♦ 1 Fremont St (between S Main and S First Sts). 382.3510, 800/426.0521

Within the Golden Gate:

San Francisco Bar $ For more than 40 years this Old West–style snack bar with wooden seats has served nearly 26 million giant shrimp cocktails. The "giant" refers not to the size of the shrimp or the San Francisco baseball team, but to the quantity of little crustaceans in this inexpensive dish. No lettuce, celery, or other garnishes go in the cup, though you can get crackers and lemon wedges for a nominal extra cost. The long lines are a testament to its popularity with locals and tourists alike. ♦ American ♦ Daily dinner. 382.6300

4 Coin Castle This slot closet will do just about anything short of kidnapping to get you inside. Ballyhooers in vests made of US currency entice you to spin the wheel out front, ply you with "Crazy Cash," and pilot you to the back of the casino, where you trade in your coupons for a "funbook" full of free food and drink offers. While you wait for the lone cocktail waitress to bring you beer, nachos, popcorn, and the like, staff with advanced degrees in marketing put you through the hard sell to pull the idiot handles. It's almost worth it, as long as you can resist the exhortations to feed, feed, feed the slots until the cocktail waitress (hopefully) returns. ♦ Daily 24 hours. 15 E Fremont St (between S Main and S First Sts). 385.7474

5 Pioneer Club Iconic "Vegas Vic," the neon cowboy, stands 50 feet tall, puffs a hand-rolled cigarette, waves (when his elbow joint is functioning), bellows "Howdy pardner, welcome to Las Vegas" (if his voice box is working), and calls this club home. The casino is a big, roomy grind joint (meaning it caters to low rollers), with quarter craps and roulette, $2 blackjack, rows of reel slots, and a **Carl's Jr** fast-food joint. ♦ Daily 24 hours. 25 E Fremont St (at S First St). 386.5000

Restaurants/Clubs: Red	Hotels: Blue
Shops/ 🍷 Outdoors: Green	Sights/Culture: Black

6 Stoney's Loan and Jewelry The oldest hock shop in the city, and the centerpiece of **Pawn Shop Plaza,** publishes a little brochure that documents the unusual history of the pawnbroker as a lending institution. The pamphlet doesn't mention, however, that Nevada law permits pawnbrokers to charge a monthly six-percent interest on their merchandise, which explains why most pawned goods are rarely reclaimed. If you're in the market, you can pick up used guns, cameras, furs, TVs, luggage, jewelry, and binoculars here at not unreasonable prices. ◆ Daily. 126 S First St (at Carson Ave). 384.2686

7 Golden Nugget Hotel $$$$ Downtown's largest and classiest hotel is, and almost always has been, the showcase of Fremont Street. Rather than glaring neon, the exterior is distinguished by polished white marble and gold fixtures. The lobby is graced with etched-glass doors and leaf-glass chandeliers, and the floors, columns, and front desk are made of marble. An awe-inspiring display of—what else?—gold nuggets features two dozen of the world's largest sparklers, including a 61-pound monster found with a metal detector behind a trailer court in Wetterburn, Victoria, Australia.

When the hotel opened in 1946 it boasted Las Vegas's largest casino, brightest neon sign, and fanciest decor. But after 25 years of setting superlative standards, the luster faded. It took a visionary new management nearly two decades to restore the resort's prestige.

Today the 1,907 rooms and suites are spread over two full city blocks (the most far-flung is a good 10-minute hike from the front desk) and are the most expensive accommodations downtown, as well as the most comfortable. The beauty parlor and spa are among the finest in town, offering exquisite pampering. The pool in the central courtyard can float scores of swimmers with room to spare. Kids will enjoy the video gameroom. ◆ 129 E Fremont St (between S First St and S Casino Center Blvd). 386.8121, 800/634.3454; fax 386.8362

Within the Golden Nugget Hotel:

Golden Nugget Casino Downtown's high rollers are magnetically attracted to this casino by $25 video-poker machines (9/6/$100,000, meaning a full house returns nine coins, a flush returns six, and a royal flush returns $100,000), $100 slots, and high-minimum blackjack tables sharing the baccarat pit. It's

always rammin' and jammin' at the 40 additional blackjack tables, 7 crap tables, and 1,000 slot machines, all poshly appointed with white leather, crystal, and bright brass. ◆ Daily 24 hours. 385.7111

California Pizza Kitchen ★$$ Cooked in wood-fired ovens, the gourmet pies served here are famous from Hawaii to Washington, DC. Exotic toppings include Peking duck, rosemary chicken, Caribbean-spiced pork, and goat cheese. Traditionalists can always opt for mushrooms and pepperoni. You can also partake of delicious salads, pasta, and Häagen-Dazs ice-cream sundaes. ◆ Italian ◆ Daily lunch and dinner. 385.7111

Lillie Langtry's ★★$$$ The decor is spectacular, with a dramatic black-and-white color scheme and bold patterning; the intimate private dining room features the **Nugget**'s signature brass and glass. The cooking is primarily classic Cantonese, with a little Szechuan spice adding a gustatory bite. Sake and plum wine complement all the dishes. ◆ Chinese ◆ Daily dinner. Reservations recommended. 385.7111

Stefano's ★★★★$$$ The marble-tiled courtyard, trompe l'oeil ceiling, bubbling fountain, and exuberant waiters who spontaneously burst into arias set quite a stage for an exemplary Northern Italian menu. Try the veal scallopini, shrimp *fra diavolo* (sautéed in olive oil and garlic with tomatoes), cioppino, or any of the pasta dishes to see for yourself why this place has garnered a reputation for outstanding preparation, presentation, and palatability of a wide diversity of dishes. ◆ Italian ◆ Daily dinner. Reservations recommended. 385.7111

The Buffet ★★$$ This smorgasbord is tops in steam-table cuisine, and compared to most restaurants of this genre, is in an attractive room. The scrumptious bread pudding is home-style consolation for those temporarily down on their luck. Clever diners eat here on Sundays, when free champagne bolsters the usual breakfast, lunch, and dinner entrées. ◆ American ◆ Daily breakfast, lunch, and dinner. 385.7111

8 Four Queens Hotel $$ Home to Big Bertha, the world's largest slot machine, according to the **Guinness Museum,** the "Queen of Fremont Street" is also the only hotel in town with 24-hour security: Guards posted by the elevator politely but firmly check for room keys; if you don't have one, a registered guest must come to the lobby to collect you. The 720 rooms are large but somewhat plain, and you can request a mini-refrigerator. Surprisingly, there's no swimming pool. A high-rise garage behind the hotel provides ample parking. ◆ 202 E Fremont St (between S Casino Center Blvd and S Third St). 385.4011, 800/634.6045; fax 383.0631

Within the Four Queens Hotel:

Four Queens Casino The "Queens Machine," Big Bertha stands 18 feet long and nine feet high, has eight reels, and seats six unselfconscious players. You play one to three dollar tokens in a terminal. An employee pulls the handle, and the symbols—bars, cherries, plums, watermelons, queens—must line up consecutively from either end of the display to win. The terminal lists the payout and spits out the coins. The casino takes an innovative approach to business, and continually introduces new games and gambling promotions. Multiple Action blackjack, in which players bet on three hands against the dealer's single up card, was created here and has spread quickly through Nevada. The casino is also famous for its token giveaways: Coupons are redeemed for slot and video-poker tokens, which you play in machines that pay back in real quarters—a favorable rate of exchange indeed. ♦ Daily 24 hours. 385.4011

Hugo's Cellar ★★★$$$$ For a restaurant situated right off a busy casino, the brick-and-brass ambience here achieves a remarkably secluded effect. Romance is enhanced by the fresh long-stemmed rose presented to every woman who walks through the door. The service is a big part of the pleasure, with waiters skillfully tossing salads tableside and palate-cleansing sorbet served between courses. The sommelier, one of only three in town, is especially attentive and instructive. Duck rubbed with anise and flamed in Grand Marnier is the delectable specialty, but you can't go wrong with the crab-stuffed shrimp, Indonesian lamb, filets and prime ribs, or lobster. ♦ Continental ♦ Daily dinner. Reservations required; jacket requested. 385.4011

French Quarter This lounge is the sole survivor of the hotel's original New Orleans theme. The Monday night Bourbon Street jazz sessions are a long-standing tradition and have been broadcast live around the country. Otherwise, the music leans toward the Big Band sound. There's a two-drink minimum, but since the lounge is open to the casino, you'll be well entertained at the slots, where you can drink for free. Pick up a few pointers at the lounge's daily gambling lessons. ♦ Two-drink minimum. Daily 24 hours. 385.4011

9 **Clark County Courthouse** More than 75,000 marriage licenses are issued annually in Las Vegas, every one of them inside the big **Marriage License Bureau** room right off the main lobby. Over New Year's Eve and Valentine's Day weekends, more than 2,000 applications are processed, and the wait can be hours-long. The rest of the year, however, the procedure is a breeze. No blood test is required, and there's no waiting period. Two people 18 or older, two IDs, and $35 are all that's asked. ♦ M-Th 8AM-midnight; F-Su 24 hours. 200 S Third St (between Carson and Bridger Aves). 455.4415

10 **Office of the Civil Marriage Commissioner** If you don't want a Las Vegas wedding-chapel ceremony and prefer to let a justice of the peace do the joining, till death or divorce do you part, walk a block south of the courthouse to the civil marriage office, where a deputy commissioner will hook you up in no time flat. ♦ M-Th 8AM-midnight; F-Su 24 hours. 309 S Third St (between Bridger and Lewis Aves). No phone calls

11 **Fitzgeralds Casino/Hotel** $$ At 34 stories, this 655-room hotel is the second-tallest building in Nevada. And with a color scheme that's an interesting mix of Irish and cash, this is the greenest building in the state as well. Clip the four-leaf-clovered coupon from the freebie visitors' magazines to receive the house "funbook" (one of downtown's better vouchers) and a free souvenir (a wristwatch, cap, or mug) at the second-floor **Welcome Center**. The rooms are medium-size and clean. There's an international restaurant, coffee shop, **McDonald's**, lounge, and small exercise facility on the premises. ♦ 301 E Fremont St (between S Third and S Fourth Sts). 388.2400, 800/274.5825; fax 388.2181

Within Fitzgeralds Casino/Hotel:

Fitzgeralds Casino Oversize leaves of funny money hanging from concrete trees shade the main pit. Odds-watchers will heed the signs posted with the name, number, and return percentage (if it's more than 100 percent) of the top 20 $1 slot machines. The craps layouts are unique, displaying complete wagering instructions, handy for helping figure the odds. ♦ Daily 24 hours. 388.2400

12 **Las Vegas Western Village** Subtle it's not: The neon nuggets in the pan held by the prospector who towers over the entrance of this granddaddy of Fremont gift shops flash a message Midas would understand: gold, gold, gold. Inside are all the cheesy souvenirs one expects in this den of depravity: Las Vegas back scratchers, glitter-filled paperweights, shot glasses, mugs, towels, caps, salt and pepper shakers, toothpick holders, dice clocks, personalized matchbooks, and "Are We Rich Yet?" T-shirts. The shop adds a twist to the tack and sells moccasins, miniature tepees, and even synthetic coonskin caps. ♦ Daily; Tu-Sa until 11:30PM. 323 E Fremont St (at S Fourth St). 386.6933

13 El Cortez Hotel $ Fremont Street was but
a half-paved path in 1941, when this hostelry
opened way out here. Soon after the asphalt
was poured, Bugsy Siegel and his cronies
became the dominant players. The jumbo
neon sign and block-long marquee appeared
in the early 1950s. The casino—now arguably
the oldest in the country—has had very few
alterations, other than some cosmetic touches
to the exterior of the original wing. Current
proprietor Jackie Gaughan took over in 1981,
adding the 14-story tower and expanding
the gaming facilities. The tower houses 200
"mini-suites"—surprisingly roomy digs with
king-size beds and couches, at reasonable
rates. This is one of the best budget hotels
downtown. ♦ 600 E Fremont St (at N Sixth St).
385.5200, 800/634.6703; fax 385.1433

Within El Cortez Hotel:

El Cortez Casino Although this casino is a
bit beyond Glitter Gulch proper, it's still a
popular place to play and is almost always
crowded with locals and regulars. The gambling house is known for a lottery-type drawing
with keno-size payoffs; winning combinations
correspond to your social security number
(bettors fill out a form that includes their social
security number; winning forms are drawn
from a drum). The casino is known for introducing new games, so you might find something novel happening in the gaming rooms or
around the pit in the cramped old wing. The
expanded gaming facilities in the new, airier
wing include a poker room and a race and
sports book. ♦ Daily 24 hours. 385.5200

Roberta's ★$$ Discover one of the greatest
meal deals this side of an Eskimo cookout: a
big plate of Alaskan king crab legs for a price
so low that you'll get change back from a
Jackson. You can also subtract some crab and
add a New York steak for the same pittance.
The decor is nothing to write home about, and
the tables are as crowded as they are small.
But neither the cramped quarters nor the out-
of-the-way location discourage the crowds
from queuing up for the fine and inexpensive
food. ♦ Steak house ♦ Daily dinner.
Reservations recommended. 385.5200

**14 Jackie Gaughan's Gold Spike Hotel &
Casino** $ Each of the 109 medium-size
rooms at this place costs no more than a
minimum bet at a baccarat table. (It's a good
idea to make reservations at least six months
in advance.) There's a two-night minimum on
weekends. The amenities are basic Vegas: a
small parking lot, an archetypal snack bar, and
a casino that's always bustling with natives
and devoted visitors. ♦ 400 Ogden Ave
(between N Fourth St and Las Vegas Blvd N).
384.8444, 800/634.6703; fax 384.8768

Within Jackie Gaughan's Gold Spike Hotel &
Casino:

Gold Spike Casino Low rollers who enter
here are transported to heaven. Even on a busy
Saturday night, there's usually only one $5
blackjack table; the other six host $1 and $2
games. The place is jammed with nickel slots
and video poker. But the unique attraction is
the array of penny video-poker machines. You
can play up to one hundred pennies, and the
royal flush on the max bet pays 10,000 coins
($100). The action is fierce, a veritable video-
poker back-wall battle, with 13 warriors locked
in combat with the machines, marked by the
occasional desperate cry to the change woman
for more ammunition. When one challenger
bows to defeat, another rushes in to pick up
the cause. If you haven't been through basic
training, you might want to steer clear of this
trench. ♦ Daily 24 hours. 384.8444

15 Sam Boyd's Fremont Hotel and Casino $
In 1956, this 452-room, 15-story hotel was
the tallest building in the state, rising a full six
floors above anything on the Strip. Unusual for
down-town, this place has such amenities
as elevators, showrooms, and a rooftop swim-
ming pool. Of all the neighborhood establish-
ments, this one weathered the longest under-
world involvement: Meyer Lansky's name
was overheard by an FBI wiretap in the 1970s.
Today, it's a typical thirty-something Las
Vegas hotel, a little faded but still vital thanks
to its prime location in Glitter Gulch. There's
a big and bold Western mural in the poker
room—where aspiring cardsharps can take
lessons in the mornings—and some model
Conestoga wagons in the **Overland Coffee
Shop.** ♦ 200 Fremont St (at N Casino Center
Blvd). 385.3232, 800/634.6182; fax 385.6270

The giant gold nugget on display at the Golden
Nugget Hotel & Casino is called "The Hand of
Faith." Melt it down and you could make 12,000
18-karat gold rings.

Within Sam Boyd's Fremont Hotel and Casino:

Second Street Grill ★★★$$$ Formerly the hotel's lounge, this casual but elegant dining room has been refurbished into an attractive, intimate space, with dark inlaid woods; Art Deco–style fixtures; and comfortable, heavy wooden chairs. The fine fare includes such exotic and tasty Pacific Rim foods as bamboo-steamed Hawaiian snapper, grilled veal chops with soy-ginger sauce, and a crispy honey duck salad. Desserts range from a ginger crème brûlée to a macadamia nut cheesecake. ♦ Pacific Rim ♦ Daily dinner. Reservations recommended. 385.6277

16 Binion's Horseshoe Hotel and Casino $$
A literal wealth of Las Vegas legends are associated with this place. Of all the rough characters who ever owned a Las Vegas casino, the late

Benny Binion, an urban cowboy, bootlegger, and gambler from Dallas, was the roughest. Benny made no bones about having killed people, nor did he pull many punches when it came to cheaters, welshers, freeloaders, card counters, and the like. A statue of the old man astride his trusty steed stands at the corner of Ogden and First Streets (overlooking what used to be Block 16). Benny Binion died in 1989 at the age of 84; his family still owns the lodging.

The older section of the hotel houses 80 rooms, all comped to high rollers, and the neighboring 25-story west wing has 300 newer and larger guest rooms. Together, they form a city block, and the two Ogden Street parking structures occupy another block. There's a pool and spa on top of the newer building.

A hundred $10,000 bills are on display in the old wing, and though the stash is advertised as one million dollars, the old currency, out of circulation for decades, is worth far more than its face value. Go ahead—have your picture taken in front of all that beautiful money. ♦ 128 E Fremont St (between N Casino Center Blvd and N First St). 382.1600, 800/237.6537; fax 384.1574

Easy Come, Easy Go: Marriage and Divorce in Nevada

Never mind poker, baccarat, or blackjack. Each year, thousands of Las Vegas visitors choose to play the ultimate game of chance: matrimony. Approximately 80,000 marriage licenses are issued annually in Clark County—which includes Las Vegas and the southern tip of Nevada—alone. And while they probably don't realize it, this legion of lovers is supporting a business that's been inextricably tied to Nevada's gaming tradition for more than 60 years.

Las Vegas's wedding industry owes its existence largely to a 1931 state statute (ironically, it was passed at the same time as legislation that legalized gambling) that liberalized the state's marriage and divorce laws. Couples were now able to obtain a divorce after a mere six weeks' residency in the state. Reno-area resorts, sensing a financial gold mine, nationally touted the locale as the ideal place where the soon-to-be-separated could spend their time (and money) in comfort and style, while fulfilling the letter of the law.

In Las Vegas, some token efforts were made to follow suit. But—call it sentimental, call it romantic, or just call it a stroke of opportunistic marketing savvy—southern Nevada entrepreneurs decided to focus on the other side of the connubial coin. They made a name for themselves by capitalizing on the lenient law's waiver of a blood test and waiting period for prospective newlyweds. In short order, wedding chapels sprouted up all over the Las Vegas Valley, and the city rapidly established a reputation as the place for quick, hassle-free nuptials.

That image has been enhanced over the years by the eclectic roster of celebrities who have decided to tie the knot in Las Vegas. Among the notables to have walked down the aisle here are: Mickey Rooney, Judy Garland, Joan Collins, Michael Jordan, Bruce Willis and Demi Moore, and Richard Gere and Cindy Crawford (there's no insurance against splitting up provided). Las Vegas weddings also appeal to ordinary folk who are looking to keep the affair low-key.

If you're scheduling your own nuptials, try to avoid Saturdays, holidays (particularly Valentine's Day and New Year's Day), and three-day weekends, as the town is virtually guaranteed to be booked up. The typical ceremony takes anywhere from a few minutes to a half hour—the quicker to get back to the tables. In keeping with the relaxed attitude of the ordinance, those presiding tend to be amenable sorts who aren't pushy about inserting religious references into vows for couples who don't want them. Some vows are by-the-book traditional, while others resemble the results of a high school creative writing project.

In addition to being convenient, a wedding is one of the city's best bargains, costing as little as $25 (not including the license, which currently runs $35). A donation to the officiant— usually $25 to $50—is customary. For an additional fee, most facilities can also provide such extras as music, flowers, photo and videotape services, and even tuxedos.

Within Binion's Horseshoe Hotel and Casino:

Binion's Horseshoe Casino Tables and slots pack the original casino, outfitted with dark wood and Western-style chandeliers. Ten tables comprise the big crap pit. But the newer west wing—decked out in brass and glass—holds the busiest poker pit in town, and the world's biggest names in poker are its habitués.

This is the joint with no house limits and where it is not uncommon to see a one-million-dollar bet placed at craps. The annual World Series of Poker—sponsored by the hotel—is held here every May; to compete for the million-dollar first prize, simply ante up $10,000. You may not win, but if you play here at least they'll feed you well; the place has a reputation for doling out some of the best meal comps in the business. ◆ Daily 24 hours. 382.1600

Coffee Shop $ The line forms a half hour before the 10PM serving time for the $3 New York steak dinner with all the trimmings. Be prepared to wait anywhere from 45 minutes to 1.5 hours. The steak is excellent, a loss leader for the casino. If you're still in the casino at 5:45AM, you can queue up for Benny Binion's Natural—the $2.50 ham and eggs breakfast. Be patient: Dinner and breakfast have been popular downtown staples for years—but you only need arrive 10 minutes ahead of time for lunch. ◆ American ◆ Daily 24 hours. 382.1600

Deli ★$ The bagels and lox and heaping pastrami, corned beef, and brisket sandwiches served here earn the approval of experienced noshers. And of course, kosher dills are served on the side. ◆ Deli ◆ Daily breakfast, lunch, and dinner. 382.1600

Snack Bars $ The 24-hour snack bars in each wing of the hotel both offer the same menu. Scrambled eggs, sausage, and a biscuit set you back just one buck between 6 and 11AM. Many residents claim to have lived through lean times on the hearty ham-and-bean soup with a big piece of corn bread. The turkey sandwiches are piled high with breast meat, carved from a fresh bird roasted daily. ◆ Daily breakfast, lunch, and dinner. 382.1600

Binion Ranch Steak House ★★$$$$ The ascent in the glass-enclosed elevator to this 25th-floor aerie is the best joyride downtown. Known far and wide for its beef, which comes from the family's own Montana ranch, recom-mended dishes include the outstanding prime ribs and 25-ounce porterhouse. The lamb chops are also winners. Or you can just come up for a drink at the quiet bar, with its wide-angle view of the city. ◆ Steak house ◆ Daily dinner. Reservations recommended. 382.1600

Restaurants/Clubs: Red   Hotels: Blue

Shops/ ♥ Outdoors: Green   Sights/Culture: Black

17 Sassy Sally's Just like its sister casino (the Coin Castle), this downtown slot joint will do anything to lure you inside. Some outlandish character—a woman wearing a 55-gallon Styrofoam hat and size 23 plastic cowboy boots or a guy in horse-riding gear—is bound to be stationed out front doing something outrageous to lure your attention, like enticing you to try your luck at the "Crack-the-Safe" device: Punch in your numbers, turn the dial, and, if the door opens, you'll be $5,000 richer. The whole place has a strange amber glow, and the ambience can be a bit overwhelming, with flashing lights; scores of shrieking, clanging reel slots; and an army of hucksters hassling you to play. ◆ Daily 24 hours. 32 E Fremont St (between N Main and N First Sts). 382.5777

18 Girls of Glitter Gulch "Vegas Vickie," a neon cowgal, sits pretty on top of the marquee at this strip club. Despite the unanimous opposition of the mayor and other city officials, as well as the majority of downtown casino managers who are convinced that Las Vegas is now a family destination, the business remains open. Although pedigree isn't usually a factor in these enterprises, this one's sort of the "Tonight Show" of jiggle joints. It was voted Las Vegas's number-one topless club by the *Las Vegas Review Journal* in 1994. ◆ Cover. Daily 9AM-1AM. 26 E Fremont St (between N First and N Main Sts). 385.4774

LAS VEGAS CLUB

19 Las Vegas Club Hotel and Casino $$ The hall leading from the casino to the front desk of this hotel is studded with vintage sports memor-abilia. The centerpiece is Maury Wills's bronzed spikes from the 1962 baseball season, when he broke the stolen-bases record with 104. Among the balls, bats, and trophies, the blown-up aerial photos of stadiums provide an unusual perspective. The 224 guest rooms have been redecorated with a Southwestern touch. The upper floors of the 16-story tower have prime views of the glittering streets below. ◆ 18 E Fremont St (between N Main and N First Sts). 385.1664, 800/634.6532; fax 387.6071

Within the Las Vegas Club Hotel and Casino:

Las Vegas Club Casino Dating back to the early days of legalized gambling, this casino is a high-ceilinged, spacious affair, affording elbow room uncommon in downtown. Huge signs over the pit spell out the most liberal blackjack rules in Vegas: double down on two, three, or four cards; split and resplit pairs, including aces; six cards that don't bust automatically win; surrender first two cards for half your bet. The basic strategy is a bit more advanced due to the six-card and surrender, but this is the best six-deck game anywhere. ◆ Daily 24 hours. 385.1664

Child's Play

For decades, Las Vegas has enjoyed a reputation as the playground for adults. But whether in response to baby boomers with babies in tow or simply trying to shed its anything-but-PG rating, southern Nevada is increasingly designing attractions specifically with children in mind. From animal displays to water parks, Las Vegas is doing its best to provide parents with ammunition to stave off the inevitable mid-vacation "What do we do now?" blues.

Of course, gambling areas remain strictly off-limits to kids, even those accompanied by adults. But, in a growing number of casinos, youngsters are seldom far from games, shows, and other on-site activities tailored to provide them with a few lasting memories of their trip.

And unlike grown-ups, kids don't have to blow their allowances to have fun.

Bonnie Springs Ranch/Old Nevada
(on Bonnie Springs Ranch Rd, 1 mile west of Hwy 159, 875.4191) offers a petting zoo with a full complement of the usual creatures (including rabbits, deer, a donkey, baby goats, and a buffalo), a duck pond, an aviary, horseback riding, and exhibits highlighting the history of this stopover point for California-bound wagon trains during the mid-1800s. Adjacent to the ranch, **Old Nevada** is a sort of wild West theme park, complete with gunfights, outdoor performances (a hanging or a melodrama), saloons, stagecoaches, a general store, and other tidbits of bygone days. Separate admission is charged for each. Both are open daily.

Circus Circus (2880 Las Vegas Blvd S, at Circus Circus Dr, 734.0410), the circus-themed hotel-casino and the granddaddy of child-friendly Las Vegas venues, designed two ways to keep the children happy. There's **Grand Slam Canyon** (open daily until 5PM with additional evening hours on Friday and Saturday), an exciting five-acre indoor amusement park complete with water rides, a roller coaster, gondola, and lots to eat, plus a large selection of games with stuffed animal prizes. Or there's the second-story **Midway,** entertaining kids just a floor above their parents, who are busy playing adult games on the main floor of the casino. Kids will find video games and a variety of carnival activities (basketball tosses, pitching games— the usual amusement park mainstays), and approximately twice an hour, aerialists, acrobats, and other circus performers display their skills. Strolling clowns and entertainers

add to the big-top ambience. The **Midway** is open Monday through Friday 11AM to midnight, Saturday and Sunday 10AM to 1AM.

Excalibur Hotel/Casino/Las Vegas (3850 Las Vegas Blvd S, at Tropicana Ave, 597.7777), **Circus Circus**'s corporate cousin, has a medieval motif, featuring **Merlin's Magic Motion Machines.** Riders are strapped into bleacher-style seats that rise, fall, bank, and dip in sync with a movie depicting either an equilibrium-destroying bobsled run or a spin on a roller coaster. Sufferers of motion sickness are forewarned: The attraction convincingly conveys the visceral sensations of these romps. The hotel also offers "King Arthur's Tournament," a lavish Olde English feast accompanied by a show starring the world-famous Royal Lippizaner stallions (daily 6PM and 8:30PM); kids especially enjoy the jousting knights. Admission is charged for the ride and the tournament.

Guinness World of Records Museum (2780 Las Vegas Blvd S, between Circus Circus Dr and E Sahara Ave, 792.3766) is weird even by Vegas standards. Exhibits here document the biggest, smallest, tallest, shortest, and the most absurd accomplishments of both nature and humankind. Don't miss the video of the falling-dominoes record, set by English engineering students in 1988 with 1,380,000 dominoes. Well-designed exhibits and computer databases allow the curious to call up bizarre bits of arcana at the touch of a button. Admission is charged to the museum, which is open daily 9AM to 9PM.

Imperial Palace Auto Collection (Imperial Palace Hotel & Casino, 3535 Las Vegas Blvd S, at Flamingo Rd, fifth floor of the parking garage, 731.3311) tributes America's favorite machine. It's a grease monkey's dream come true, with more than 200 classic and antique cars culled from nearly every era of automotive history, from the early 1900s to the 1960s, with a few later models for good measure. Car buffs can see such motoring memorabilia as a 1947 Tucker (one of only 51 in existence), the world's largest collection of Model J Duesenbergs, Benito Mussolini's 1939 Alfa Romeo, Dwight D. Eisenhower's 1952 Chrysler Imperial limousine, and Adolph Hitler's custom-built 1939 Mercedes-Benz. Admission is charged. The collection is open for viewing Monday through Friday 9:30AM to 11:30PM.

Las Vegas Natural History Museum (900 Las Vegas Blvd N, between E Washington Ave and E Bonanza Rd, 384.3466), a local favorite, offers tableaux of stuffed animals ranging from antelope to yaks, a collection of wildlife art and wood carvings, and a room devoted to birds. The centerpiece of the *Prehistoric Life* exhibit is an animated dinosaur, which emits an impressive roar with ear-numbing frequency. Aquariums teeming with live sharks are crowd-pleasers in the **Marine Life** gallery, although quirkier visitors might prefer the display of items found in the stomach of a single tiger shark (including a California license plate, a doorknob, a running shoe, and a full bottle of white wine). It's open daily, and admission is charged.

Las Vegas Stars (Cashman Field Center, 850 Las Vegas Blvd N, between E Harris and E Washington Aves, 386.7200), the **San Diego Padres**' Triple-A farm team, play from April to Labor Day in what is generally considered one of the cleanest and best-designed minor-league ballparks in the country. With showmanship worthy of its hometown, the front office is adept at attracting fans, scheduling team merchandise giveaways or special events such as fireworks displays or rock concerts at just about every game at **Cashman Field.** And the club isn't a bunch of benchwarmers—they play some pretty good ball. Tickets can be purchased at the box office or by calling **Ticketmaster** (474.4000).

The Liberace Museum (Liberace Plaza, 1775 E Tropicana Ave, at Spencer St, 798.5595) is, depending on your point of view, either a fascinating collection of artifacts from Liberace's career or an exercise in kitsch. But for some reason or another, kids love it. The rotating displays showcase the pianos he played, the cars he drove, and the jewelry and costumes he wore with such élan. (If you're lucky, the 1971 red, white, and blue hot pants ensemble will be available for viewing.)

A special section is devoted to gifts sent to the entertainer by faithful fans; check out the teeny piano made of matchsticks. A souvenir shop is located on the premises, and all proceeds go to the Liberace Foundation for the Performing and Creative Arts, a nonprofit group that awards scholarships to music students around the country. Open Monday through Saturday, and Sunday afternoon, the museum charges admission.

Lied Discovery Children's Museum (833 Las Vegas Blvd N, between E Washington Ave and E Bonanza Rd, 382.3445) is a place children and parents will love. The museum, which is open Tuesday through Saturday, plus Sunday afternoon, features more than 50 hands-on exhibits that illustrate principles of nature and science. Kids—and adults who aren't afraid of acting like kids—can construct buildings out of cardboard boxes, encase themselves in giant bubbles, play "Jingle Bells" by jumping on giant pieces of carpeting marked with musical notes, draw pictures using computers, buy "groceries" by withdrawing money from a pretend automated teller machine, spin in a gyroscope chair, and design and fly paper airplanes. Who says science isn't fun? Admission is charged.

MGM Grand Adventures Theme Park (3799 Las Vegas Blvd S, at Tropicana Ave, 891.1111) features seven rides, including the **Lightning Bolt, Deep Earth Exploration, Backlot River Tour, Parisian**

Taxis, Haunted Mine, Over the Edge (sawmill), and **Grand Canyon Rapids.** There are also theaters, arcades, restaurants such as **Kenny Rogers Roasters** and **Burger King,** and retail shops.

On the **Lightning Bolt,** a thrilling indoor roller coaster, a futuristic motion simulator takes the riders on a fantastic voyage deep into the earth's core; dazzling special effects amaze riders on the **Backlot River Tour.** An abandoned mine haunted by an old Indian chief's spirit, a ride on the swirling white-water rapids in an inner tube, and the bump-em **Parisian Taxis** all provide excitement for the price of admission daily.

The Mirage Hotel & Casino's Tigers and **Dolphins** (3400 Las Vegas Blvd S, between Spring Mountain Rd and Dauphine Way, 791.7111) are two separate exhibits. The white felines belong to magicians Siegfried and Roy, whose show has been packing **The Mirage** since it opened in November 1989. When the Bengals aren't working in the duo's act, they are on view at no cost 24 hours a day, lazing, prowling, and otherwise doing typical tiger things in a glassed-in habitat off the main casino. Admission is charged to view the dolphins, who cavort in a series of pools behind the building. Refreshingly, they don't perform tricks or put on shows, and visitors can watch them up close through underwater windows. A guide is available to answer questions. Tours leave every five minutes from back of the pool area daily.

Omnimax Theater (Caesars Palace, 3570 Las Vegas Blvd S, between Dauphine Way and E Flamingo Rd, 731.7900), a supermarvel of theater technology, allows people to watch movies that are larger and louder than any they've seen before. The curved Omnimax screen measures 82 feet high and 82 feet wide, and audio is provided through 89 hi-fi speakers, enveloping the audience in sight and sound. Films cover subjects as visually compelling as the history of flight and the geological and volcanic wonders of Yellowstone Park. Admission is charged. Call ahead for show times.

Santa Fe Hotel and Casino Ice Arena (4949 N Rancho Dr, between Lone Mountain Rd and I-95, 658.4900), located in one of Las Vegas's newest casinos, usually offers (depending on hockey league practice and game schedules) at least two public skating sessions each day. It's your chance to escape the hot sun, work off all those buffets, or just watch your kids have some fun on ice. A fee is charged.

Scandia Family Fun Center (2900 Sirius Ave, just west of I-15, off Spring Mountain Rd, 364.0070), a local hangout, provides numerous ways to spend a bit of spare change and a few hours. A video arcade, three miniature golf courses, softball batting cages, slot cars, and bumper boats are among the diversions offered at relatively inexpensive prices. Family discount passes are available. It's open daily from 10AM to 10:30PM, Friday and Saturday until 11PM.

Southern Nevada Zoological Park (1775 N Rancho Dr, at Melody La, 648.5955), Nevada's only zoo, is home to more than 150 species of plants and animals from around the world: monkeys, a llama, a Bengal tiger, a mountain lion, coyotes, desert tortoises (a threatened native species), and an extensive flock of exotic birds, including several proprietary peacocks that wander freely around the three-acre property, a King vulture, and a toucan. A small petting zoo gives kids a chance to feed little critters, providing parents

with photo ops galore. Admission is charged. The zoo is open daily.

Sports Memorabilia Display at the Las Vegas Club Hotel and Casino (18 E Fremont St, between S Main and S First Sts, 385.1664) is an inspiring collection open to all comers 24 hours a day. Included are a program from the **1934 World Series** (St. Louis vs. Detroit), a football signed by **Green Bay Packer** greats Vince Lombardi and Bart Starr, photographs autographed by such immortals as Bob Feller and Gale Sayers, and even a bank of six green wooden seats rescued from Chicago's old Comiskey Park. All at no charge, which makes this one of the best deals in town.

Wet 'n Wild (2600 Las Vegas Blvd S, between E Sahara Ave and Riviera Blvd, 737.3819, recorded information 734.0088) is an aqueous oasis at the northern end of **the Strip** and the perfect remedy for Las Vegas's hellish desert afternoons. Open daily from early April to early October, it features more than a dozen water rides for persons of all ages and thresholds of fear, from a gently flowing stream that takes inner-tube cruisers around the perimeter of the park to some very high, truly gut-twisting water slides and chutes. At least one major ride is added every summer, and the designers seem to have a knack for treading the thin line between excitement and abject terror. Afternoon discounts and two-day passes are available.

20 California Hotel and Casino $$$
Although this hotel opened in 1975 with a Southern California theme, the clientele always has hailed overwhelmingly from the Aloha State. The owners took the cue and decided to add a distinctly tropical ambience to the place, with vibrant Hawaiian prints everywhere and the **Aloha Specialties** store and restaurant. The shop sells dried fruit and nuts in bulk, while the eatery serves such traditional Hawaiian plate lunches as *saimin* (noodle soup), teriyaki chicken and rice, beef stew curry, and stir-fried vegetables. Less discerning palates go for the Spam *musubi* (rice and Spam wrapped in nori seaweed). **Dave's Bar** affects a thatch-roofed, Waikiki look, and the lounge is sometimes filled with islanders jamming on ukuleles and guitars. If it wasn't for the mural of the Las Vegas banana wearing neon sunglasses, you might think you're at a luau. The Hawaiian theme carries over into the casino—a colorful room offering the basic craps, roulette, and blackjack games. There's a pool on the third floor of the west wing. An overpass connects the main building with the **Main Street Tower** for those who prefer a turn-of-the-century ambience. Altogether the hotel provides 1,000 clean, comfortable, and commodious rooms. ♦ 12 Ogden Ave (between N Main and N First Sts). 385.1222, 800/634.6255; fax 388.2670

Within the California Hotel and Casino:

Pasta Pirate ★★★$$ The design-your-own pasta dishes offered in the hotel's Italian-American eatery are huge (even the kids' plate). The fish is fresh and the surf 'n' turf combos are great to split. But the big winner here is the daily special, usually a filet mignon or top sirloin with a pair of baby lobster tails. If quantity is a major concern, you won't be disappointed; generous meals come with a house salad topped with bay shrimp, garlic bread sticks, vegetable, a side order of pasta, and a glass of wine. ♦ Italian/American ♦ Daily dinner. Reservations recommended. 385.1222

21 Downtown Transportation Center Two bus lines and a trolley come and go from this attractive, convenient local transportation hub. **CAT** buses serve the valley, **Las Vegas Transit** vehicles run up and down the Strip, and the trolley meanders around downtown. Inside are a ticket counter, helpful personnel, a small snack bar, and a security office. ♦ Daily 5:30AM-10PM. 300 N Casino Center Blvd (at Stewart Ave). CAT 228.7433, Las Vegas Transit 384.3540

22 Las Vegas City Hall This 10-story semicircle of polished beige marble, designed by **Daniel, Mann, Johnson & Mendenhall** and built in 1973, stands proud and confident at the edge of downtown. The office tower overlooks a circular courtyard that's ringed by two levels of walkways, giving the public easy access to the space. (Note: Weddings are not performed here.) ◆ M-F. 400 Stewart Ave (at Las Vegas Blvd N). 229.6011

23 Central Fire Station A postmodern, peeled-back portico of glazed brown tile frames the entrance to the administrative offices of this station, designed in 1984 by **Harris Sharp Associates.** The garage is in the rear of the building, and the communications center for Clark County's fire services is tucked beneath a raised forecourt. It's an impressively bold statement for a civic institution. ◆ Bonanza Rd and N Fourth St

24 Las Vegas Public Library Las Vegas's fabled architectural context—or lack thereof—is tested by this library, designed by **Antoine Predock** and completed in 1990. A dynamic assemblage of such simple geometric forms as cubes, cones, and a 112-foot-tall cylinder renders the sandstone structure into an aesthete's playground (not an inappropriate analogy since the building also houses a children's museum). Numerous picture windows flood the rooms with natural reading light. The myriad channels and chambers promote an ongoing architectural exploration of the interior. Upstairs is the **Young People's Library,** with a circular-plan reading room and computer terminals. **Predock,** an Albuquerque-based architect, received the American Institute of Architects' Award of Excellence for this project. ◆ M-Th 9AM-9PM; F-Sa 9AM-5PM; Su noon-5PM. 833 Las Vegas Blvd N (between E Washington Ave and E Bonanza Rd). 382.3493

Howard Hughes isn't the only aviation billionaire to shape Las Vegas history. Business tycoon and pilot Kirk Kerkorian built the International (now the Las Vegas Hilton), which was the world's largest resort when it opened in 1969. He followed that with the MGM Grand Hotel (which is now Bally's) and then once again topped the record with the MGM Grand Hotel and Theme Park, which opened in 1993.

The Las Vegas area is the site of the first two ghost towns in Nevada: Pueblo Grande, abandoned by the Anasazi in the year 1000, and the Old Mormon Fort, which the Latter-day Saints deserted in 1858.

Within the Las Vegas Public Library:
Lied Discovery Children's Museum With 130 participatory exhibits that teach children about the world around them, the rpms (revelations-per-minute) here thrust kids' kinetic needles right into the red zone. Some displays are just for fun, like the *Toddler Towers, Bubble Pavilion,* and musical hopscotch. Others stimulate young imaginations with activities exploring technology, natural science, and art. ◆ Admission. Tu, Th-Sa 10AM-5PM; W 10AM-7PM; Su noon-5PM. 382.3445

25 Las Vegas Natural History Museum After the kids have exhausted the **Lied,** and before they've exhausted their parents, a visit to this modern and well-laid-out wildlife museum is a must. Large galleries of taxidermied North American predators and African ungulates, sharks, birds, and dinosaurs fascinate young and old. A hands-on room has a fossil sandbox, a dinosaur "horn" (you have to see—and blow into—it to appreciate it), and more. Combining art and nature, the halls are adorned with paintings and sculptures of fauna. ◆ Admission. Daily. 900 Las Vegas Blvd N (between E Washington Ave and E Bonanza Rd). 384.3466

26 Old Mormon Fort Latter-day Saint missionaries and homesteaders attempted to colonize the Las Vegas Valley in 1855. They built a large stockade to protect their possessions and gardens against the Paiute Indians—unnecessarily, it turned out, since the indigenous Las Vegans were a hospitable bunch. But the fortress was no match for the forces of nature, and in only a couple of years the Mormons abandoned the settlement to the desert elements. The oldest historic site in southern Nevada, this prosaic little adobe shack has not only endured 140 years of modern Las Vegas history, it also survived the demolition of the rest of the stockade by the fraternal society of Elks (who owned the property) in 1963. Uncharacteristically, the city rallied to rescue the structure, and today it's the only trace of Las Vegas's prerecreation, prerail-road, even preranching past. ◆ Donation requested. Sa-Su. E Washington Ave and Las Vegas Blvd N (at the Cashman Field parking lot). 486.3511

Restaurants/Clubs: Red   **Hotels:** Blue
Shops/ ⚑ Outdoors: Green   **Sights/Culture:** Black

27 Cashman Field Center One of three major Las Vegas convention venues, this one also has a playful side, doubling as a sports facility. The **Las Vegas Stars**—the Triple-A **Pacific Coast League** team affiliated with the **San Diego Padres**—hold their home games here from early April through Labor Day. The center was built in 1983 to blueprints by **George Tate & Associates.** Two exhibition halls provide 100,000 square feet; there's also a 1,940-seat theater. The baseball stadium seats 10,000 fans. The public is invited to peruse the exhibit halls and theater even when there are no special events. ♦ Hours vary; call ahead. 850 Las Vegas Blvd N (between E Harris and E Washington Aves). 386.7100; Stars ticket information 386.7200; tickets at the box office, or call Ticketmaster 474.4000

28 Las Vegas Academy of International Studies and Performing Arts Elaborate detailed reliefs of flora and fauna and a frieze of heroic figures bedeck Las Vegas's only example of Art Deco architecture. A state historic landmark listed on the National Register of Historic Places, the building was designed by **Ferris & Sons** (Reno-based architects descended from the inventor of the Ferris wheel) and constructed in 1931. ♦ 315 S Seventh St (at Bridger Ave). 871.7208

29 Andre's ★ ★ ★ ★ $$$$ This award-winning French restaurant is housed in a former residence in a historic part of the city. Owner-chef Andre Rochat is in the kitchen, but makes frequent forays into the cozy dining rooms to visit with guests. Ask to tour the extensive wine cellar that includes vintages dating back to 1830, or attend one of the spectacular Thursday night wine maker dinners held several times a year. The menu changes with the seasons, but always features *escargots de Bourgogne* (snails in garlic butter) and various presentations of smoked salmon and *coquilles St. Jacques* (scallops in the shell), plus creative preparations of fillet of beef, veal (loin, chop, and medaillons), lamb, fresh fish, poultry, and stuffed pork tenderloin. The exquisite desserts served here are legendary.
♦ Continental ♦ Daily dinner. Reservations recommended. 401 S Sixth St (between Bridger and Lewis Aves). 385.5016

30 Mad Dogs and Englishmen ★$ Sporting a dart room and dark wood bar, this is as close to an English pub as you can hope to find in the American desert. Bartenders with rugby player physiques sport big handlebar mustaches. Wash down the Lancashire hot pot (beef stew) or shepherd's pie with a draught of Taunton cider, Bass Ale, Watney's Red Label, or Guinness Stout. ♦ English ♦ Daily 24 hours. 512 Las Vegas Blvd S (at Clark Ave). 382.5075

31 Gambler's General Store Here lies your one-stop shop for every kind of gambling gadget known. The smallest item in stock is an eight-millimeter, two-ounce die. The largest is a walk-in "money chamber" (popular for check-cashing promotions). Contestants attempt to grab fistfuls of bills swirling inside the enclosure and then push them through a narrow slot. Also here are hundreds of antique and video slots, roulette wheels, blackjack tables, bulk chips and dice, king, queen, and joker directors' chairs, watches, neckties, two big walls full of books and tapes, even a dice-inlaid toilet seat (only $279). This is indisputably the best spot in town to find an authentic souvenir of a sojourn to the gambling capital of the world. ♦ Daily. 800 S Main St (between Gass St and Garces Ave). 382.9903

32 El Sombrero ★$ If you glance at this squat adobe cantina and think that it's been around for a while, you're right. In operation since 1951, it's the third-oldest restaurant in Las Vegas. The whole place seats only 30 people, though the reverberating, high-volume jukebox might be more suited to a stadium. This is the real thing—mounds of Mexican food at prices that are a bargain even for this town. ♦ Mexican ♦ M-Sa lunch and dinner. 807 S Main St (between Gass St and Garces Ave). 382.9234

A group of eight Las Vegas Hilton baccarat dealers pooled $80 at the beginning of the 1992 football season and planned on betting one game a week for 15 weeks, or until they lost. They won an incredible 12 games in a row, but lost the 13th—for $103,000. The odds against winning 15 straight football bets are about 33,000 to one. If they had succeeded, they would have made $1.3 million.

33 Chicago Joe's ★$ Not all dining arenas in Las Vegas are coliseum-size; these two rooms in a tiny brick house on the fringe of downtown have just 12 tables. Lunch, with a menu of various pastas and meatball sandwiches, is quick but not too rushed. Veal, fish, chicken, and eggplant are served at dinner, but the way to go at this joint is some straight-up, down-home macaroni and marinara, with a glass of house red. ◆ Italian ◆ Tu-F lunch and dinner; Sa dinner. Reservations recommended. 820 S Fourth St (between Hoover Ave and Gass St). 382.5637

34 Doña Maria's ★★$ This Las Vegas–Mexican-food institution serves as good tamales as any you'll find north of the border; try them enchilada-style with green or red salsa. Chips, a beer, and an à la carte taco will set you back less than a minimum blackjack bet on the Strip and will fill you up until breakfast (whenever that is). ◆ Mexican ◆ Daily breakfast, lunch, and dinner. 1000 E Charleston Blvd (at Las Vegas Blvd S). 382.6538

35 Gambler's Book Club If your brother-in-law's system crashes or your lucky numbers fail, consult the experts. Anything that you might need to know about every aspect of gambling is right here. The stacks are conveniently organized into categories: card and dice games, sports and the horses, probability theory, casino management, the mob (no connection implied!), gambling economics, dealer's manuals, and more. Also sold here are videotapes and software and a giant mail-order catalog published by the store. ◆ M-Sa. 630 S 11th St (at Charleston Blvd). 382.7555, 800/634.6243, 800/522.1777

36 Swiss Cafe ★★★$$$ Reminiscent of a Swiss chalet, this restaurant is decorated with loads of collectibles—pepper mills, old cake molds, lots of plants—and Old World charm. The Haubolds (chef-owner Wolfgang and hostess-owner Mary) make the visit to their intimate 40-seat hideaway a delightful experience. Specialties include veal Zurich (sautéed veal scallopini and mushrooms in bordelaise sauce), duck with raspberry sauce, and tournedos Cafe de Paris (filet mignon topped with herb butter, all served with spaetzle). ◆ Continental ◆ M-Sa lunch. Reservations recommended for dinner. 1431 E Charleston Blvd (between E 14th and E 15th Sts). 384.6807

Bests

Lance Burton
World Champion Magician/Headliner, Hacienda

The **Red Rock Scenic Loop, Lake Mead/Hoover Dam,** and **Valley of Fire** are the classic "out for a drive" things to do. All with good reason. The Lake Mead water in August is heaven. Rent a boat at one of the marinas and drive out to see the dam. Race up toward the dam, then do a steep turn, spraying a rooster tail of water high into the air. You'll be the envy of all of the tourists standing on the hot asphalt. Then leap into the water (stop the boat first or you'll look like an amateur).

If you go to the Valley of Fire there are great petroglyphs just off the beaten path. The petroglyphs near the signs are tortured by young lovers demonstrating their commitment to each other by scratching or painting their names on ancient artifacts, or by people who don't get enough attention at home. However, a short hike will take you to many that are beautiful and undamaged (apparently vandals don't hike much). Valley of Fire is just the name of the place. Although in the summer it reaches hundreds of degrees, there is nothing actually burning; it's all sand. On the Red Rock loop take some time to hike into the canyon at the Sandstone Quarry pullout. Five minutes puts you into some great scenery right up against the cliffs. There are usually rock climbers in this area, and that's something worth watching a bit of. Be careful not to get hit by falling people.

Cafe Nicolle and **Cafe Michelle West** are good, nice-weather hangouts offering decent food. By coincidence, both are on Sahara Avenue and have outdoor dining. Both of these places have mist systems to keep them fairly tolerable in the summer.

At night a drive down the **Strip** with the windows open is a must-see for first-time visitors. Waving out the windows and shouting at people on the sidewalk is mandatory. A walk from the volcano at **The Mirage** to the **Forum Shops at Caesars** is a fun thing to do, too. And then there are cool clothes and good food at **Boogie's Diner** in the **Forum Shops** (for those of you concerned about the name, I've been assured that they use no "boogies" in the cooking process).

If Kristine and the Sting, Earl Turner, or Santa Fe are playing at any of the lounges, get out to see them.

If you're looking for some great late-night entertainment, a lot of show people see the Lon Bronson All Star Rhythm and Blues Band at the **Riviera**'s **Bistro Lounge.** The show starts at 1AM Saturday and Monday. With a big horn section and lots of guest singers from around town, it's a party.

The Las Vegas of the '90s is no longer the Las Vegas

of the '50s and '60s. It's not just for high rollers any more; the city has become a first-class, worldwide destination resort for the whole family.

D.R. McBride
Horror Novelist/Las Vegas Native

Buildings appear and disappear in Vegas so fast, it's a pleasure to find something wonderfully bizarre left from the 1950s or 1960s.

Las Vegas Boulevard: It's only the south end of this street that's known as the **Strip** and gets to be in all the movies. But keep going north past **Sahara Avenue** and you'll slip into a time tunnel of Vegas's past: from the 1990s to the 1930s. You'll end up at **Woodlawn Cemetery,** where a lot of Vegas legends are buried, including Jimmy the Greek. This is the part of Vegas Kirk Kerkorian and Steve Wynn don't want you to know about—pawn shops, Cuban cafes, rip-off check-cashing joints, flophouses, and biker bars. I think this end of town is a lot more fun than the part littered with pyramids, castles, and fiberglass Roman gods.

The **Golden Gate** hotel and casino downtown at **Fremont** and **Main Streets.** They claim a founding date of 1906, which is bogus except that this corner has been occupied since then. But I like the **Golden Gate** because it has the classiest logo of any hotel-casino in town.

I don't eat much, but when I go out for supper I like the seafood *diablo* at **Carluccio's** behind **The Liberace Museum.**

Flamingo Wash: This flood channel cuts right through the middle of Vegas and fills with muddy water every time it rains. People drown in it. There's always a trickle in the bottom, and you can watch minnows darting around the busted slabs of concrete and asphalt and the twisted wrecks of grocery carts half-buried in the gravel. There are crayfish and squirrels, abandoned house cats, mesquite bushes, cattails, cottonwoods, and salt cedar. Jimson weed grows wild all over the wash: The botanical name is *datura inoxia,* but they call it "locoweed" in Texas, and it's the stuff Don Juan taught Carlos Casteneda to process. Jimson weed has enormous white flowers that bloom at night, and they look like faces in the dark.

Finally, a true gem right on the Strip: the stained-glass window hidden inside the **Barbary Coast Hotel** on the west wall of the casino. It's called "The Garden of Earthly Delights," and there are all kinds of secret things worked into the design: mysterious faces, devils, dragons, toads. Few people look up from their video-poker machines long enough to see it, but it's very apropos of Vegas—nothing about it is what it seems to be.

Claire Harris
Las Vegas Resident

In the winter one can jump into a car and within an hour be skiing on **Mount Charleston** to the west or visiting **Lake Mead** and the **Hoover Dam** to the east. Many people spend their weekends driving to **Death Valley** in a 4×4, while others drive to **Red Rock Canyon** and **Bonnie Springs Ranch,** which are only 30 minutes away.

I prefer going to a local poker room. Unfortunately, the average visitor only knows about the **Strip** and downtown and sees the lights, the shows, the volcano, and the new theme parks springing up all around us. However, the growing population consists of workers and retirees who see the other attractions, many of them similar to those in cities all across the country.

Las Vegas's natural scenery is outstanding, since it's in a small desert surrounded by mountains. It isn't surprising to drive along and see snow on Mount Charleston when the valley's temperature is 80 degrees. Desert blooms (don't touch!) are breathtaking in April and May.

You can gamble 24 hours a day, pick from many four-star restaurants, or eat a buffet dinner that costs from $4.95 to $14.95. Vegas offers the best value for food in the US.

Many visitors bring their youngsters in the summer. Some hotels have fabulous pools, and the city has video arcades, a year-round circus (**Cirque du Soleil**), and three new hotels, one with a massive theme park, another with a pirate theme (complete with outdoor gun battles), and the third with a pyramid.

Tourists looking for a low-budget nongambling day should start early, eat a nice breakfast buffet, hop into a rental car, and drive east through Red Rock Canyon to be greeted by the wild burros (please don't feed them) and marvel over the unusual rock formations and blooms. Drive up to **Mount Charleston Lodge** for a light meal, then head back to the hotel for a swim, followed by a great buffet dinner. Then, take a ride downtown and walk **Fremont Street** to check out the lights. After you have seen the sights (and walked off dinner), drive down the Strip and park at **Caesars Palace** to wander through the new **Forum Shops.** At **The Mirage,** watch the volcano erupt then head inside to see the white tigers.

Riqui Leon
Freelance Publicist

Monday night jazz at the **Four Queens:** There's no cover charge to watch the top names in jazz. Order the shrimp cocktail with your drinks, or if you're too hip to hang out, you can hear the tunes while playing in the casino.

The **Forum Shops at Caesars:** Spectacular shops and a free hourly laser-and-talking-statue show. Pass through the casino on your way out and stop in for the 30-minute Omnimax movie (best when you're stoned).

Rio Casino: Great variety of video-poker machines, colorful and upbeat ambience, and drop-dead gorgeous cocktail waitresses.

Part of the fun of Vegas is always being in action. Don't dine anywhere you can't play keno or drink at bars without poker machines.

Bring money!

The Strip

The Las Vegas Strip is a monument to the doctored maxim "nothing succeeds like excess." Home to nine of the world's 10 largest hotels, this five-mile corridor—spanning **Las Vegas Boulevard South** from **Sahara Avenue** to **Hacienda Avenue**—also boasts the longest and brightest stretch of neon and the most extensive gambling opportunities on any single street on the planet. Notched into a vast, monochromatic desert, shimmering through the heat and dust, the Strip defies categorization; simultaneously inviting and intimidating, it blurs the distinction between fact and fiction.

The story of the Strip has been one of risk takers and rivalries involving entrepreneurial players from both sides of the law. In the 1940s, the Strip was a primitive gravel road (then called **Highway 91**) linking Los Angeles and Salt Lake City to Las Vegas; the town itself was little more than a collection of rooming houses and saloons surrounded by vacant, arid wasteland.

In 1941, the owner of a large chain of motels—a new type of accommodation in those days—visited Las Vegas and decided to try his luck at the casino business. Thomas Hull opened his **El Rancho Vegas** just beyond the city limits in April of that year: a 100-room structure with Spanish Mission overtones, a big parking lot, and a swimming pool strategically placed along the highway. Its instant popularity with tourists seeking comfortable, commodious lodging in the desert caught the attention of like-minded Texas movie theater mogul D.W. Griffith, who built his own 100-room motel, christened the **Last Frontier Hotel,** just a few miles down the road.

Benjamin "Bugsy" Siegel showed up a few years later, on hiatus from his East Coast gangster haunts to avoid a murder rap. After living the high life for several decades in New York, Miami, and Los Angeles, he wanted to build a suitably classy joint from which to oversee the syndicate's West Coast operations. Hollywood's interpretation of events in the film *Bugsy* to the contrary, Bugsy did not invent the Strip; he simply gave the nouveau West a certain amount of polish. The criminal's success in procuring a gambling license from the county and opening the **Fabulous Flamingo** demonstrated to his partners and other interested observers the beauty in legalized gambling and the importance of personal legitimacy. Not long after Bugsy took a couple of fatal slugs, four more mob-owned and -operated hotels opened on the Strip.

A mere decade after **El Rancho Vegas** broke ground, seven hotels populated old Highway 91. Similar in style and substance, they all faced a common dilemma: how to rise above the competition. With the advent of the cheap, highly visible neon sign, this identity crisis came to an end, and the fledgling Strip lit up the sky.

The nine-story **Riviera Hotel** opened in 1955, introducing a modern, luxurious character to the Strip. Between then and 1973, another 10 hotels were built, each one upping the architectural ante with a bravado that had become synonymous with the city. First, the **Stardust** opened with 1,000 rooms. Then the **Tropicana** built the fanciest lobby, replete with mahogany paneling and crystal chandeliers. **Caesars Palace** went on to pioneer the theme concept, with its wholesale transplant of the Roman empire. And in 1973, the **MGM Grand** (now **Bally's**) cracked the 2,000-room mark.

Though many of the existing hotels expanded during the 1970s and late 1980s, no new lodgings opened on the Strip during these years. Critics crowed that Las Vegas was overbuilt, the market had peaked, and no one could ever top the **MGM Grand.** They should have hedged their bets. Visitors continued to stream to the city at an accelerating pace, attendance increasing by a million each year (by 1994, the annual draw reached 23.5 million). Hotels were always filled to capacity.

In 1989, the 3,000-room **Mirage** materialized, its smoldering, six-story volcano, rain-forested lobby, and high-roller appeal sounding the first salvo in the current building boom. Four years later, the new 5,000-room **MGM Grand** opened, bringing a billion-dollar boost to the local economy.

At press time, a number of expansion plans for Las Vegas were on the drawing board: In the summer of 1996, Mirage Resorts Inc. is slated to open two 3,000-room hotels—the **Beau Rivage** and another tentatively called **Victoria.** They will be set around a 14-acre artificial lake on the former **Dunes** property on the Strip south of **Caesars Palace.** And on an 18-acre lot across from the **MGM Grand,** scheduled to open simultaneously with Mirage's new kids on the block, is the 5,119-room **New York-New York** complex. The $300-million resort will attempt to re-create the best of New York restaurants, theater, and entertainment, and will include an Empire State Building complete with a climbing King Kong. The **Las Vegas Hilton** is scheduled to open a 70,000-square-foot multimillion-dollar entertainment complex with a "Star Trek" theme in late 1996. There will be interactive video and virtual reality stations, where visitors can assume the identities of Starfleet- or alien-crew members aboard the *Enterprise;* a 24th-century Cardassian restaurant will complete the experience. Such rabid development and speculation can be likened to a spinning roulette wheel; for now, at least, the stakes continue to climb, and the game continues to make big payoffs for visitors and Las Vegans alike.

A word to the wise: The city's scale can be deceptive. Individually, each of its 38 amenity-packed resorts is manageable; collectively, they converge into a destination of daunting proportion. Savvy visitors explore small sections of the town at a time. But with a landlocked riverboat moored up the street from a 50-foot cowboy near the pyramid of Cheops, the nature of the city delightfully defies conventional touristic logic, and encourages all comers to indulge in its carefully cultivated fantasy.

1 Olympic Gardens This is the classiest burlesque show in town, a real gentlemen's—and ladies'—club (there's a private room where women can take in a show by male performers), where all the dancers are in admirably good shape. The audience is generally well dressed, well mannered, and well entertained. The drinks are noted for their fair weights and measures, and are often on special. ♦ Admission. Daily 2PM-6AM. 1531 Las Vegas Blvd S (between E Oakey Blvd and Paradise Rd). 385.9361

2 Pamplemousse ★★★★$$$ An attractive wine cellar at the entrance is the first indication of wonderful things to come at this charming, intimate French country restaurant. There's no menu—waiters recite the evening's offerings and describe their preparations and sauces. Specialties include veal medaillons with baked apples, many varieties of fresh fish, and sliced duckling imaginatively presented. Be sure to save room for dessert—profiteroles and *coupe maison* (ice cream topped with mixed fruit and whipped cream) are two outstanding choices. ♦ Continental ♦ Tu-Su dinner. Reservations recommended. 400 E Sahara Ave (between Paradise Rd and Maryland Pkwy). 733.2066

3 The Flame ★★$$$ Those searching for the red-and-blue neon flame that flickered on Desert Inn Road for 32 years will now have to head a few blocks east. Not to worry: The new place continues to serve steaks grilled to perfection. Steak sandwich, steak and eggs, lobster tail, orange roughy, ribs, and a few children's portions are also offered, along with slots and video-poker machines. ♦ Steak house ♦ Daily lunch and dinner. Reservations recommended. 1243 E Sahara Ave (at Maryland Rd). 735.4431

4 Holy Cow! Casino If you're in the moo-d, head for this popular casino and micro-brewery, under the same ownership as **Big Dog's Bar and Grill.** A 10-foot black-spotted cow with pink neon sunglasses grazes above the front door. In fact, everything here is colored holstein black on white. Check out the Cow History of Moovies posters: *Amoodeus, Termoonator, Dr. Zhivacow, Cowsablanca, Ben Herd. . . .* The micro-brewery bucks the mixed drink convention—it's the only place like it in Las Vegas and one of only two in all Nevada. As you might guess, the grill serves specialty hamburgers. ♦ Daily 24 hours. 2423 Las Vegas Blvd S (at E Sahara Ave). 732.2697

5 Bonanza Gifts The big sign out front claims that this is the "World's Largest Gift Store." Las Vegas hype notwithstanding, it might very well be. If you can't find a souvenir from among the address books, eyeglass holders, change purses, R-rated towels, T-shirts, place mats, picture books, fans, bells, bowls, mugs, shot glasses, piggy banks, plastic cups, sunglasses, earrings, shopping bags, hats, ashtrays, hot plates, party napkins, dice clocks, chips, cigarette lighters, tie tacks, and pill boxes, then you aren't really trying. ♦ Daily 8AM-midnight. 2460 Las Vegas Blvd S (at W Sahara Ave). 385.7359

6 Tony's Greco-Roman Restaurant ★$$$ A genuine hole-in-the-wall restaurant sitting only two blocks off the Strip, both its Greek and Italian dishes are highly praised by discriminating diners, not only for their preparation but for the large portions. The avgolemono (lemon-rice) soup is a meal in itself, or try it with *taramasalata* (a spread of fish eggs) or *tsatziki* (garlic dip) or Greek salad with feta cheese and olives. The entrées aren't fancy, just tasty and plentiful. Such staples as stuffed grape leaves, moussaka, *spanakopita* (spinach pie), and leg of lamb, along with eggplant parmigiana, veal piccata, and fettuccine Alfredo are sure bets. The only nod to decor here are the big fire engine red Naugahyde booths in the main dining room. ♦ Greek/Italian ♦ Daily lunch and dinner. 220 W Sahara Ave (between Las Vegas Blvd S and Industrial Rd). 384.5171

7 Golden Steer ★$$$ This institution has corralled its share of famished masses since 1962. Don't let the prosaic exterior put you off; inside you'll find a typically overblown, over-scaled Las Vegas eatery. The immense lounge is filled with cushy high-backed chairs and has a massive wood bar featuring one of the best-looking liquor displays in the state. The labyrinthine Western-decorated dining rooms can seat nearly 300 at one time, often feeding a thousand diners a night, especially when a big convention is in town. The brawny brass bovine by the door does clue you in on the menu. Massive cuts of beef are the specialty, though you can also order quail, pheasant, rock partridge, frogs' legs, and Italian-style chicken and veal. ♦ Steak house ♦ Daily dinner. 308 W Sahara Ave (between Las Vegas Blvd S and Industrial Rd). 384.4470

♠ SAHARA

8 Sahara Hotel & Casino $$ The sixth hotel to open on the young Strip was built in 1952 by the Del Webb Construction Company, a Phoenix-based firm that had worked on the **Flamingo Hotel** for Bugsy Siegel a few years earlier. Webb had learned a lesson or two on the previous project and garnered 20 ownership points in exchange for undertaking this one. Over the next few years, and under

changing ownership, the hotel was expanded on several occasions.

Today a pastiche of new and old—a common combination in the Strip's original hotels—at press time it boasted the tallest freestanding sign in the world (222 feet), counting more than 3,000 lightbulbs in its lettering alone. The original garden rooms (low-rise and bungalow style) are often among the most reasonably priced in town, and in slack periods, even the tower rooms can be a great bargain. Only a two-minute cab ride away from the **Convention Center**, it's especially popular during trade shows and can be hard to book. ♦ 2535 Las Vegas Blvd S (at Sahara Ave). 737.2111, 800/634.6666; fax 731.6636

Within the Sahara Hotel & Casino:

Sahara Casino This is Valhalla for video-poker players, with high jackpots on the progressive machines. There are also several four-coin machines scattered around the casino (most machines require five coins for you to qualify for the big royal-flush jackpot; a four-coiner eliminates 20 percent of your risk). The slot club offers excellent perks, and the special gambling promotions—which change frequently—can be quite enticing; ask for the latest details. ♦ Daily 24 hours. 737.2111

House of Lords ★★★$$$$ English decor and a classic London-style bar set the mood for this elegant gourmet restaurant. The chef's specialty here is veal, so be sure to try the succulent veal chop. Also scrumptious are the Dover sole Brittany (sautéed with lemon butter, shrimp, and capers), 26-ounce porterhouse, and rack of lamb. ♦ Continental ♦ Daily dinner. Reservations recommended. 737.2111

Turf Club Deli ★$ Chicken soup with matzo balls is the star of the menu at the most authentic kosher-style deli in a Las Vegas hotel. The mile-high cold-cut sandwiches, with names like Maven, Monte Cohen, and Abba, appear on light or Russian rye, pumpernickel, or a bagel. ♦ Deli ♦ Daily breakfast and lunch. 737.2111

Guy McAfee, a Los Angeles gambling operator, came to Las Vegas in the mid-1930s and invested in clubs in the downtown area and way out along Highway 91, the road to Los Angeles. He traveled back and forth so often that he began calling the highway "the Strip," after the Sunset Strip in his hometown. The nickname stuck.

9 Corner of the Strip and Sahara Avenue
Vacant for 35 years, the southwest corner of the Strip and Sahara Avenue is the former site of **El Rancho Vegas,** the first hotel-casino on the highway beyond the city limits. The resort was erected in 1941 and endured a number of mobster bosses, including Bugsy Siegel himself. In 1960, it burned to the ground in a spectacular—and suspicious—fire. A decade later Howard Hughes bought the lot, and his Summa Corporation still owns it. Believed to be one of the most valuable pieces of real estate in the country, if not the world, its future has been widely discussed. And, though no opening date had been set at press time, in January of 1995 Major League Properties signed an agreement with St. Andrews Golf Corporation to operate **Slugger Stadium** and **All American Family Sports Park** on this spot. The stadium is slated to include 17 batters' boxes and seven on-deck circles, with a choice of baseballs or softballs pitched at three different speed intervals. Plans for the sports park include a golf driving range.

10 Wet 'n Wild This splashy amusement park is just the thing for kids who are bored with video arcades and the hotel pool. A dozen rides, slides, and tides include **Der Stuka,** a 75-foot near-vertical drop; **Blue Niagara,** a six-story, 300-foot-long blue water tube; a **Wave Pool** with four-foot swells; the 300-yard-long **Lazy River;** and more. ◆ Admission. Daily early Apr-Oct. 2601 Las Vegas Blvd S (between E Sahara Ave and Riviera Blvd). 737.3819, recorded information 734.0088

11 Guinness World of Records Museum
The quite astounding collection displayed here features freaks of nature, quirks of fate, and extremes of physiology, behavior, topography, and human endeavor. For example, the world's heaviest man tipped the scales at a stout 1,069 pounds, while the heaviest woman weighed 840 pounds. The oldest man lived for 121 years. The most-often-married man went to the altar 28 times, a feat that undoubtedly puts a gleam into the eyes of this city's wedding chapel owners. Video loops show the highest shallow dive and 1,380,000 dominoes falling in perpetuity. There's an interesting Las Vegas exhibit, with historical black-and-white photos, tapes of local world records being set, and other trivia. ◆ Admission. Daily. 2780 Las Vegas Blvd S (between Circus Circus Dr and E Sahara Ave). 792.3766

Restaurants/Clubs: Red   **Hotels:** Blue
Shops/♥ Outdoors: Green   **Sights/Culture:** Black

12 Circus Circus $ In 1968 this circus pulled into town with just a big top and a casino geared toward high rollers; it nearly went bankrupt in the first few years. Today a resort with 2,800 of Las Vegas's gaudiest guest rooms, it caters to cautious gamesters and families, practically gives away food, and is owned by the most profitable casino corporation in the world. In fact, the family formula has been so successful that similar theme hotels and amusement parks are sprouting all over Las Vegas. But this extravaganza will not be overshadowed. The massive portico is billion-bulb brilliant. Behind it stands the pink-and-white candy-striped **Big Top,** housing the 100,000-square-foot casino and circus stage. The **Midway** features shooting games, knockdown doll games, and balloon and dart games with stuffed animals as prizes. The neon "Lucky the Clown" presides over a 50-ton marquee; his crazy expression is a perfect reflection of the bedlam within.

The world's largest permanent circus rocks 'round the clock, packed with more fun seekers at one time than an average county fair might see in a month. Trapeze and high-wire acts, dancing poodles, motorcycle daredevils, jugglers, acrobats, and the like perform on the mezzanine stage. The shows, which run continuously from 11AM to midnight every day, consistently win the "Best Free Show" award in the *Review-Journal*'s annual reader poll. Knock over the bottles, watergun races, shooting galleries, and other carnival games surround the stage. The buffet is always overrun with masticating hordes. ◆ 2880 Las Vegas Blvd S (at Circus Circus Dr). 734.0410, 800/634.3450; fax 734.2268

Within Circus Circus:

Circus Circus Casino Attention tight wads! This is the joint for you. Blackjack games with two-dollar minimums abound, nickel slots are the status quo, and you can play keno all night long with a $20 bill. That is, if you can find a parking space within walking distance, an empty seat at a 21 table, or a slot machine that's not being jealously played or guarded. ◆ Daily 24 hours. 734.0410

Steak House ★★$$$ This is the one tranquil corner in the **Circus** madhouse: a subdued dining room with a dark-wood interior that wouldn't be out of place in an English manor. A glass-walled refrigerator stores a ton or two of beef sides, which are cut into slabs and grilled on a mesquite broiler in the center of the room. Top sirloin, filet mignon, and porterhouse steaks, prime rib, surf 'n' turf, swordfish, and chicken are among the choices, all accompanied by big, fat baked potatoes. ◆ American ◆ Daily dinner. Reservations recommended. 794.3767

Behind Circus Circus:

Grand Slam Canyon Sitting on five acres, this amusement park features a 15-story mountain peak punctuated with re-creations of Anasazi cliff dwellings presiding over a 90-foot waterfall. A (high) roller coaster with four vertiginous loops and a corkscrew is intertwined with an 800-foot water ride. There are also other rides and win-the-furry-stuffed-animal games. ◆ Admission. Daily from 10AM; closing time changes with the seasons. 734.0410

Adjacent to Circus Circus:

Circusland RV Park The resort's 35-acre campground can accommodate 421 RVs of all sizes and still has room for all the comforts of home: a disposal station, grocery store, laundry facilities, two pools, a sauna and Jacuzzi, recreation room, and playground. ◆ Reservation deposit required. 500 Circus Circus Dr (at Las Vegas Blvd S). 794.3757

13 Riviera Hotel $$$ In 1955 this was the first high-rise on the Strip—then nine stories tall. The dubious beneficiary of several decades' worth of expansions and renovations, an amalgamation of tacked-on towers has turned the hotel into a maze, and your room can be a mile from your car. But there's so much happening on site that this might not be an inconvenience after all. There are five restaurants, a good buffet, sprawling fast-food court, and choice of four shows. There's always a show-and-dinner tandem ticket—one of the most affordable nights out in town. When you're not living the lush life you can lounge at the pool, work out at the health club or on the tennis courts, shop at the upscale stores, taste wines from Nevada's only vineyard, or, if the chance presents itself, get married in the wedding chapel. ◆ 2901 Las Vegas Blvd S (at Riviera Blvd). 734.5110, 800/634.6753; fax 731.3265

For only four bucks a ticket, you could have seen the Beatles perform at the Las Vegas Convention Center in August 1964. The group played two concerts and earned $25,000—60 percent of the total admission receipts.

Within the Riviera Hotel:

Riviera Casino At 125,000 square feet, this was the largest casino in the world—until the 171,000-square-foot **MGM Grand** opened. The behemoth still has a wide assortment of games as well as a lively lounge featuring Monday night jazz. ◆ Daily 24 hours. 734.5110

Ristorante Italiano ★★$$$ Transport yourself to Venice simply by stepping into this Northern Italian dining room. Though it's sequestered deep in the hotel, the trattoria has windows that magically look onto the charms of Venezia—via murals of the Rialto, the Bridge of Sighs, and St. Mark's Square. Of course the food is also evocative of Italia. The *pasta e fagioli* (with beans); black-and-white fettuccine with shrimp, garlic, white wine, and sweet cream; veal chop stuffed with spinach and gorgonzola cheese served in a sweet madeira wine sauce; and tiramisù will elicit a *"delizioso"* from all. ◆ Northern Italian ◆ Daily dinner. Reservations recommended. 734.5110

Rotisserie Buffet ★$ A good alternative to the **Circus Circus** buffet across the street is this all-you-can-eat smorgasbord. Fresh rotisserie-cooked chicken, pork loin, ribs, and beef roasts are featured. All the traditional buffet items are also there for the taking. Breakfast spreads include eggs, pancakes, bacon, sausage, and an assortment of rolls. ◆ Daily breakfast, lunch, and dinner. 734.5110

Mardi Gras Food Court $ Possibly the most intense concentration of fast food under one roof, among the array of familiar places to grab a quick bite here are: **El Pollo Loco, Taco Rico, Wienerschnitzel, Forenza Pasta and Pizza, La Patisserie, New York Deli, Burger King, Baskin-Robbins,** and **Dunkin' Donuts.** ◆ Daily breakfast, lunch, and dinner

The Riviera's Shows The **Riviera** is the entertainment center of the Entertainment Capital. *Splash!,* which ran for 10 years (from 1985 to 1995), was to Las Vegas production shows what **The Mirage** volcano is to hotel facades—wet, blinding, and in a word, eruptive. The diving and synchronized swimming executed in the 20,000-gallon tank, the numerous shower heads drenching the dancers (and the front-row audience), the motorcycle daredevils, and speed jugglers all created one wild ride in the fast lane. *Splash II —The Next Wave* is slated to open at the end of 1995. Billed as the voyage of a lifetime, it will whisk showgoers into the theater in a cruise ship that travels across a glass-bottom bridge. Ticket buyers will have to choose between coach, business class, and first class in the 1,000-seat theater. And 200 of the seats will be equipped with a joystick to provide an interactive relationship between audience, performers, musicians, and lighting effects! You can also take in top comedians at the

Riviera Comedy Club. Dragsters do their turns on Madonna, Joan Rivers, Cher, Tina Turner, Bette Midler, and even a chorus line in *An Evening at La Cage*. And for some nearly naked bump-and-grind antics, check out *Crazy Girls*. ♦ 794.9301

14 Slots A Fun Next door to the **Big Top**, this is about as close to a downtown grind joint (one that caters to low-stakes players) as you'll find on the fancy Las Vegas Strip. A four-reel, one-dollar slot machine is so close to the street you can almost pull the handle from your car window. The minimum bet on the crap table is *raised* to two dollars for the Saturday night crowd. The blackjack tables remain a buck all week long. The snack bar also appeals to penny-pinchers, handing out free popcorn and serving shrimp or crab cocktails, waffles, big bowls of sauerkraut, hot dogs, chicken wings, pizza by the slice, tacos, and strawberry shortcake for a pittance. ♦ Daily 24 hours. 2880 Las Vegas Blvd S (between Circus Circus Dr and Stardust Rd). 734.0410

15 Peppermill Cafe and Lounge ★$$ Anyone familiar with the **Peppermill**'s psychedelic casinos in the border burgs of Mesquite, Wendover, and Reno is in for a surprise upon entering this understated restaurant and bar. The dining room resembles a **Denny's,** but thanks to the trademark silk plants and flowers it has the upscale air of a faux fern bar. It's an excellent asylum (so to speak) from the lunacy of the Strip, with plush carpeting, commodious velour couches, and coffee tables providing privacy and tranquillity perfect for a close encounter. Offerings include a large selection of burgers, sandwiches, steaks, seafood, and chicken; all entrées are accompanied by a fresh spinach salad or soup. The burgers are a hefty half pound, and the steak is all USDA choice. Traditional desserts include peach melba; peach, cherry, or apple deep-dish cobbler; and an incredibly creamy cheesecake. ♦ American ♦ Daily 24 hours. 2985 Las Vegas Blvd S (at Convention Center Dr). 735.4177

The worst flash flood in Las Vegas history occurred on 4 July 1975. When it was over, cars were stacked five deep in the Caesars Palace parking lot.

Restaurants/Clubs: Red   **Hotels:** Blue
Shops/ ♥ Outdoors: Green   **Sights/Culture:** Black

15 Silver City The table limits are low, and the food and drinks are very inexpensive at this casino. The mining theme, with some serious excavation action taking place above the aptly named "pit," is a nod to the seminal event of Nevada's history: the 1859 discovery of the Comstock Lode, the largest silver and gold deposits ever found in the continental US. The casino is named after the town of Silver City, which sits atop the Comstock, 15 miles east of Reno. ♦ Daily 24 hours. 3001 Las Vegas Blvd S (at Convention Center Dr). 732.4152

16 Westward Ho Hotel & Casino $$ This sprawling complex of two- and four-story courtyard units constituting 1,000 rooms stretches all the way from the Strip to Industrial Road. The room rates are a delight to the frugal, and there's a wing of two-bedroom, one-bath apartments with a living room, TV, minibar, and refrigerator, also at a reasonable tariff. Also available are seven swimming pools, a free airport shuttle, a coffee shop, a lunch and dinner buffet, and a popular slot club that packs the small casino with handle-pullers and button-pushers; the 9/6 progressive video-poker machines often yield player-positive results. Split the snack bar's renowned two-pound strawberry shortcake. ♦ 2900 Las Vegas Blvd S (at Convention Center Dr). 731.2900, 800/634.6651

17 Stardust Resort & Casino $$$ When this refuge opened in 1958, it was accompanied by the requisite slew of superlatives: the largest casino, neon sign, theater stage, and swimming pool in the world. That same year, the *Lido de Paris* show began its record-setting 33-year run here and baccarat made its first Nevada appearance in the casino. Over the next decade, however, the resort lost some of its luster. One of the last of the 1950s hotels to undergo an expansion, it regained much of its former glory after the addition of a 1,500-room tower in 1990. ♦ 3000 Las Vegas Blvd S (between Stardust Rd and Fashion Show Dr). 732.6111, 800/634.6765; fax 732.6296

Within the Stardust Resort & Casino:

Ralph's Diner $ A fun place for a bit of nostalgia, this neo-1950s diner sports black and white tiles, and individual jukeboxes in the booths. Breakfast is served all day (the omelettes are four-egg affairs). Burgers and such dominate the menu, but there are also blue-plate specials and a full soda fountain with floats, sundaes, shakes, and malts. The waitresses' uniforms are apropos the period, as are their attitudes—often boogying to your table to the oldies' beat. Management's motto? "If you're not served in five minutes, you'll get served in eight or nine, maybe 12." Relax! ◆ American ◆ Daily breakfast, lunch, and dinner. 732.6111

Enter the Night This production is Las Vegas's attempt to be avant-garde. The show is presented as a dream, or at least a waking tribute to twilight and the passions it conceals and reveals. A seamless fusion of such disparate elements as erotic and tap dancing, gymnastics and skating, laser effects and costuming, the pace is languid and the entertainment is concentrated, enhancing the originality of this surprisingly thought-provoking performance. ◆ Admission. M, Su 8PM; W-Sa 8PM, 10:30PM. 732.6111

18 Nippon ★★$$ With *shabu-shabu* and sushi bars, a serene dining room, a solicitous staff, and excellent food, you'd think this Japanese jewel would always be crowded. But except when the nearby **Convention Center** is hosting an out-of-town entourage (when the restaurant is jammed), meals here are quiet and leisurely. The *yaki udon* (buckwheat noodles in broth) served in a big black kettle will satisfy those who haven't yet developed a taste for the seafood nibbles. ◆ Japanese ◆ M-F lunch and dinner; Sa-Su dinner. 101 Convention Center Dr (between Paradise Rd and Las Vegas Blvd S). 735.5565

19 Debbie Reynolds Hotel/Casino, Movie Museum $$ The energetic actress has brought Hollywood to Las Vegas. Not only does her 200-room hotel (plus some time-share suites) display authentic props and costumes from such films as *Tammy, Singing in the Rain, Cleopatra,* and *The Wizard of Oz,* but, on many Monday afternoons, such stars as Ann Miller, Jane Powell, or June Allyson meet with guests between showings of films from the Golden Age. The casino—also decorated with movie sets, props, and posters—features craps, 21, slots, video poker, and a piano player. The **Hollywood Cafe** is an ideal spot for casual dining. ◆ 305 Convention Center Dr (between Paradise Rd and Las Vegas Blvd S). 734.0711, 800/633.1777; fax 734.2954

20 Piero's ★★★$$$$ Celebrities and sports figures always find their way to this popular restaurant. Former **UNLV** basketball coach Jerry Tarkanian is a regular, with a cozy room named for him. For private dining, ask for seating in one of the many alcoves or dimly lit booths; if you're more of a party animal, there's also a massive bar. The service is excellent, and the wine list extraordinary. Among the special-ties are *zuppa di pesce* (lobster, clams, mussels, shrimp, scallops, and calamari in light fish broth with a touch of tomato), veal chop *Gran Duca D'Alba* (sautéed with mushrooms in a creamy brandy sauce), whole kosher chicken, osso buco, and such creative pastas as *linguine all'aragosta* (with fresh lobster in a light tomato sauce) and *fettuccine puttanesca* (with capers, olives, anchovies, and oregano in a tomato sauce). ◆ Italian ◆ Daily dinner. Reservations required. 355 Convention Center Dr (at Paradise Rd). 369.2305

21 Alpine Village Inn ★★$$ Recalling the town square of a Bavarian village, the main dining room here is replete with quaint street scenes on the walls. The waiters wear lederhosen, the waitresses are in dirndls, and the table service is primarily pewter. Entrées—Wiener schnitzel, beef fondue, sauerbraten, and steaks—are accompanied by a loaf of bread, as many tureens as you can eat of chicken soup, green beans, sauerkraut, potato pancakes, and dessert. Downstairs at the **Rathskeller,** you can enjoy a more casual menu of burgers, pizza, and sandwiches, as well as a piano sing-along. ◆ German ◆ Daily dinner. Reservations recommended. 3003 Paradise Rd (between Riviera Blvd and Convention Center Dr). 734.6888

22 Las Vegas Hilton $$$ When this hotel opened in 1969, Las Vegas had never seen a property with a 2,000-seat theater, 3,000 employees, and more than 1,500 rooms. For a while, Kirk Kerkorian, who financed the $60-million price tag out of his own pocket, stole the spotlight from Howard Hughes, who was in the middle of his own legendary spending spree. When Hilton purchased the property two years later, it became the first major hotel corporation to enter the casino business.

Another 1,500 rooms were added in 1973, making it the largest resort hotel in the world, a title it held until it was eclipsed in 1990 by the **Flamingo Hilton** and then again in 1993 by the new **MGM Grand Hotel and Theme Park.** Today the second runner-up is right next door to the **Las Vegas Convention Center,** and primarily caters to business-people attending the 600 conventions and trade shows that descend here each year. With 250,000 square feet of meeting space, a dozen restaurants, a 10-acre third-floor recreation deck (with a 385,000-gallon pool), a **Youth Hotel** with all-day and all-night baby-sitting services, a theater that's been playing Andrew Lloyd Webber's *Starlight Express* since 1993, and two shopping promenades, guests needn't stray any farther than the immediate vicinity for work or pleasure. The different sections of the hotel are clearly articulated: The vast meeting spaces and ballrooms are connected by a walkway to the **Convention Center,** and the hotel and casino have their own entrances. ◆ 3000 Paradise Rd (between Riviera Blvd and Convention Center Dr). 732.5111, 800/732.7117; fax 794.3611

Within the Las Vegas Hilton:

Las Vegas Hilton Casino This casino is huge: 85,000 square feet filled with thousands of slots and hundreds of table games. The race and sports room is so large it's called a super book; its walls are lined with 46 TV screens. ◆ Daily 24 hours. 732.5111

Benihana Village ★★★$$$ In the most exotic corner of the otherwise ordinary hotel, this popular chain restaurant inhabits a stylized Japanese village, with a trio of dining rooms and bars. The meat, fish, and vegetable dishes are prepared at the table hibachi-style in the main room; Japanese grilled seafood is served in the **Seafood Grille;** and Chinese food is offered in the excellent **Garden of the Dragon.** ◆ Asian ◆ Daily dinner. Reservations recommended. 732.5454

Le Montrachet ★★★★$$$$ In a sophisticated break with the quick-and-copious dining-out theory that rules Las Vegas, this place embodies the essence of French cuisine, European elegance, and artistic attention to detail. Flowers are everywhere, and the table settings are extravagant. The menu is seasonal, and everything—from the pheasant-breast mousse appetizer to such entrées as veal chops with mussel puree to the Swiss chocolate soufflé dessert—consists of only the freshest ingredients prepared with a distinctly French flair in the seasonings and sauces. The sommelier can help you choose one of 400 wines to enjoy with your dinner. ◆ French ◆ Daily dinner. Reservations recommended; jacket required. 732.5454

The Tropicana hotel was the sole anchor of the south end of the Strip for more than three decades, but the intersection of Tropicana Avenue and Las Vegas Boulevard South has been built up considerably recently. With Luxor, MGM Grand, Excalibur, and Hacienda joining Tropicana, the five hotels within walking distance contain nearly 16,000 rooms and approximately the same number of employees. On a busy weekend, the population of this crossroads is greater than that of Carson City, the capital of Nevada.

23 Las Vegas Convention Center This town has been a convention destination since 1935, when 5,000 Southern California Shriners converged here. As early as the mid-1940s, local boosters realized that conventions could fill hotel rooms and casinos during weekdays and low seasons, as well as help Las Vegas improve its image as a place where respectable people could hold business meetings. The Clark County Fair and Recreation Board was established in the boom year of 1955 to supervise events and encourage conventions. It took another four years for the site selection, design, financing, and construction of the convention center to be completed. The $5.3-million complex consisted of a 20,000-square-foot rotunda and a 90,000-square-foot exhibit hall. In 1959, fewer than one hundred conventions took place in Las Vegas, with a total attendance of roughly 50,000.

The current convention center, a 10-minute walk from the Strip, was most recently expanded in 1992. The 33-year-old rotunda was torn down and replaced with a fifth hall, giving the center a total of 1.6-million square feet of exhibitor space. The second-largest show facility in the country, more than 600 conventions and trade shows are held here each year. From the 2,500-participant American Association of Meat Processors to the 130,000 attendees of the Construction Manufacturers Association gathering, conventions pump more than a billion dollars into the Las Vegas annual budget, overcrowd the town in a single bound, and inflate accommodation prices by as much as 300 percent. When you're planning a visit to Las Vegas, you should first find out how many conventioneers will be in town at the time of your trip. ◆ 3150 Paradise Rd (at Convention Center Dr). 892.7550

24 Sun Harbor Budget Suites $ This large and centrally located motel features 639 two-room units with kitchenettes (you'll have to supply your own plates, pots, and silverware). These mini-suites are especially popular with travelers staying a week or longer—the weekly rates further discount the already budget prices. Another plus: It's on the corner of Industrial Road, which is the only westside shortcut to the busy Strip and interstate. ◆ 1500 Stardust Rd (at Industrial Rd). 732.1500

Tricks of the Trade:
Nevada's Adult Entertainment Industry

No wonder visitors to Las Vegas aren't sure how much sin is legal in Sin City. Whether by design or lack of diligence, the city, county, and state governments send mixed messages—from the legality of prostitution to how closely patrons can get to the topless dancers in the area's dozen or so joints.

North Las Vegas, for instance, allows the ladies of the palatial **Palomino Club** to dance totally nude while the clientele partakes of favorite libations within grabbing distance. On the other hand, Clark County, which has jurisdiction over most of the area's topless bars, has determined that alcohol and nude dancing don't mix. Consequently, clubs such as **Cheetah's** and the **Crazy Horse Too** are free to serve booze, as long as dancers keep their panties on and don't make physical contact with customers. Then there's **Henderson,** the booming suburb on the south side of Las Vegas, which requires topless dancers to wear pasties while they work. Despite rumors to the contrary, strippers who work in local topless bars generally draw the line at what they call a "table dance" (essentially a more personalized version of what they do on stage, except that it can cost customers upward of $20 a song).

For those who come to town seeking hands-on experience with the seedier side of Las Vegas, local authorities would like to make a few things clear. First, prostitution is illegal in Clark County, which contains Las Vegas and covers the southern tip of the state. It also is prohibited in four other Nevada counties: Washoe, which contains Reno; Douglas, home of Lake Tahoe; Lincoln, which outlawed prostitution by vote of the people; and Carson City, the state capital and its own county.

That leaves the so-called "Cow Counties" (the 16 rural counties between Las Vegas and Reno), where Nevada's 30 or so legal brothels have become an accepted fact of life. From the infamous **Mustang Ranch** (claiming the longest and most sordid history of the state's brothels) a few miles outside of Reno, to the **Chicken Ranch** near Pahrump (about 65 miles northwest of Las Vegas), as many as 300 working girls ply their trade. The brothels—open 24 hours a day, seven days a week—provide a sure thing for men who can afford their services, which start at $50. Most bordellos even sell T-shirts and other souvenirs. The Nevada Brothel Association, an industry organization that acts as a lobbying arm, boasts that the Silver State's legal prostitutes are less likely to spread sexually transmitted diseases than streetwalkers found in most resort towns, including Las Vegas. State law requires every legal prostitute to register with the state and submit to weekly exams for most sexually transmitted diseases and monthly tests for syphilis and HIV, the virus that can cause AIDS. No applicant can work in a bordello until she has been given a clean bill of health. After more than six years of testing, state health officials claim they have yet to find a prostitute working in one of Nevada's legal brothels infected with HIV.

Of course, none of these controls applies to the illegal prostitutes who have patrolled Las Vegas since it began as a railroad watering hole in 1905. Back then, men frequented what locals called Block 16, the town's original red-light district, which was bordered by First and Second Streets and Ogden and Stewart Avenues. Prostitution thrived in this area until the military moved to town during World War II.

The crude wooden cribs where prostitutes serviced their customers on Block 16 are a distant memory. But the oldest profession, though illegal, is still alive and well in Las Vegas. Instead of working the streets around downtown and along the **Strip,** as hookers did until the early 1980s, most Las Vegas ladies of the evening have merely moved into the massive hotels. For proof, look no further than the Yellow Pages of the local phone book, where you'll find more than 20 pages of suggestive advertisements under the heading "Entertainers." Expensive full-page pitches promote businesses such as Swinging Suzy's and Satisfaction Guaranteed, each one promising to deliver the hottest male and female "dancers" and "entertainers" direct to your hotel room, 24 hours a day.

These businesses are typically nothing more than fronts for pimps and prostitutes. The vice/narcotics bureau of the Las Vegas Metropolitan Police Department has conducted hundreds of undercover sting operations in an attempt to control the pesky call-girl services and has yet to find one that is legitimate. However, the operators usually escape prosecution by claiming that the prostitutes were working on their own—not as their employees.

Of even greater concern to local law-enforcement authorities is the handful of "sex-tease" clubs that have surfaced in recent years. Police say these places, with names such as Black Garter and Nastys, lure lonely men with the promise of sex, force them to purchase nonalcoholic drinks for hundreds of dollars a pop, and then fail to deliver on their sexual promises. Although local laws require such establishments to post signs stating that prostitution is illegal in Clark County, police say that the scantily clad ladies usually give their sales pitch with a wink and a suggestive smile. When the con is complete—or when the sucker comes to his senses—the would-be client is often escorted out by beefy bouncers who do their best to discourage complaints. In fact, few victims of this hustle ever report it. After all, who wants to admit that he was swindled while trying to pay for sex, much less that he struck out in Sin City?

25 Las Vegas Sporting House Covering 65,000 square feet, this is an impressive athletic club. You can work out on dozens of cardiovascular and fitness machines, sign up for an aerobics class, play full-court basketball, volleyball, racquetball, squash, or tennis, run on an outdoor track with parcourse stations, swim laps in the 25-meter indoor pool, or repair to the Jacuzzi, sauna, or steam bath. ♦ Admission. Daily 24 hours. 3025 Industrial Rd (at Stardust Rd). 733.8999

26 Sheraton Desert Inn $$$$ When the original **Desert Inn** (often called the "D.I.") opened in 1950, it was the fifth hotel on the Strip and was known as "Wilbur Clark's joint." Clark started out as a busboy in San Diego restaurants and a crap dealer on gambling ships off the coast of Southern California, and worked his way up to building his dream hotel-casino. But before it was even half finished, Clark ran out of money, and he sweated for two years until Moe Dalitz, underworld boss of Kentucky and Ohio, agreed to complete the job—with Clark remaining on as the law-abiding front man. Once Dalitz had shown how the transition from gangster to executive could be made, mobsters nationwide began migrating to Las Vegas with a vengeance.

Today, with the resort's glass facade, 821 luxurious rooms—including 95 suites—a high-caliber showroom (*Guys and Dolls*, starring Jack Jones as Sky Masterson, Frank Gorshin as Nathan Detroit, and Maureen McGovern as Adelaide opened at press time), huge golf course, complete health club, tennis courts, and award-winning restaurants, it is certainly among the most elegant hotels in town. ITT Sheraton Corp. purchased the complex for $160 million (in cash) in 1993 and at press time had plans to build a 3,500-room, billion-dollar resort–theme park on the adjacent property. ♦ 3145 Las Vegas Blvd S (at Desert Inn Rd). 733.4444, 800/634.6906; fax 733.4676

The MGM Grand, the largest hotel in the world, has 93 elevators; 2,300 miles of electrical wiring; and 15,500 exterior concrete slabs. Some of the hotel's contractors nicknamed it "Monty Hall's Nightmare" because it has 18,000 doors.

Within the Sheraton Desert Inn:

Sheraton Desert Inn Casino Come here to hobnob with the nabobs: A chic clientele glides through the casino, laying down stacks of blacks ($100 chips) at craps and blackjack tables with aplomb. Though the table limits are normally $5,000 per bet, if you want to go higher (and bet $10,000 or even $25,000 at a hand of cards or a roll of the dice), just ask. ♦ Daily 24 hours. 733.4444

Portofino ★★$$$ Even though this restaurant is situated on the open balcony over the casino, its marble floors, black velvet booths, and lush potted foliage create an air of quiet luxury. The menu caters to most pocketbooks and all tastes, offering such affordable dishes as tortellini in vodka-spiked tomato sauce, herb-ricotta–stuffed shells, and bow tie pasta with sweet peppers and pine nuts, as well as the very expensive chateaubriand, rack of lamb with an herb-mustard crust, and lobster tail. ♦ Northern Italian ♦ Tu-Sa dinner. Reservations recommended. 733.4495

Monte Carlo ★★★★$$$$ This is one posh and pricey restaurant—French oil paintings and gilded mirrors on the walls, crystal on the chandeliers and tables, and furniture befitting Versailles set the scene. Plan on killing half a night in these luxe surroundings from the time the appetizers (including littleneck clams, pâté, oysters Rockefeller, clams casino, and seafood crepes with lobster sauce) arrive until you polish off dessert. All is served with a dramatic continental style by suitably snooty waiters. For the main course, choose from such haute dishes as Canadian salmon with lemon-caper butter; fresh Florida stone crabs; filet mignonette sautéed with truffles and goose liver; duck in orange or cherry sauce; or Nevada quail with wild rice. ♦ French ♦ M, Th-Su dinner. Reservations recommended; jacket required. 733.4524

27 Frontier Hotel & Gambling Hall $$ The name of this establishment has undergone a witty evolution. The **Last Frontier** opened in 1942, the second hotel on the infant Strip and the last to embrace a Western motif. The building was razed in 1955 and replaced with the **New Frontier**, which, in the spirit of the times, had an outerspace theme; it was demolished in 1966. A year later Howard Hughes bought it and gave birth to the rein-carnated hotel with its present moniker. The Elardi family took over in 1988, and opted to retain the name.

In addition to the original 500 rooms, there

are 500 more in the modern **Atrium Suites Tower**—15 floors of reasonably priced two-room suites overlooking a picturesque lagoon and courtyard. ♦ 3120 Las Vegas Blvd S (at Fashion Show Dr). 794.8200, 800/634.6966; fax 794.8326

Within the Frontier Hotel & Gambling Hall:

Frontier Gambling Hall This casino is a favorite haunt of old-timers, who gamble here like in the good old days—before the MBAs, CPAs, and PhDs started running the show. It sports one of the only bingo rooms on the Strip. Single-deck blackjack is the norm. This is also the last joint in town where you can take 10 times odds on a one-dollar pass-line bet (you can get 10 times your money back on a $1 bet). ♦ Daily 24 hours. 794.8200

Margarita's ★$$ Warm-from-the-griddle tortillas (not chips), along with guacamole, bean dip, and salsa, are brought to your table when you sit down, possibly to fuel the decision-making process of selecting an entrée from the extensive menu. Tacos, burritos, enchiladas, tostadas, fajitas, and tamales are served, and the *especiales* include *carne asada* (steak with spices), chile Colorado (chunks of beef cooked in a red-chili sauce), and *camarones* (shrimp). If you're really hungry, try one of the special-plate dinners. *Margaritas grandes* come in 45-ounce stemmed glasses (which you're free to keep). ♦ Mexican ♦ Daily breakfast, lunch, and dinner. Reservations recommended. 794.8200

St. Thomas Seafood Grotto ★$$$ Water rushes over a rocky scarp, and stone walls enclose a small brook and ponds teeming with colorful carp: This is as close to creekside dining as you'll get in the Mojave Desert. The fare features steamed clams, with linguine or casino-style (on the half-shell with bacon, herbs, tomato, and parmesan cheese), along with smoked salmon, oysters, *coquilles St. Thomas* (scallops, crab, and shrimp in a mushroom-cream sauce), stir-fried shrimp or scampi, sesame-ginger chicken, and steaks. A wide variety of fresh fish is offered, including blackened ahi, fresh halibut, mahimahi, charbroiled trout, sea bass, and snapper. ♦ Steak/Seafood ♦ Daily breakfast, lunch, and dinner. Reservations recommended. 794.8200

28 Fashion Show Mall If the retail anchors of this mall—**Neiman Marcus, Saks Fifth Avenue, May Company, Dillards,** and **Bullocks**—don't have what you're looking for, one of the 145 boutiques surely will. **Mr. Boxer** sells boxer shorts, **Mr. Hat** hawks you-know-what, and the **American Sock Company**'s wares are equally predictable. **West of Dallas** features Southwestern art and artifacts. The **Antique Emporium** has an eclectic collection of jukeboxes, Coke and slot machines, gas pumps, cash registers, old neon, and more. And the **Disney Store** is full

of cartoon paraphernalia. For a mildly intellectual thrill, check out the **American Museum of Historical Documents**' presentation of important papers—for example, a handwritten letter from Albert Einstein explaining the theory of relativity, which sells for a cool $1.2 million. ♦ M-F 10AM-9PM; Sa 10AM-7PM; Su noon-6PM. 3200 Las Vegas Blvd S (at Spring Mountain Rd). 369.8382

Within the Fashion Show Mall:

Chin's ★★★★$$$ Featuring modern decor designed by **Jim Cheng,** an award-winning architect, and incredibly satisfying food, this gourmet Chinese restaurant has a loyal following of locals and visitors. Hong Kong–born owner Tola Chin's imprint is on every dish. Recipes she invented, such as shredded chicken salad or crispy pudding, are often copied in other restaurants. Dim sum is offered at lunch, or you can choose from a menu that features shrimp puffs, crispy duck, lobster with mushrooms, and vegetables with meat or seafood. Special dishes are prepared on request. A piano player provides entertainment in the lounge. ♦ Chinese ♦ Daily lunch and dinner. Reservations recommended. 3200 Las Vegas Blvd S (at Spring Mountain Rd). 733.8899

Morton's ★★★★$$$ This branch of the Chicago-based steak house is regarded as one of the best restaurants in Las Vegas. The men's club atmosphere has been retained with a polished oak barroom, comfortable booths, and a paneled boardroom for large parties. Of course steak is the raison d'être here. But the broiled sea scallops wrapped in bacon, whole Maine lobster, and lemon-oregano chicken are also scrumptious. If you still have room after downing the hearty portions, the strawberries with sabayon sauce will do nicely. ♦ Steak house ♦ Daily dinner. Reservations recommended. 3200 Las Vegas Blvd S (at Spring Mountain Rd). 893.0703

The Circus Circus buffet serves more than 12,000 meals a day, making the hotel the world's largest commercial eating establishment.

Howard Hughes purchased the Desert Inn in 1967 after his famous stay in the resort's top-floor penthouse: He checked in and simply wouldn't leave. Then Hughes, bothered by the lights from the Silver Slipper Hotel & Casino sign across the street, asked the management to dim the sign at a certain hour. When they refused, he bought that hotel, too.

Restaurants/Clubs: Red   **Hotels:** Blue
Shops/ ♦ Outdoors: Green   **Sights/Culture:** Black

Working the Main Room

Elvis. Frank. Sammy. Dean. Liza. Wayne. Siegfried . . . and don't forget Roy. The Las Vegas showroom legends need only a first-name introduction, their presence looming larger than life on casino marquees visible a mile away.

Celebrity acts were part of the Las Vegas formula from the earliest days of the **Strip.** The **Flamingo Hotel**'s infamous founder, Benjamin "Bugsy" Siegel, ignored the city's Western frontier-town image when he opened his dream hotel in late 1946. He wanted to impress his Hollywood and East Coast gangster pals by building a ritzy "carpet joint" to rival the casinos in Havana. This feat required stars. Jimmy Durante and Lena Horne were the first **Flamingo** headliners.

In short order, Las Vegas was the self-proclaimed "Entertainment Capital of the World," a billing that publicity types still perpetuate. The city didn't claim more stars in residence than New York or Chicago; it was simply a novelty to have so many greats playing in this remote desert location. Hotel owners forked out ridiculous amounts to book big names, knowing the attendant media hype would lure high rollers to the gaming tables and thus make it worthwhile: Liberace set a well-publicized record when the **Riviera** paid him $50,000 per week to perform at the hotel's opening in 1955.

Over the years, certain stars came to define a genre of entertainment known as the "Vegas style." Some seemed particularly attuned to the Vegas milieu; comedians Durante, Phil Harris, and Joe E. Lewis flourished disproportionately to their popularity elsewhere. They were "down-front entertainers," as Sammy Davis Jr. put it, and they knew how to work the room, interacting with the audience and making everyone feel as if they were witnessing a unique event. As longtime *Las Vegas Review-Journal* columnist Forrest Duke defined the scene in the early 1960s: "These are primarily nightclub performers, their fans are nightclub patrons, and people who can afford to go to a nightclub usually can afford to drop some money in the casino on the way out."

By 1960, the **Sands Hotel** had a lock on the biggest names. Frank Sinatra was a heavyweight draw on his own, but the hotel capitalized on current headlines, presenting "The Summit at the Sands." The entire "Rat Pack" (Sinatra, Davis, Dean Martin, Peter Lawford, and Joey Bishop) held court in the **Sands's** showroom for three weeks while in town filming *Ocean's Eleven* (VIPs in the audience included presidential hopeful John F. Kennedy). The town would be the Rat Pack's turf from that day on: Martin opened the **MGM Grand Hotel** (now **Bally's**) in 1973 and played there until health problems forced him to quit in 1992. Sinatra celebrated his 77th birthday at the **Desert Inn.** When Davis died in 1990, the hotels on the Strip dimmed their lights in tribute for 10 minutes.

As the 1970s approached, Las Vegas was changing—growing bigger and more outlandish. Nightclub acts seemed like tea parties compared to the garish "feather shows" that had been getting more extravagant every year since they had first been imported from France in 1958. When the **International** (now the **Las Vegas Hilton**) opened in 1969, Barbra Streisand christened the **Showroom.** But she returned to her movie career, and management was desperate for a bigger star than the usual to fill the 1,500-seat theater—then the city's largest. Coincidentally, rock singer Elvis Presley was seeking a new direction for his career. It was the perfect marriage.

In the eyes of young people caught up in the 1960s revolution, Elvis had degenerated from the dangerous rebel of the 1950s to B-movie square. Instead of trying to establish himself with a new generation, Presley chose to reconnect with his following from the 1950s by donning a sequined jumpsuit, beefing up his rock combo with a full orchestra, and choreographing a few karate moves into his act. The rest is show biz history. More than 25 million people saw The King play 837 dates at the **Hilton** through 1976, and hotel officials claim there was never an empty seat. Indeed, it's reputed that fire inspectors were bribed to look the other way while an extra 500 fans were stuffed in for each show. In return, the hotel had no qualms about giving its top star the 5,000-square-foot apartment on the 30th floor: the **Elvis Suite.**

Meanwhile, the **Hilton** had another star who wasn't shy about upping his level of tastelessness to match the city's garish persona: Wladziu Valentino Liberace—known by his surname to the public and as "Lee" to his friends. He was a natural; back in 1952, Liberace made waves by trading in his black tux for a gold lamé smoking jacket. By the 1970s, Vegas had become synonymous with kitsch, and Liberace was welcomed into the fold, fueling the image with his floor-length furs, rhinestone jackets, and a harness rigging that allowed him to "fly" across the stage. The flamboyant pianist, who died in 1987, left behind costumes and custom-made pianos that are enshrined in the museum that bears his name (see page 78).

This first wave of headliners hit the Strip with some degree of star power already in place, but a story of the rags-to-riches variety also happened in Las Vegas during this period. Siegfried (Fischbacher) and Roy (Horn) first came to the **Tropicana Hotel**'s *Folies Bergere* as a specialty magic act in 1966, then secured a longer spot in the **Stardust Hotel**'s *Lido de Paris*. (The two had met several years earlier on a German cruise ship. Siegfried was the ship's magician; Roy, a homesick cabin boy who volunteered his pet cheetah for the act as an excuse to smuggle it on board.) They discovered that simply exchanging the traditional rabbit for a more exotic animal made the illusions more dramatic and added an aura of danger.

The duo hooked up with Irvin Feld, who had turned the **Ringling Brothers and Barnum & Bailey Circus** from a dying tradition into a million-dollar enterprise. First Feld signed them up for two **NBC**-TV specials in 1979. Then, having won their trust, he pitched a brilliantly simple plan: The Strip had stars, and it had production shows. Why not have both in one? *Beyond Belief* opened at the **Frontier Hotel** in late 1981 and made stars of Siegfried and Roy, who played an estimated 3,500 performances through 1987.

By then the team had a new gimmick—rare white tigers—and a deal to go to **The Mirage,** where their act raised the standards of showroom spectacle from near-naked women, circus trappings, and hyperactive musical numbers to a symphonic score and tasteful Broadway production values assimilated from the director of *Les Misérables* and the production designer of *Cats.*

A self-made product of the Vegas star machine, Wayne Newton was only 15 and needed a work permit to perform in the **Fremont Hotel** when he came from Phoenix with his brother Jerry in 1957. Newton might have been trapped in the lounge caste system forever had it not been for a booking on "The Jackie Gleason Show," which led to a meeting with Bobby Darin, who supervised the recording of Newton's 1961 breakthrough hit "Danke Schoen." Throughout the next 10 years, there were other chart-toppers for Wayne, but his bankability came from the reputation he built for having *the* must-see show on the Strip, performing 40 weeks a year at the **Sands, Desert Inn,** and **Frontier.**

When Elvis died in 1977, Vegas needed a star to fill the void. Newton was happy to take over not just the **Hilton** showroom, but to expand on the King's musical arrangements and his performance style as well. Elvis never landed onstage in a flying saucer, but Newton did, to the strains of "Thus Spake Zarathustra," zipping off his space suit to reveal a natty tuxedo jumpsuit. Leading his 36-piece orchestra through a distilled history of American music—from "Shenandoah" to "Bridge Over Troubled Water"— each show seems like the performance of his lifetime. Nearly every song is extended with an extra reprise, just in case the audience feels like giving him a standing ovation. And by the time he's played a plethora of instruments in one tune and implored the

ushers to "lock the doors because this crowd is so hot tonight," they have dutifully given him several.

Today, the stars that helped build the town are now a niche market, and headline acts are but a shadow of the standard established during the glory days of the 1960s and 1970s. As the city zeroes in on families, showroom entertainment is becoming an endangered species. The downswing really began more than a decade ago, when hotel owners failed to groom a new generation of performers to take over from the aging perennials; simultaneously, rock 'n' roll's youthful audience turned away from the lounge lizards who made the city famous. The economics of the music business changed as well. Performers with clout can make much more money playing a one-night gig in a sports arena than from an extended run in a 1,200-seat showroom. The majority of Las Vegas visitors may still be over 40, but they prefer such classic rockers as Eric Clapton over crooners like Engelbert Humperdinck.

By 1993, only three celebrity rooms were still operating: **Bally's, Caesars Palace,** and the **Desert Inn.** Today, **Caesars** does not book an act every weekend, and the **Desert Inn**'s status as the last refuge for veteran Vegas mainstays such as Sinatra and Liza Minelli has been lost. But the **MGM Grand Hotel and Theme Park**—with its 650-seat room—has taken the **Desert Inn**'s place and kept the count at three.

While it may be harder to find the stars on certain weekends, they're not likely to totally disappear. Everyone from Noel Coward to Cheech & Chong has played Vegas, and the modern-day Strip still has a reserve of dependable headliners. Tom Jones's and Engelbert Humperdinck's sex appeal has spanned several generations. Don Rickles has trod the boards in Las Vegas every year since 1959, and such younger comedians as Dennis Miller, Louie Anderson, and Rita Rudner have become steady draws. Pop illusionist David Copperfield is so successful in Las Vegas he built a mansion here. And the city has embraced the country music boom, reaching out to stars such as Willie Nelson, Reba MacEntire, and George Strait. A showroom full of cowboy hats might seem odd at first, but it does take things full circle to the town's frontier origins.

ART BY ROLANDO CORUJO

29 Treasure Island $$$ With swaying palms atop cliffs bordering the "ocean" and a colonial Polynesian village, this $300-million, 3,000-room megaresort is a veritable South Pacific island unto itself. Every hour and a half from 3:30PM to 10PM, a lifesize pirate schooner sails into the bay and engages a British frigate in a dramatic battle, a cannonade causing impressively major damage to both ships. The crews patch up their battered craft, sail back to their respective corners, and repeat the Sisyphean performance an hour and twenty minutes later. ♦ 3300 Las Vegas Blvd S (at Spring Mountain Rd). 894.7111, 800/944.7444; fax 894.7414

Within Treasure Island:

Buccaneer Bay ★★★★$$$ With many nooks and alcoves for intimacy, the decor at this dramatic restaurant includes treasure chests, exotic cabinets, and simulated foot-thick windows overlooking **Treasure Island**'s "Bay"—complete with battleships. Not only do guests hear the guns roar, but they also feel the heat as flames break out on the ships. The theme-inspired menu covers a unique selection of seafood, beef, lamb, and desserts. Among the house specialties are Buccaneer clams (casino) and oysters topped with smoked salmon and hollandaise, lobster bisque under a puff-pastry dome, smoked salmon Napoleon (smoked salmon and herbed cream cheese between layers of fine pastry), and Pirate's Plunder for dessert— an amazing chocolate treasure chest filled with coconut rum mousse, a white chocolate treasure map, and dark chocolate cake. ♦ Continental ♦ Daily dinner. Reservations recommended. 894.7111

Cirque du Soleil Circus Circus it ain't! This nouvelle experience is a combination of theater, dance, music, comedy, and acrobatics. The whole wild show takes place in a single ring, without animals or spoken communication, and involves the audience to an unprecedented degree. As at *Siegfried & Roy*, money can't be an object to audience members (tickets are the *second* most expensive in town); if it isn't, this is a Las Vegas must-see. (For more details, see "A Review of Revues," page 50.) ♦ Tu-Su 7:30PM, 10:30PM. 894.7722

30 Sands Hotel $$$ Pachyderms and pyramids be damned! Resisting the theme trend of other places on the Strip, this place has steadfastly held onto the grandeur of its glory years—the 1950s and 1960s—when Frank Sinatra and Dean Martin owned points in the joint and the "Rat Pack" jammed in the **Copa Room.** Carrying the torch for the time when Las Vegas was a brash young boomtown and you could rub elbows with a famous gangster or two, the brass porte cochere was the ne plus ultra in glitz almost three decades ago. The 720-room hotel last expanded in 1965 with a 16-story cylindrical tower addition. Besides the elegant eateries (**Xanadu** and the **Regency**), the **Garden Buffet** serves breakfast, lunch, and dinner all-you-can-eat style and the **Shangri-La** coffee shop is open around-the-clock. At press time, *Glitz*, a new show starring Marty Allen and Steve Rossi and mounted by the same producer as the long-running *Legends in Concert* (at the **Imperial Palace**), was scheduled to open in the **Copa Room.** Billed as a spectacular based on the history of Las Vegas entertainment from the Rat Pack days to the present, it is meant to be a show for the whole family, featuring a three-screen, multimedia background, a new group of Copa Girls, plus singers, specialty acts, and a live band. ♦ 3355 Las Vegas Blvd S (at Sands Ave). 733.5000, 800/634.8901; fax 732.1047

Within the Sands Hotel:

Sands Casino Affording the little guy a chance to sit in the big pit and feel like a high roller, the baccarat minimum here is only $5. There are 28 blackjack tables, a few with $2 and $3 minimums, but mostly $5 and $10; maximums top off at $2,000. This gambling house's offerings are completed by four crap tables, three roulette tables, and 800 slot machines. ♦ Daily 24 hours. 733.5000

Xanadu ★★★$$$ The menu bears the title, "A mildy wild steak house," and the highly original dinner menu covers the gamut, from an 11-ounce New York strip to a tenderloin of beef stuffed with roasted red peppers, mushrooms, other vegetables, and provolone cheese. Seafood includes pan-seared scallops and salmon sautéed with fresh herbs and a zinfandel sauce. Breast of chicken is stuffed with lobster, crab, and roasted red pepper and served with *español* sauce, or filled with wild rice, prosciutto, and garlic-herb butter. A hot chocolate fondue, served with skewered fresh strawberries and melon slices, and surrounded by billows of simulated fog complete the fixed-price dinner. ♦ Steak/Seafood ♦ M-Tu, F-Su dinner. Reservations recommended. 733.5453

Frank Sinatra first played in Las Vegas at the Desert Inn in 1951.

Restaurants/Clubs: Red   **Hotels:** Blue
Shops/♀Outdoors: Green   **Sights/Culture:** Black

Regency Ristorante ★★★$$$ Regal decor and a traditional gourmet menu provide elegant dining at this establishment. The Italian sampler for two includes fried mozzarella, stuffed mushrooms, shrimp scampi, and fried zucchini. The pasta selection features shells filled with veal, beef, sausage, spinach, and ricotta cheese; linguine with clams; and baked *mostaccioli* (short pasta in a casserole with ricotta and mozza-rella cheeses topped with marinara sauce). The chef's specialty is *vermicelli bella vista,* with a sauce of shrimp, crab, prosciutto, and julienne vegetables. Lobster *française,* broiled lamb chops, and seafood lasagna are also terrific. All this and imaginative preparations of seafood, veal, fowl, and creamy, classic desserts. ♦ Continental/Italian ♦ W-Su dinner. Reservations recommended. 733.5453

31 Casino Royale Formerly **Denny's, Travelodge,** and the old **Nob Hill Casino** next door, this joint is now a 150-room hotel with a 60,000-square-foot casino and a six-story, 300-car garage. Its small pit is filled with one- and two-dollar blackjack tables, along with the usual craps and roulette tables, slots, and video poker. Visitors in the know head for the upstairs lounge and snack bar when hunger strikes. Big burgers, chili dogs, Belgian waffles, shrimp cocktails, sandwiches, break-fasts, and draft beer can all be had for a song. The five window tables (plus four seats at the small counter) directly face **The Mirage,** so if it's after dark and the winds are calm, you can eat, drink, and have a ringside seat at one of the best shows in town. ♦ Daily 24 hours. 3411 Las Vegas Blvd S (between Sands Ave and E Flamingo Rd). 737.3500

Harrah's

32 Harrah's Hotel $$$ The riverboat facade adds a folksy element of Americana to the urban hubbub of hotel-casinos surrounding this lodging. The Mississippi delta theme is judiciously invoked inside, the lounge and restaurants generating a congenial New Orleans ambience without becoming mawkish. The two towers (connected via circuitous hallways) feature 1,700 sizable quarters with free Showtime movies; the rooms fronting the **Captain Tower** have a magnificent view of the Strip and **The Mirage**'s volcano. For entertainment, there's the 580-seat **Commander's Theatre,** featuring *Spellbound,* "a concert of illusion", as well as the 300-seat **Evening at the Improv** comedy club. ♦ 3475 Las Vegas Blvd S (between Sands Ave and E Flamingo Rd). 369.5000, 800/634.6765; fax 369.5008

Within Harrah's Hotel:

Harrah's Casino Friendly dealers and pit bosses are the rule here, more so than at most other Strip casinos. At one group of blackjack tables known as the "Party Pit," the dealers are creative jokers who clown around with the players, encouraging such silliness as clanging a bell when someone hits a natural. This conviviality, as well as the excellent cocktail service and some two-dollar minimums, always assures a crowd at the table games. Slot players will never feel left out: There's one automated opponent for every room in the hotel. ♦ Daily 24 hours. 369.5000

Joe's Bayou ★$$ The Cajun theme reigns supreme at this eatery with its tin walls and authentic Louisiana home cookin'. Oyster shooters, hot and spicy Cajun wings, Louisiana gumbo, barbecued chicken, pork chops, blackened snapper and halibut, shrimp Creole, and jambalaya—all hearty, stick-to-the-ribs fare—and it comes with an extra helping of Southern hospitality. ♦ Cajun ♦ Daily dinner. Reservations recommended. 369.5000

"I personally own about 40 years of great Las Vegas memories. If I were to pick a favorite, it would probably be our series of summit meetings for Jack Entratter at the Sands in the '50s—Frank Sinatra, Dean Martin, Peter Lawford, Joey Bishop, and myself. We were all in town at the same time, making a picture or just hanging out.

"Each of us was supposed to take a different night, but every night turned out to be everybody's night. Danny Thomas would drop in; people working at other hotels would fall by. After the second show, the action would move into the casino where we would all deal blackjack or craps, then wind up the early morning by taking over the lounge.

"How will they ever be able to top this? It would be like having Bruce Springsteen, Prince, Michael Jackson, and Sting on stage at the same time in a nightclub room that seats fewer than 500 people. It could never happen again."

Sammy Davis Jr., 1984

Court of Two Gators This skylighted lounge is set in a four-story courtyard with Vieux Carré overtones: wrought-iron railings on the balconies, louvered doorways, and bands providing the *bon temps* for dancers from 8PM all through the night. ♦ Free. Daily 24 hours. 369.5000

33 The Mirage $$$$ No doubt about it. With its fire-breathing volcano, indoor rain forest, white-tiger and dolphin habitats, huge aquarium, the *Siegfried & Roy* extravaganza, high-roller casino, and overall opulence, this 3,000-room resort is the ultimate in Vegas overkill. It's also the top tourist destination in the city.

Enter these grounds and you leave the desert far behind. A dozen waterfalls flow into a giant lagoon, ringed by hundreds of towering palm trees. A 54-foot waterfall cascades over the volcano, which punctually erupts nightly every half hour (if the wind is too strong, red lights signal the volcano's temporary dormancy). The lush tropical understory grows more and more convincing as time goes by. Beyond the four bronze dolphins standing sentry at the front door, the theme continues beneath a 100-foot-high glass dome. A thick canopy of palms presides over more waterfalls and tropical foliage. After a drink in the **Lagoon Saloon**, take a peek at the 57-foot-long, 200,000-gallon aquarium full of colorful ocean life behind the registration desk. Whitewashed rattan and caning lend a light accent to the rooms' bright color scheme. Allow plenty of time to explore the seemingly unending amenities: The resort encompasses three million square feet. ♦ 3400 Las Vegas Blvd S (between Spring Mountain Rd and W Flamingo Rd). 791.7111, 800/627.6667; fax 791.7446

Within The Mirage Hotel:

The Mirage Casino The action here is rammin' and jammin', with more money passing back and forth on the craps and baccarat tables in a month than some banks, even countries, see in a year. The atrium across from the **Caribe Cafe** features $500 slot machines and $100 video poker (9/6 with a $150,000 royal jackpot on the max $500 bet). ♦ Daily 24 hours. 791.7111

KOKOMO'S

Kokomo's ★★★$$$ Add a few Mai Tais to the tropical foliage and longhouse decor here and you might actually believe you're in Fiji. The menu changes seasonally, and highlights might include broiled sea bass West Indies (served on a bed of wilted spinach with mustard, butter-cream sauce, and sautéed shiitake mushrooms), shrimp and scallop fettuccine, sautéed garlic shrimp, grilled swordfish, lemony herb-crusted roasted half chicken, smoked roast-pork loin, and steaks. The desserts are always sinful. ♦ American ♦ Daily lunch and dinner. Reservations recommended. 791.7111

Moongate ★$$$$ Passing through the restaurant's eponymous entryway, a footbridge takes you to a tranquil courtyard containing a pagoda shaded by the graceful spread of a maple tree. It's not worth the big bucks, but if shark's fin is your thing, order the soup made with shark's fin, crabmeat, and shredded chicken in a light chicken-based broth. Or try the salt-and-pepper shrimp, soothing *moo shu* plates (stir-fried vegetables and meat served with crepes), whole steamed fish, Peking duck, walnut chicken, and more. ♦ Chinese ♦ Daily dinner. Reservations recommended. 791.7111

Mikado ★★$$$$ The decor here is the yang to **Moongate**'s yin: square, powerful, and commanding. Bright acrylic Japanese murals grace the walls. Appetizers include sashimi, sushi, shiitake mushrooms, yakitori, and deep-fried tofu. All entrées, such as seafood tempura, vegetarian delight, and steaks, are served with a shrimp appetizer, miso soup, Mikado salad (iceberg lettuce, red cabbage, and tomatoes topped with ginger dressing), vegetables, tea, and sherbet. ♦ Japanese ♦ Daily dinner. Reservations recommended. 791.7111

Bistro ★★$$$$ Under a stained-glass ceiling and overlooking the casino, this is the place **The Mirage** high rollers come for classic French fare. Though the menu changes seasonally, some of its highlights include venison, lobster *en croute* (in a pastry shell) with truffles and spinach, pheasant, sirloin roquefort, rack of lamb Melba, and Lake Superior whitefish. ♦ Continental ♦ Daily dinner. Reservations required. 791.7111

Lounge acts may be a dying tradition, but they helped put Las Vegas on the map in the 1950s. The biggest lounge star at that time was singer and trumpeter Louis Prima, who put on "The Wildest Show in Vegas" from midnight to 6AM. Prima first teamed up with his wife, singer Keely Smith, and saxophonist Sam Butera at the Sahara's Casbar Lounge in 1954. Prima died in 1978, but Butera and Smith still perform together.

Dolphins Imported from various marine facilities, these six Atlantic bottle-nosed dolphins now call the big pools in back of the hotel home. Escorted tours are conducted in a glassed-in viewing area; the underwater scene is accented with recorded clicks, squeaks, and whistles of dolphin talk. There's a short video of the 1991 birth of Squirt, being helped to the surface by his mama for his first breath of air. At the end of the tour, you're free to wander around the pool area, have a bite at the **Dolphin Snack Bar**, or peruse the souvenirs at the **Dolphin Shop.** ◆ Admission. Tours leave every five minutes M-F 11AM-7PM; Sa-Su 9AM-7PM. Behind pool area. 791.7111

Tigers These rare, royal white tigers are descendants of the felines donated to the US in 1958 by an Indian prince. Their habitat artistically reflects their heritage: white palms, a colorful tiled mural, elephant statues, and a big pool that the cats frequently dip into. A tape, produced and narrated by Siegfried and Roy (who own the tigers and use them in their illusion act), runs continuously on screens above the large glass viewing windows, and acts as a video biography of the big cats. ◆ Free. Daily 24 hours. 791.7111

Siegfried & Roy It's fitting that the world's preeminent illusionists stage their show at an establishment named **The Mirage.** The extraordinary sets, stunning costumes, and, of course, action-packed and theatrical illusions simply must be seen to be believed. (And even then, you never know when to trust your eyes.) When a mechanical dragon lifts Roy in its bionic claw, deposits him in a metal container 20 feet in the air, and then crushes it like a tin can, you're simply stunned. And when Siegfried is impaled by a spear, you'll have experienced "shock magic" firsthand. Note, however, that tickets not only are the most expensive in town (they're triple the price of other shows), but also the most difficult to procure. If you're not a guest at the hotel, line up at 6:30AM at **The Mirage** box office up to three days prior to the show of your choice, and wait, wait, wait, wait. ◆ M-Tu, Th-Su 7PM, 10:30PM. 792.7777

34 Imperial Palace $$$ Nevada's only casino with an Asian motif boasts 2,700 hotel rooms, a 70,000-square-foot casino, five restaurants, and two buffets. But the real entertainment here is automotive: 200 antique, classic, and special-interest cars that span a century of vehicular history are featured in a superb display. The hotel is the state's largest employer of people with disabilities, and wins considerable recognition for its personnel policies. It has an abundance of facilities for physically impaired guests, including 30

rooms with roll-in showers and transfer wheelchairs, a hydraulic lift at the swimming pool, and an infrared transmitting system for sound enhancement in the showroom. ◆ 3535 Las Vegas Blvd S (at E Flamingo Rd). 731.3311, 800/634.6441 outside Las Vegas; fax 735.8578

Within the Imperial Palace:

Imperial Palace Casino At first glance, this is a routine casino, with the usual table games in a big pit and slot and video-poker machines crowding the rest of the floor. But look around and you'll notice the confluence of Asian elegance and technological sophistication. Hissing dragon heads leap out from the carved beams overhead. The sports book is unique, consisting of six levels of tiered clubhouse-style seating—with an eight-inch color monitor at each chair for close-up views of the big screens. ◆ Daily 24 hours. 731.3311, 800/351.7400 outside Las Vegas

Embers ★★$$$ Oysters with creamed spinach, prosciutto, and hollandaise is the specialty at this dining spot above the lobby. Rich, burgundy-striped walls, a recessed ceiling, and tufted booths create a comfortable atmosphere in which to enjoy a wide range of menu items. Good choices are the pasta, chicken, and steak preparations, as well as Alaskan king crab and charbroiled salmon that's tender, juicy, and tasty. There's also a comfortable piano bar that offers a fine selection of wine by the glass. ◆ Continental ◆ W-Su dinner. Reservations recommended. 731.3311, 800/751.3400 outside Las Vegas

"One night at a dinner in Los Angeles, sometime in 1946, a friend of mine said to me, 'Why don't we run up to Vegas and look at this new town?' I said, 'For what?' He said, 'Let's just look around.' The next day we jumped aboard a DC-3 and landed at McCarran Field, hired a car, and proceeded to drive around. There was nothing. Not even a coyote. We stopped at a corner where there was a sign stuck in the ground that said 'For Sale.' My friend went to a phone, called the number on the sign, and found out what it was all about. It turned out to be a piece of property containing a thousand acres at one dollar an acre. So, the great wheeler and dealer that I was, I said to my friend, 'What the hell are we gonna do with it?' He replied, 'Let's hang on to it, it's cheap enough.' I said, 'Don't be ridiculous!' We never made the deal.

"Cut . . . dissolve . . . The property still exists across the road from the Tropicana. Never had courage enough, up to this day, to ask any real estate person what it is worth, knowing the answer might give me a heart attack." (Across from the Tropicana today are the MGM Grand Hotel and Theme Park and the Excalibur Hotel/Casino/Las Vegas.)"

Frank Sinatra

Auto Collection This 250-car collection consists of rare, famous, and infamous automobiles, trucks, tractors, motorcycles, and fire engines. The **Duesenberg Room** houses $50-million worth of the Model J Doozeys. A half-dozen presidential conveyances are in residence, including FDR's unrestored 1936 V-16 Cadillac. Elvis's 1976 Cadillac, Al Capone's bulletproof 1930 Cadillac, and W.C. Fields's 1938 Cadillac are on display, as are the King of Siam's 1928 Delage, an 1898 Haynes-Apperson that runs on cleaning fluid, and one of only 51 1947 Tuckers ever manufactured. ◆ Admission (coupons for free entry are available). Daily 9:30AM-11:30PM. Fifth floor of parking structure

Legends in Concert In this G-rated, good-natured production, eight or so uncanny impersonators take the stage each night out of a cast of two dozen late and living luminaries: Cher, Michael, Madonna, Dolly, Kenny, Elton, Tom Jones, Buddy Holly, et al. The Elvis look-alikes are the best of the weird wannabes. But Liberace impersonator Daryl Wagner steals the show. Your senses are guaranteed to be assailed by the 24 projectors flashing 1,000 slides and video on three screens, strobes, lasers, and a live six-piece band. Headphones are available for the hearing impaired. ◆ M-Sa 7:30PM, 10:30PM. 731.3111, 800/351.7400 outside Las Vegas

35 **Flamingo Hilton** $$$ For those who saw the movie *Bugsy*, be forewarned: Don't come here expecting to find nostalgic remnants of the past. Ben "Bugsy" Siegel's venerable rose garden, planted by the gardening gangster himself, was paved over in 1990. And his penthouse was demolished in 1993 when the original **Oregon Building** made way for the new water park. The only nod to the hotel's founder is his name, in lights, on the **Celebrity Theater**. Now a Hilton property, the five towers contain a grand total of 3,450 rooms, making it the third-largest hotel in town (and the fourth in the world). ◆ 3555 Las Vegas Blvd S (between Sands Ave and E Flamingo Rd). 733.3111, 800/732.2111; fax 733.3528

Within the Flamingo Hilton:

Flamingo Casino This casino not only sprawls from one end of the building to the other, but bridges a side alley. During one of the hotel's expansions, a motel and its parking lot were torn down and **O'Sheas Casino** went up in their place. Between the main joint (with the higher limits) and the smaller **O'Sheas** (with the lower), there's gambling for all budgets. ◆ Daily 24 hours. 733.3111

Beef Barron ★★★$$$ A rare occurrence on the modern Strip, this 250-seat room has retained the atmosphere of the Old West. A number of guns from Barron Hilton's collection, plus longhorn chandeliers and mounted deer heads decorate the walls. A crackling grill provides the sounds and smells of prime ribs being prepared much as they were 100 years ago during the famous cattle drives. The tradition of serving the cowboys as soon as they are seated is preserved here: "Texas caviar"—black-eyed peas marinated in oil and vinegar, spiced with green pepper and pimento—is presented almost immediately. Among other specialties are black bean soup with sherry, sirloins, filet mignon, porter-house, double lamb chops, a steak and lobster combination, chicken, ribs, roast duckling, and rack of lamb. ◆ Steak house ◆ Daily dinner. Reservations recommended. 733.3502

Alta Villa ★★$$ A truly Tuscan environment awaits diners here, the stone floor and ivy-covered trellis creating a rustic respite from the town's glut of glitzy restaurants. The risotto (with fish or vege-tables) is superb, and the eggplant Florentine appetizer is a meal in itself. The minestrone is ladled from a 25-gallon kettle simmering in front of the exposed kitchen. Veal is the specialty; order a cutlet, or have it prepared *alla milanese* (breaded and fried). Other fare includes *chicken piccata* (sautéed in lemon and butter), salmon, calamari, pasta, and pizza. Save some room for the fruit-topped zabaglione for dessert. ◆ Italian ◆ Daily dinner. Reservations recommended. 733.3111

The Great Radio City Music Hall Spectacular Starring the **Radio City Rockettes** and Susan Anton, this lively show celebrates the greatest stage productions from the legendary theater's long history, including the famous "Parade of the Wooden Soldiers" from the "Christmas Spectacular." (See "A Review of Revues," page 50) ◆ Daily 7:45PM, 10:45PM. 733.3111

Robert Goulet married his third wife, Vera Novak, on 17 October 1982 in the Little Chapel of the West located on a landscaped plot in front of the Hacienda Hotel. Glenn Ford "gave her away," and Wayne Newton was best man.

Restaurants/Clubs: Red   **Hotels:** Blue
Shops/ ❦ Outdoors: Green   **Sights/Culture:** Black

⟨A⟨SARS PALA⟨⟨

36 Caesars Palace $$$$ Before **The Mirage** came along in 1989, this hotel-casino reigned supreme in sheer opulence and sky-high wagering limits. But though its splashier contender has volcanoes and rain forests, **Caesars,** now an ITT-owned property, still has a loyal following.

And the competition has actually made it easier to get here: The moving sidewalk that delivers people from the south exit of **The Mirage** back to the Strip conveniently ends a few steps away from one that whisks visitors into the **Forum Shops at Caesars.** On the next, less-traveled people mover, experience the $2-million holographic *World of Caesar,* where miniature Dionysian dancers and a toastmaster appear in an exquisitely rendered Roman city. Next, pause on the overlook to view the incongruous but impressive *Brahma Shrine,* a replica of an original statue cast in Thailand to improve the *feng shui* (vibes) of a Bangkok hotel.

The 1,670 rooms (in four towers, of various designs, but all with expensive furnishings and oversize baths and showers) are concealed behind lacy sun screens which at night filter the light into a beautiful pastel-blue haze that envelops the buildings. Wandering the sculpture-strewn hallways (which include a full-size reproduction of Michelangelo's *David*) you'll encounter two casinos—the **Caesars Palace Casino** and the **Olympiad; Cleopatra's Barge** (a lounge sitting in water); a slew of fancy shops along the **Appian Way;** the 1,200-seat **Circus Maximus** headliner room; six restaurants; a buffet and food court; the "Garden of the Gods" pool area; the 550-seat **Olympiad Sports Book;** and some of the swankiest citizenry of the empire. ◆ 3570 Las Vegas Blvd S (between Spring Mountain Rd and W Flamingo Rd). 731.7110, 800/634.6661; fax 731.7172

Within Caesars Palace:

Caesars Palace Casinos No longer the exclusive high-roller territory it once was, the hotel's original casino has had to lower its legendary standards slightly to compete for the middle gambling trade. At the south end of the hotel, adjacent to the **Forum Shops,** the newer **Olympiad Casino** reflects the compromise between elegance and egalitarianism. Its interior imperial splendor—soaring ceiling, heroic marble columns and arches, and stately centurions wearing red capes, red-bristle helmets, and shiny brass shields (who hand out slot-club membership cards to the hoi polloi)—is home to humble reel slots and quarter video-poker machines. The old casino, however, is still high-roller central, and you'll rarely see higher stacks of chips on a craps or blackjack table than you will here. Souvenir seekers can get a free deck of used playing cards by asking at the cage. ◆ Daily 24 hours. 731.7110

The Palatium ★★$$ Named for the meeting place of the first academy of Roman chefs, this buffet consists of semicircular serving satellites around a central carving station. The food, though lavishly presented, is the usual steam-table fare: roast beef carved to order, cold cuts, salads, and desserts. ◆ Buffet ◆ Daily breakfast, lunch, and dinner. 731.7499

Bacchanal ★★★$$$$ Olympian meals are served under a grape arbor in this sumptuous sunken dining room around a marble-walled fountain. Enjoy a seven-course, fixed-price Roman banquet while belly dancers shimmy seductively, vestal virgins in skimpy togas pour house wine into bottomless cups, and Caesar and Cleopatra put in two appearances nightly. Dinner consists of crab cocktail, mushroom ravioli, Caesar salad, choice of entrée (chicken, duck, swordfish, salmon, filet mignon, or prime ribs), and a flaming dessert. ◆ Continental ◆ Tu-Sa dinner. Reservations required; jackets required. 731.7525

Palace Court ★★★★$$$$ The processional entrance to this superlative French restaurant is fit for Caesar: Ascend a scarlet-carpeted spiral staircase with brass balustrade (or take the crystal-and-bronze elevator), then pass the view from the arched picture windows of the "Garden of the Gods" pool area and the private gambling salon and piano bar to the peach-hued foyer. The traditional cuisine is first-rate; salmon smoked on the premises, cherrystone clams, truffled goose liver, and caviar at market price. ◆ French ◆ Daily dinner. Reservations required; jackets required. 731.7547

La Piazza $ At this fancy food court that shames its counterparts at the **Riviera Casino, Fashion Show Mall,** and **O'Sheas,** choose from American, Chinese, Italian, Japanese, Mexican, and deli fare. There's also an excellent salad bar, and an ice cream, yogurt, and beverage station. Pull up a ringside seat to the casino; at night there's live entertainment. ◆ International ◆ Daily lunch and dinner. 731.7846

Siegfried and Roy's contract with The Mirage is the largest live entertainment agreement ever signed: $57,500,000 for five years.

Forum Shops This 240,000-square-foot upscale *agora* (marketplace) has stone floors underfoot and a dusk-to-dawn sky overhead. The *Festival Fountain* features four animatronic Roman gods (lifelike robots), laser constellations, dancing waters, and fiber-optic musical instruments (shows are on the hour). There are art galleries such as **Galerie Lassen**, featuring landscapes and seascapes of Hawaii, and **Thomas Charles Gallery,** spotlighting such celebrity artists as Anthony Quinn and Tony Bennett. The 60-odd boutiques include **Armani, Cartier, Cazal, Davante, Gucci, Sudachi, Vasari, Versace,** and **Vuitton,** to name but a few of the European designers who will happily max out your credit line with a single purchase. Dine at the upscale **Palm,** with its hearty platters, or at Wolfgang Puck's imaginative, popular **Spago,** the affordable **Stage Deli,** the lively **Boogie's Diner,** the gracious **Bertolino's,** the hectic **Planet Hollywood,** or the bargain-priced, friendly **La Salsa** (try the refreshing *agua fresca*—sugar water blended with pineapple or watermelon juice). ♦ Daily 10AM-11PM. Entrance at west end of Caesars Olympic Casino; exit onto north people mover back into Caesars. 735.8885

37 Barbary Coast $$$ Surrounded by three towering hotel-casino competitors, this tiny 200-room hotel adopted its name and decor from the San Francisco coast once frequented by pirates. Built on the site of a small motel, its rococo architecture is eye-catching, allowing the hotel to maintain the pirate tradition by stealing customers who are staying across the way at **Bally's, Caesars,** or the **Flamingo Hilton.** The casino is small, and a tough joint to get a handle on. To its credit, the mahogany and stained glass create a tony, turn-of-the-century ambience (the *Garden of Earthly Delights* on the north wall is supposedly the largest stained-glass window in the world). And in heavy-hitter tradition, the hotel's 200 rooms are mostly reserved for its steady clientele: medium rollers who crowd the many tables, leaving the few slot machines conspicuously neglected. But there's a **McDonald's** here for tinhorns who can't go a day without a Big Mac, as well as a 24-hour Western Union office (the last resort for busted-out gamblers—or the choice of the prudent few who want to wire winnings safely home). ♦ 3595 Las Vegas Blvd S (at E Flamingo Rd). 737.7111, 800/634.6755; fax 737.6304

> A gambler hit the world-record jackpot for nickel slots, $864,554, on a Nevada Nickels progressive machine at the Stardust in 1993.

> The 1.5-million-gallon dolphin habitat at The Mirage is the largest saltwater pool in the world.

Within the Barbary Coast:

Michael's ★★★★$$$$ One of Las Vegas's top gourmet restaurants, its lump crab cocktail, baked escargots, hearts of palm, imported French beans amandine, fresh Maine lobster (flown in daily), Vesuvio chicken breast, and assorted dessert berries will please the most jaded of palates. But be forewarned: It's one of the most expensive places in town, and the menu is all à la carte. Like other Las Vegas gourmet dining venues with haute cuisine and eye-popping prices, this spot exists primarily to reward big-spending casino customers with meals on the house. For example, a dinner comp for two here might require an average blackjack bet of $100 played over an eight-hour span. By charging such exorbitant tariffs in the gourmet room, the hotel wins three ways. First, it makes the high rollers feel like they're getting "their" money's worth. Second, it gives the casino inflated comp expenses to deduct from the gross win. And third, it compels the paying customers to help subsidize the preferred customers. If you're paying for your meal, look around the room—you're picking up the tab for most of the other diners. ♦ French ♦ Daily dinner. Reservations required; jacket required. 737.7111

38 Bourbon Street $$$ A y'all-come-down, New Orleans attitude, plus good Dixieland and jazz bands enlivening the lounge, are two of the draws at this tiny, 150-room hotel. But what really keeps this off-Strip joint packed is its liberal low-roller gambling policies. If you're looking for unbeatable deals in nickel slots, free tournaments, and low-limit blackjack, this is the scene. The **French Market** serves American and French cuisine. There's no pool here, but guests can take a dip next door at the **Maxim.** ♦ 120 E Flamingo Rd (between Las Vegas Blvd S and Koval La). 737.7200, 800/634.6956; fax 794.3490

39 Maxim $$ This low-key hotel-casino is just far enough off the beaten path that it has to try a little harder to compete, much to its guests' advantage. The 800 rooms in the twin 17-story towers are consistently among the least expen-sive and most available, even on weekends and during conventions (though the decor is a little tatty). With a reputation far and wide for dealing the best multideck blackjack game in town, the casino occasion-ally invites card counters to come and play! How? By advertising that they're dealing single-deck games down to the very last card—unheard of in Las Vegas. The 200-seat showroom is the perfect venue for an intimate comedy club; the buffet-comedy package is a popular night out for locals. ♦ 160 E Flamingo Rd (between Las Vegas Blvd S and Koval La). 731.4300, 800/634.6987; fax 735.3252

BALLY'S

40 Bally's Las Vegas $$$$ Even by Vegas standards, this resort is big. It was big when it opened in 1973 as the **MGM Grand,** and since then it's doubled in size. The portico could shelter a shipyard, and the casino could encompass a Super Bowl stadium.

It is also the site of the city's worst disaster—a terrible fire in 1981 closed the place for nine months. Rebuilt, fireproofed, and expanded, the hotel today features 3,000 guest rooms, a 1,400-seat headliner venue, four restaurants and a buffet, 10 lighted tennis courts, and well-appointed health clubs for men and women. A recent upgrade included refurbishing the guest rooms and parking and pedestrian facilities, and the unveiling of the $14.5-million **Bally's Plaza,** where four 200-foot walkways move guests between the Strip and the casino. Every 20 minutes after dark, a five-minute light-sound-and-water show erupts. At press time, more ambitious trailblazing is afoot (or rather, aloft): A mile-long monorail is being planned in a joint venture with the **MGM Grand** to shuttle visitors between the properties. ◆ 3645 Las Vegas Blvd S (between E Flamingo Rd and E Harmon Ave). 739.4111, 800/634.3434; fax 739.4432

Within Bally's Las Vegas:

Bally's Casino Size is again the object. With 88 blackjack tables, 12 crap tables, 10 roulette wheels, and 1,000 slot and video-poker machines, this gambling hall is one of the most extensive in the world. ◆ Daily 24 hours. 739.4111

Seasons ★★★★$$$$ The menu—as one would gather—changes four times a year to keep current with the harvest. Offerings might include fresh ahi with lotus chips, grilled boneless capon breast, roast duckling Grand Marnier, roast loin of venison with a pistachio-pepper crust, or ballotine of rabbit with roasted pine nuts. The environment is elegant with draped dining alcoves, crystal chandeliers, and gilt mirrors. ◆ French ◆ Tu-Sa dinner. Reserva-tions recommended; jacket required. 739.4651

Las Olas ★★$$$ Tex-Mex enthusiasts can tuck into the reasonably priced burritos, fajitas, seviche, tamales, enchiladas, and *chiles rellenos,* or sample more unusual dishes, like *queso fundido* (melted cheese with chorizo and green chilies). You can also enjoy such *nueva cocina* as broiled salmon topped with jalapeño hollandaise, grilled halibut with avocado-cilantro cream sauce and mango-papaya salsa, and filet mignon with green tomatillo sauce. A mariachi band serenades diners with traditional, sprightly tunes. ◆ Mexican ◆ M-Tu, F-Su breakfast, lunch, and dinner; W-Th breakfast and lunch. Reservations recommended. 739.4111

Big Kitchen Buffet ★$ Though the Great Buffet Debate is ongoing—and at times ferocious—this place is a consistent contender for the steam-table title. The serving area is the kitchen of a previously existing restaurant. In one corner is **Wong's Wok,** where a dozen Chinese dishes are prepared. The line features the customary comestibles: steak and potatoes, baked potato bar, prime rib carved to order, fresh salads, etc. To reach the room, head south inside the main entrance and take the escalator to the buffet. The second-floor dining area is comfortable and roomy. ◆ Buffet ◆ Daily brunch and dinner. 739.4930

Al Dente ★★★$$$$ Chef Michael Pergolini, formerly of Los Angeles's Il Fornaio, creates the unique Italian specialties found here. The dining room is decorated with colorful, modern plastic sculptures, the cuisine is light and imaginative. Popular meals include *melanzane al formaggio di capra* (grilled eggplant); *lattughe al sapor d'uva* (mixed baby greens); *focaccia al formaggio* (thin pizza crust filled with mozzarella); osso buco with polenta; *salsiccia e peperonata* (Italian sausage and peppers); and dessert ravioli stuffed with candied fruit, pine nuts, chocolate, and ricotta and topped with crème fraîche. ◆ Italian ◆ Tu-Sa dinner. Reservations recommended. 739.4111

Sterling Brunch ★★★$$$$ A new standard for Las Vegas's Sunday champagne extravaganzas is set here: The attentive waiters sport white gloves. Offerings include a sushi and sashimi bar, imaginative salads, smoked fish, and gourmet entrées that change each week. A sample menu might feature seared black tiger shrimp with peach and peanut chutney, loin of venison with fresh chanterelle mushrooms and green peppercorn sauce, and smoked marinated chicken with *pancetta* (Italian bacon) and wild rice linguine. French pastries and fresh berries are among the delectable desserts. ◆ Continental ◆ Su brunch. Reservations recommended. 739.4111

The highest price ever paid for land on the Strip was $1.75 million an acre when Kirk Kerkorian purchased the 18-acre vacant lot across from the MGM Grand Hotel and Casino in 1992. The total tab: $31.5 million.

A Review of Revues

The images assault you as soon as you step off the plane. From posters at **McCarran International Airport,** billboards along every major roadway, and postcards in gift shops along the **Strip,** leggy women in sequins, feathers, and those impossibly tall headpieces summon you like sirens.

The dancers, and the variety revues they star in, are synonymous with Las Vegas. Never mind that the concept originated in France (floor shows such as *Lido de Paris* were imported intact in the late 1950s to further the city's reputation as a glamorous and slightly naughty desert hot spot). While the sight of topless women parading in feathers and sequins seems less exotic now, the basic production formula remains unchanged: musical numbers interspersed with specialty acts such as jugglers, acrobats, and magicians. In the 1960s, Las Vegas was just one of several outlets for Ed Sullivan–style entertainment. Today, it's the leader of the last bastions for such extravaganzas, which harken back to the heyday of Broadway spectacles, circa Flo Ziegfeld. About 41 percent of Las Vegas visitors find time for a show, and, with the number of solo celebrity attractions dwindling, most opt for one of the big stage shows.

But with such generically exclamatory titles as *EFX* and *Jubilee!,* how can you tell them apart? Use this brief overview of the more spectacular and most enduring shows on the Strip as a guide.

The smaller rooms seat about 400 people, the larger ones, more than 1,200. Most are laid out in tiers, each containing a row of booths and several long tables—a holdover from the days when most shows included an evening meal. Today, only four serve dinner regularly: the **Flamingo Hilton**'s *Great Radio City Music Hall Spectacular,* the **Rio**'s *!Conga!,* **Tropicana**'s *Folies Bergere,* and **Excalibur**'s *King Arthur's Tournament* (a medieval-themed show at which you actually munch on Cornish hen without benefit of utensils).

Some showrooms continue to operate under the long-standing maître d' system—you call ahead to place your name on a reservations list but still stand in line (sometimes up to an hour) before curtain time. It's an unwritten custom that tipping the maître d' five dollars (or more) will improve your seating, but the hosts claim the purpose of the system is not to line their own pockets, but to allow them more flexibility in accommodating high rollers.

Today, more than half of the venues use reserved-seat ticketing, a practice familiar to the modern showgoer. Most of the celebrity rooms and some of the larger revues—including *Siegfried & Roy* and *Jubilee!*—have made the switch to tickets. Each hotel has a different policy, but most accept credit card orders by telephone as far as three months in advance or sell tickets at a box office on the premises from one to three days ahead.

Savvy patrons should ask if the advertised price includes cocktails, and whether the city's entertainment and gratuity taxes are included. *Legends in Concert* is the lowest-priced show on this list; *King Arthur's Tournament, The Great Radio City Music Hall Spectacular,* and *!Conga!* are in the midrange; and *Siegfried & Roy* commands the Strip's top dollar.

Hotels can be helpful about telling you whether their show is acceptable for children or has early performances in which the female dancers are "covered" with bras they shed for the later shows.

A final tip: If you opt to use a ticket broker (they usually sublet booths at casinos in hotels that don't have their own shows), take their recommendations with a grain of salt. They tend to promote the lower-budget revues because they often receive an "incentive" from the producers.

Cirque du Soleil **(Treasure Island)** is understated and distinctly European in tone—a complete departure from anything previously associated with Las Vegas. The audience is seated close to a circular stage where the emphasis is on human acrobatics (no animals are used) integrated with mime and a moody New Age score. Felliniesque clowns, or *flounes,* entertain before the show and serve as stagehands for trapeze artists, foot jugglers, teenage contortionists, and a near-naked flying man, who soars to the top of the big top and performs an aerial ballet while hanging by wrist-straps. The show is a clever solution to the problem of entertaining international visitors, since the only "language" spoken is the *flounes'* comic gibberish.

!Conga! **(Rio Suite Hotel & Casino)** is a lively Latin romp, with dinner integrated into the show: Each scene introduces a course. To begin, dancers wearing costumes depicting lettuce, tomatoes, onion, and garlic and following the lead of Chef Rico swirl around the 430-seat room as the wait staff serves crispy spinach salad. Female lead Rio Rita presents a Carmen Miranda routine, followed by a staff of chefs and dancers in vegetable costumes; and the entrée is served as Rico demonstrates his juggling ability. The strawberry Napoleon dessert is offered after being paraded around the room; guests are then invited to join the cast in the grand finale conga line.

EFX **(MGM Grand Hotel and Theme Park)** stars Michael Crawford as the Effects Master who transforms himself into four legendary characters: Merlin, the Master of Magic; P.T. Barnum, the Master of Laughter; Harry Houdini, the Master of the Spirit; and H.G. Wells, the Master of Time. This original $30-million production is staged in the 1,700-seat **Grand Theatre** and includes a cast of 70, plus animatronic technology similar to the robotic characters on display throughout the hotel.

Enter the Night **(Stardust Resort & Casino)** debuted in 1991 in an attempt to reinvent the Vegas spectacular with a Broadway aesthetic. In this $10-million production, topless female dancers in sleek and contemporary costumes abound. The original score is dynamic and engaging, performed by live musicians and leads who actually sing, rather than mouth the songs. In some numbers, the cast even interact as characters instead of simply serenading the audience. A few of the high-tech touches truly dazzle, particularly the laser number set to music

reminiscent of arrangements by the Alan Parsons Project.

Folies Bergere **(Tropicana Hotel & Casino)** is the Strip's longest-running show and the last of the French revues: It debuted at the **Tropicana** in 1959, and the show still has the most legitimate choreography on the Strip, with such traditional numbers as the cancan finale standing up to the test of time. Indeed, the Vegas version has outlasted its Parisian counterpart, which closed in late 1992.

The show cultivates a stylish French flavor from the opening number—a "living postcard" of the bawdy Gallic music halls of the 1900s—to the "Grand Ladies of Paris" segment. The pièce de résistance comes when the dancers lie down on a turntable and contort into kaleidoscopic formations à la Jackie Gleason's **June Taylor Dancers.** In light of the high-tech competition from such newcomers as **Luxor** and the **MGM Grand Hotel and Theme Park,** sentimentalists might want to catch this piece of vintage Vegas before the **Tropicana** decides it's too much of an anachronism.

The Great Radio City Music Hall Spectacular **(Flamingo Hilton),** starring the **Radio City Rockettes** and Susan Anton, is a new addition to the show scene. The world's most famous precision dance troupe takes the audience on a magical journey through Radio City's treasure chest of spectacular entertainment. More than 10 numbers are presented, including the **Rockettes'** famous "Parade of the Wooden Soldiers," Gershwin's "Rhapsody in Blue," and Ravel's "Bolero," backed by an all-male drum ensemble. And Susan Anton laments in song that she's "Too Tall" to be a Rockette.

Jubilee! **(Bally's Las Vegas)** is a Las Vegas warhorse. For better or for worse, there will never be another show like it. Hydraulic lifts sink the *Titanic* right on cue on the custom-built stage, and the epic "Samson and Delilah" number brings down the house—or at least the temple—every night. This is the only enduring work of producer Donn Arden, who came to town with the opening of the

Desert Inn and eventually staked his claim as a cross between Busby Berkeley and Cecil B. DeMille. *Jubilee!* opened in 1981, but its sexist clichés and downright hokey lyrics—"(Delilah's) got the hots for a guy named Sam/He thinks the chick is wild!"—are decades behind the times. The idea of a foxy female passenger causing the *Titanic* disaster by distracting the men in the control room seems like Mel Brooks material. None-theless, the spectacle still impresses all but the most callous audience.

King Arthur's Tournament **(Excalibur Hotel/Casino/Las Vegas)** came to the Strip in 1990. It's family entertainment in the oval, dirt-floor arena in the basement of the medieval-themed hotel. Knights charge one another on horseback, and the audience cheers on their favorites as they clash and joust. Merlin the Magician narrates the sketch of a plot, which barely elevates the show a level above Arthurian professional wrestling.

Legends in Concert **(Imperial Palace Hotel & Casino)** spawned a cottage industry in 1983—packaging celebrity impersonators into a Vegas revue. "Living Legends" such as contemporary entertainers Neil Diamond and Michael Jackson counterbalance the emphasis on such nostalgic personalities as Judy Garland and Nat King Cole. The "cast" rotates, but there's usually a Marilyn Monroe and a patriotic Elvis finale. Even those who find the concept more tasteless than tributary will have to admit the show offers fast-paced fun with a live band and no lip-syncing. It's a true variety show, respectful enough for those who take the premise seriously and wacky enough for those who appreciate its camp quotient.

Siegfried & Roy **(The Mirage Hotel & Casino)** is the most expensive ticket in town. It is also the show that brought the Las Vegas revue into the present when it opened in 1990. These two magicians have been repackaging the same basic repertoire of tricks on an increasingly

grander scale since the 1960s. For instance, the stock illusion of "impalement" is now done on the horn of a giant mechanical dragon, a showstopping firebreather that comes to life midway through the act.

The spectacle begins with the room itself: The stage is an immense crescent with ramps encircling part of the audience, putting them right in the middle of the action. Production designer John Napier says he's striving for a tone that combines Pink Floyd, Wagner, and Marvel Comics. Indeed, the first half of the show casts the two magicians as superheroes combatting the evil queen of a fantasy world. The recorded score is dense and operatic.

One cannot argue that the performers have single-handedly raised the standard of Las Vegas entertainment, yet it is easy to understand the minority who feel the act is too dark, cold, and pretentious. Those few will prefer the latter part of the show, during which the pace slows down sufficiently for the duo to schmooze with the crowd, chat about their careers, and let their affable, slightly goofy personalities shine through. If price is no object, this is the best Las Vegas has to offer.

Starlight Express **(Las Vegas Hilton)** turned Elvis's famous showroom into a customized theater neither the King nor his minions would recognize. The $12-million production of Andrew Lloyd Webber's pop musical on roller skates features a banked dome and a stage with ramps leading into the audience. Performers donning skates portray trains in a high-tech version of "The Little Engine that Could."

The musical was not a Broadway hit on the scale of Webber's *Cats* or *Phantom of the Opera,* and the Las Vegas effort didn't benefit by being trimmed down to 90 minutes. But the marriage of spectacle and legitimate theater is a step in the right direction for the Strip. Besides, *Starlight* seems more at home in Vegas's family environ-ment than in front of a New York audience.

Jubilee! Get a glitz fix at this $12-million production of non sequitur spectacles and historical revisions that only Las Vegas could create. It's a great show, nonetheless, with larger-than-life sets, flamboyant costumes and special effects, and notably beautiful performers. In the first scene, Delilah seduces Samson, who then single-handedly destroys the temple; in Act Two, the *Titanic* sinks right through the stage. Interspersed are dance, variety acts, and a parade of exposed female torsos. ♦ M, Su 8PM; Tu-Th, Sa 8PM, 11PM. 739.4567

41 Aladdin Hotel $$$ "Your wish is our command" is the motto of this hotel, with its elegant porte cochere, oversized lead glass chandeliers, and 1,100 rooms, suites, and villas. The villas—each of which has a separate outdoor entrance and full kitchen facilities—are favorites of celebrities and honeymooners; both covet the convenience and the privacy.

Guests who desire musical entertainment need go no further than the 7,000-seat **Theatre for the Performing Arts,** which has hosted such big-names as Sting, Stevie Wonder, Rod Stewart, The Moody Blues, Chicago, Stevie Nicks, Alabama, Luther Vandross, and Paul Simon, plus Broadway imports *Jesus Christ Superstar, Dreamgirls,* and *Cats. Country Tonite,* voted in 1993 "best live country show in America" by the Country Music Association of America, has been playing in **The Showroom** for three years. Gustatory desires can be fulfilled in any of six eating establishments, including a snack bar, a 24-hour coffee shop, a buffet, **Wellington's Steak House, Fisherman's Port,** and **Sun Sun** (which serves Vietnamese, Chinese, and Korean cuisine). Two Olympic-size swimming pools, three lighted tennis courts, three full-service bars, and a 75,000-square-foot casino and state-of-the-art race and sports book complete the list of wishes this genie has graciously fulfilled. Under new management at press time, there's no telling what the new master will desire. ♦ 3667 Las Vegas Blvd S (at E Harmon Ave). 736.0111, 800/634.3424; fax 734.3583

42 Holiday Inn Casino Boardwalk $$$ You'd be hard-pressed to find the boardwalk at this funky little casino and 200-room **Holiday Inn.** To bring back memories of its Atlantic City counterpart, black-and-white photographs (ca. 1920 and 1930) of the East Coast ocean resort town deck the halls. It's locally revered for its budget-balancing snack bar fare: fresh doughnuts baked on the premises, hearty soups, hobo stew served in a one-pound loaf of baked bread, and tiny White Castle–style burgers. The daily dinner specials are amazingly inexpensive, and include a gratis glass of drinkable wine. Casino-chip collectors and gambling historians will appreciate the 1967 50¢, $1, $2, and $5 gaming tokens on

display at the main cage. ♦ 3750 Las Vegas Blvd S (between E Harmon and E Tropicana Aves). 735.1167, 800/635.4581; fax 739.8152

43 The Metz One of the trendiest clubs in town, this Stripside nightspot is friendly and high-tech. Neon signage, laser beams, and video screens abound; the nouveau disco platters are spun by a low-key DJ. ♦ Admission; women free on Sunday. Daily from 9PM. 3765 Las Vegas Blvd S (between E Harmon and E Tropicana Aves). 736.2228

44 MGM Grand Hotel and Theme Park $$$ The smart money says this extravaganza will be setting the pace in Las Vegas for the foreseeable future. The $1-billion building houses the largest hotel in the world, with 5,007 spacious guest rooms, including nearly 800 suites ranging in size from 675 to a palatial 6,000 square feet. The casino is a record-setter, too; its 171,000 square feet outstrip the nearest competition by almost 50,000 square feet. The 15,000-seat **Grand Garden** is the centerpiece of the five entertainment arenas. The four 30-story emerald towers contain eight restaurants; a buffet and food court; a health spa featuring massage, facials, herbal wraps, and extensive cardiovascular and weight training equipment; a 30,000-square-foot video arcade; a youth activity center; and four themed casinos with 3,500 slot machines and 165 table games. The 33-acre theme park features a multicultural mix of street scenes from Paris, New York, and Hong Kong. Rides include a Mississippi riverboat, a roller coaster through darkness, a 1,600-foot-long rapids ride, a flume with sheer vertical drops, and bumper cars. ♦ 3799 Las Vegas Blvd S (at E Tropicana Ave). 891.1111, 800/929.1111; fax 891.1000

Within the MGM Grand Hotel and Theme Park:

Charlie Trotter's ★★★★$$$$ Highly esteemed chef Charlie Trotter, whose chic Chicago restaurant has garnered raves since it first opened its doors, has alighted on Las Vegas. Though the menu is always evolving to accommodate the freshest ingredients available, there are only two options per night—the meat and seafood sampler or the vegetable sampler. Providing tastes of several of Trotter's exquisite preparations, a meat and seafood choice might include smoked Maine salmon with pulped avocado, California squab breast with foie gras, Japanese yellowtail with

red cabbage and sweet-potato gnocchi, and Colorado beef with garlic potato risotto and yellow-foot mushrooms. The vegetable selection could include such imaginative dishes as truffle potato soup with leeks, artichokes, and black Périgord truffles; root vegetables and wild mushroom ravioli with white truffle oil; quinoa, couscous, and pearled barley with roasted butternut squash; and ragout of tiny vegetables and wild mushrooms with truffle oil. Both meals are followed by a delicious assortment of sorbets and a variety of luscious desserts and petits fours. With a 6,000-bottle wine cellar, there's no shortage of liquid refreshment, either. Service is impeccable and the atmosphere is elegant and refined: Rich woods and marble surround Beidermeier furniture, Axminster carpets, and magnificent fresh flowers.
♦ Continental ♦ M, W-Su dinner. Reservations required; jacket and tie requested. 891.7337

Coyote Cafe
★★★★$$$

This replica of the original Santa Fe eatery is just one of Mark Miller's tremendously successful ventures scattered around the world. You have a choice of where to sit and savor the Southwestern food— in the informal **Cafe** or the elegant **Grill Room.** Imaginative soups, salads, entrées, and casseroles are highlighted on both of the delicious seasonal menus. Two of the **Cafe**'s more popular dishes are the blue-corn chicken enchilada and sizzling shrimp diablo. The **Grill Room**'s signature dishes are a little more upscale. Try the cowboy Angus rib chop or the skillet-seared Alaskan salmon in a pumpkin-seed crust served with butternut squash and lobster *jus.* ♦ Southwestern ♦ Cafe: daily breakfast, lunch, and dinner; Grill Room: daily dinner. Reservations required for Grill Room. 891.7349

Wolfgang Puck Cafe ★★★$$ Bright and cheerful, this popular cafe overlooking the casino is decorated with framed *Puck* magazine covers (*Puck* was a popular English humor magazine at the turn of the century) and vividly colored wall and floor tiles. Imaginative specialties prepared in the open kitchen include breakfast pizzas of focaccia with creamy scrambled eggs and cheese, roasted prime rib hash, smoked salmon plate, and a fresh fruit plate with blueberry yogurt. For lunch and dinner, choose the roasted eggplant, tomato, and fresh mozzarella salad; vegetable spring rolls with mustard plum

sauce; Barbara's fettuccine with shrimp, vegetables, and a curry sauce; Grandma Puck's linguine with chicken Bolognese; or meat loaf with port wine sauce and garlic mashed potatoes. Among the immense variety of gourmet pizzas from the wood-burning oven are herb sausage, prosciutto with goat cheese, smoked salmon with red onions, and barbecue chicken with cilantro. ♦ American. ♦ Daily breakfast, lunch, and dinner. 891.3019

Leonardo's ★★★$$ Designed to resemble an Italian vineyard, this restaurant is filled with Roman columns and grapevines woven among latticework. Slices of huge oak wine casks and attractive murals depicting Old World markets decorate the walls. But the hearty antipasto bar is the hot spot in this busy eatery. Other appetizers include *fritto misto* (fried scallops, shrimp, and calamari), *pecci alla scotadeo* (mussels in white-wine broth), *capesante alla griglia* (scallop kabob with brandy, basil, and lime-honey sauce), and prosciutto with melon. The house salad is tossed with tomato, red onion, goat cheese, Italian olives, and mushrooms. Pastas include *cappellini pomodoro* (with a sauce of tomato and basil), *linguine alla Genovese* (with basil, olive oil, and toasted pine nuts), and *ravioli di pomodoro* (spinach ravioli filled with ricotta cheese and tomato sauce). Marinated New York steak, osso buco, and *saltimbocca di vitello* (veal scallopini with prosciutto and fresh sage) are among the entrées on the extensive menu. ♦ Italian ♦ Daily dinner. Reservations recommended. 891.7331

Sir Reginald's ★★★$$$ A lifelike statue of Sir Reginald Baskerville—an imaginary aristocratic English hound who led the pampered life of nobility and had a passion for gambling and fine dining—stands guard over the entrance to this elegant restaurant. Perfect for intimate dining, the room is divided into cozy alcoves with handsome dark wood paneling. The menu includes oysters Rockefeller, gravlax, Cuban black bean soup, steaks, prime ribs, rack of lamb with ratatouille, frozen pecan soufflé in a chocolate shell with blackberry puree, and strawberries Romanoff. There's also a grandiose champagne brunch on Sundays. ♦ Steak house ♦ M-Sa dinner; Su brunch and dinner. Reservations recommended. 891.7318

Grand Garden This is the scene of *EFX,* a $30-million extravanganza that stars Michael Crawford as the Effects Master who portrays four historical characters. The show inaugurated the 1,700-seat theater in 1995 with a cast of 70, and utilizes cutting-edge animatronic technology to dramatic effect. (For more information, see "A Review of Revues," page 50.) Admission. M, W-Su 7:30PM and 11PM. 891.7777

EXCALIBUR

45 Excalibur Hotel/Casino/Las Vegas $$
This 4,032-room behemoth held the title of world's largest resort hotel until the **MGM Grand Hotel and Theme Park** across the street overtook it by almost 1,000 chambers. The medieval detail, inside and out, renders the resort a theme park in its own right, with an overblown scale and exaggerated style. Turrets, spires, belfries, and moats usher you into the castle. The bellmen wear poofy yellow-and-black knickers, white-and-gold blouses, and purple vests (the dealers used to wear the same outfits, but mercifully, theirs have been toned down). Signs around the casino direct customers to the **Jester's Lounge, Royal Royals,** and the **Medieval Slot Fantasy.** The lower level houses the **Fantasy Faire,** a sort of Sherwood Forest of midway games, featuring the Flagon Toss, Great Racing Knights, Knock Down the Knave's Teeth, and William Tell Darts. But the main draw is **Merlin's Magic Motion Machines,** an amazing show where the theaters' benches move in sync with the wild action on the screen. Don't miss it.

On the **Medieval Village** level are four restaurants and the mega-size buffet, which seats 1,500. Singers, acrobats, magicians, jugglers, and harpists hold court at the **Court Jester's Stage. Camelot,** the third level, is where you'll find ballrooms, a beauty salon, wedding chapel, and an excellent gourmet restaurant (also called **Camelot,** see below). ♦ 3850 Las Vegas Blvd S (at W Tropicana Ave). 597.7777, 800/937.7777; fax 597.7009

Within the Excalibur Hotel/Casino/Las Vegas:

Excalibur Casino Attracting a mom-and-pop crowd, this casino offers ample opportunity to do everything from feeding nickels and quarters into machines to playing $2 blackjack. It's huge—100,000 square feet—with 80 blackjack tables, six crap tables, and four roulette tables. The table minimums are kept low: $2 blackjack, $1 craps, and quarter roulette. But mostly there are slot machines everywhere—nearly 3,000 of them! The serious gamblers have plenty of other places to play in this town. ♦ Daily 24 hours. 597.7777

Lance-alotta-Pasta ★$ If the pun on the restaurant's name doesn't deter you, you'll find plenty to eat here. The menu features antipasto, fried calamari, minestrone or the *zuppa del giorno* (soup of the day), salads, and pasta galore. Choose from six sauces or toppings while a string quartet plays in the background. ♦ Italian ♦ Daily lunch and dinner. 597.7777

Sir Galahad's Prime Rib House ★★$$
At this Olde English inn, wait staff in period costumes carve the prime ribs to order—a King Arthur's or Lady Guinevere's cut—at your table. The main course is accompanied by barley soup or salad, mashed potatoes, creamed spinach, Yorkshire pudding, and whipped-cream horseradish. At the end of the meal, you'll feel as roly-poly as Friar Tuck. If you're not up to the prime rib, opt for the less filling, but equally satisfying, breast of capon harlequin (simmered in red wine sauce, garnished with pearl onions and mushrooms) or the fresh catch of the "knight," and top it all off with English trifle. ♦ English ♦ Daily dinner. Reservations recommended. 597.7777

Camelot ★★★$$$ With suits of armor flanking both sides of the entry, the Round Table theme continues. Light shines through stained-glass windows in the cocktail lounge and bar, and pewter plates and swords hang from the walls of the dining room. Such appetizers as Scottish smoked salmon with grilled onion salsa or warm quail salad with balsamic vinaigrette and strips of vine-ripe tomatoes would have been ample reward for those in service to their king. Equally delicious is Queen Guinevere's soup (creamy lobster bisque with diced lobster meat). Woodland fettuccine (with smoked quail, fresh vegetables, and pesto in a creamy game sauce) and Glendale purses (fresh ravioli with veal and herbs, surrounded by a creamy porcini mushroom sauce) may not have been staples in medieval castles, but you'll be glad they're served here. Entrées include Argyle swordfish with fresh asparagus vinaigrette, Canterbury duckling (with wild rice, crispy potatoes, and port cherry sauce), and rack of lamb King James (squash-encrusted and served with potato puree). To reach idyllic happiness, try the chocolate "decadeuce" (rich flourless chocolate cake with whipped cream) before returning to normal life. ♦ Continental ♦ Daily dinner. Reservations recommended. 597.7777

In 1960, during the filming of *Ocean's Eleven,* the movie's stars—Frank Sinatra, Dean Martin, Sammy Davis Jr., Joey Bishop, and Peter Lawford—appeared onstage nightly at the Sands Hotel's Copa Room in what's been called the "most celebrated talent event in supper-club history." Senator John F. Kennedy showed up for the festivities. In the movie, the five casinos on the Strip that the Rat Pack's characters rob are the Sahara, the Riviera, the Sands, the Desert Inn, and the Flamingo.

Restaurants/Clubs: Red   **Hotels:** Blue
Shops/ ♥ Outdoors: Green   **Sights/Culture:** Black

46 Tropicana Hotel $$$$ Though at 300 rooms it wasn't much larger than the ranch-style lodges that preceded it, this was the last, fanciest, and most expensive of the Strip hotels to be built in the 1950s. Its $15-million price tag taxed the cash capabilities of even the richest old bootleggers. Because of the state and federal heat on organized crime figures in Nevada gambling and the growing media hysteria over Las Vegas as the vice capital of the country, another new Strip hotel didn't open for nearly a decade.

It still has a lot going for it. The scenic entrance features 35-foot-tall tiki heads (delightfully grotesque Polynesian totems) and gas torches lighting the longhouse facade. A quarter-mile walkway connects the two towers, with flocks of tropical birds and coral aquariums lining the path. And the five-acre pool area is a lush and cool hideaway just out of hearing range of the Strip; the famous swim-up blackjack game is played here. ◆ 3801 Las Vegas Blvd S (at E Tropicana Ave). 739.2222, 800/468.9494; fax 739.2469

Within the Tropicana Hotel:

Tropicana Casino The main pit here is defined by a colorful 4,000-square-foot stained-glass ceiling, making the table-game atmosphere quite dramatic. Fairly innovative with gambling promotions, the casino has introduced a progressive jackpot at roulette, blackjack, and craps (won by such feats as rolling three 11s in a row). A good place to come if you're new to gaming, the casino also offers free lessons in craps and Caribbean stud poker. There are also learning tables where dealers answer questions on how to play, and the low minimums (baccarat for $5 and blackjack for $1) make it painless. While you're in the casino, sign up for a free membership in the **Island Winners Club,** and you can earn points toward dining and the *Folies Bergere* as you play table games, slots, or video poker. Cash bonuses are also awarded to slots and video-poker players. ◆ Daily 24 hours. 739.2222

El Gaucho ★★★$$$ Between wonderful fare at this south-of-the-border steak house and the view overlooking the **Island of Las Vegas** water park, you couldn't ask for a more enjoyable dining experience. Among the hearty specialties are oysters del Rio (oysters on the half shell baked in asiago cheese), swordfish Mazatlán (broiled swordfish with cilantro-lime sauce), and porterhouse steak. ◆ Steak house ◆ Daily dinner. Reservations recommended. 739.2376

Play & Eat ★★$$ This relatively recent combination casino-deli allows you to devour two-foot-long hot dogs while indulging in slots or video poker. You can even order a salad or sandwich while you bet in the sports book or sip some cappuccino to keep you playing all night in the poker room. There's

also a beautiful view of the hotel's lagoons, spas, waterfalls, and wildlife. ◆ Deli: daily breakfast, lunch, and dinner until 5PM; Casino: daily 8AM-10PM. 739.2503

Folies Bergere By far the oldest show in town, this production is a throwback to a previous generation of Las Vegas extravaganzas. Turn-of-the-century Parisian song and dance, American golden oldies, cancan chorus lines, and 1950s-style dancers appeal mostly to the sentimental. Dinner is served before the early show and included in the price of admission; cocktails only are included in the price of the late show. Backstage tours are conducted during the day. ◆ Admission. Shows: daily 7:30PM, 10:30PM. Tours: Tu-F noon, 1PM; Sa 1PM, 3PM. Tiffany Showroom. 739.2411

47 Hotel San Remo $$$ The Japanese owner of this 711-room jewel is dedicated to offering comfort and service to his guests. Those staying here need never stray far for fun. There are 50 Jacuzzi suites, a casino with blackjack, craps, keno, roulette, mini-baccarat, poker, *pai gow,* and *pai gow* poker, plus a slot club and sports book. Five restaurants on-site offer a variety of gustatory experiences. **Paparazzi** offers continental dining in an intimate, romantic setting; moderately priced Italian fare is served in a relaxed, festive atmosphere at **Pasta Remo; Luigi's Place** features deli sandwiches and pizza all day; the 24-hour coffee shop offers breakfast, lunch, and an all-you-can-eat dinner buffet; and an award-winning chef creates authentic delicacies in the **Sushi Bar San Remo** every night. In the evenings, the **Parisian Cabaret** is home to *Comedy Cabaret,* a lively romp featuring dancers reminiscent of those in the movie *Cabaret.* ◆ 115 E Tropicana Ave (between Las Vegas Blvd S and Koval La). 739.9000, 800/522.7366; fax 736.1120

48 Luxor Hotel & Casino $$$$ Trading on the appeal of both New Age and age-old pyramid power, this 30-story, $300-million bronze tetrahedron with 2,500 rooms and a 90,000-square-foot casino is a one-of-a-kind resort. Luxor was the original religious locus for the ancient Egyptian civilization of Thebes. A reproduction Nile River runs through the lobby of the pyramid, and, in a fantastic juxtaposition of technology, guests are transported by boat from the front desk to the elevators, which ascend the building at a 39-degree angle. Also featured are King Tut's tomb, seven restaurants, a 1,200-seat arena, and the New York City skyline. This hybrid of a historical theme and the comforts of a modern hotel are sure to lure even the most jaded visitors. ♦ 3900 Las Vegas Blvd S (between E Tropicana and E Hacienda Aves). 262.4000, 800/288.1000; fax 262.4405

Within Luxor Hotel & Casino:

Isis ★★★★$$$ This romantic 95-seat gourmet restaurant is set off by soft blue lights, larger-than-life Egyptian statues, and harp music. According to the embossed menus decorated with stone carvings, Isis was the ancient goddess of fertility. The appetites of guests are renewed with imaginative choices, from appetizer treasures of the sphinx to exotic desserts of the pharaohs. Among dramatically presented entrées are New York sirloin with green peppercorn sauce; lobster tail and seafood mousse in a pastry crust, topped with a white zinfandel sauce; and salmon fillet with spinach and pine nuts in papillote with lobster sauce. ♦ Continental ♦ Daily dinner. Reservations recommended. 262.4773

49 Hacienda Hotel & Casino $$ The subdued Southwestern look of this 840-room hotel is reinforced by its adobe and tile decor, and the shaded pool area reaps the benefits of 40 years of landscaping (the hotel was established in 1955) and surrounds the original motor-inn units. Other draws include the **Charcoal Room**, a well-respected steak house, and the **Little Church of the West** wedding chapel, one of the town's matrimonial hot spots. Away from the hubbub, this is one of the county's finest small hotels. When it was recently sold to Circus Circus Enterprises, magician-in-residence Lance Burton (who some say is even more proficient at his trade than the German illusionists Siegfried and Roy) bailed out for a mere $100 million. He's signed a 13-year contract with Mirage Resorts to move his show to their property, scheduled to open at the former **Dunes** location in the summer of 1996. ♦ 3950 Las Vegas Blvd S (at E Hacienda Ave). 739.8911, 800/634.6713; fax 798.8289

50 Vicious Rumors ★★★$$$ Catering to the gay community, but attracting both gays and straights, this little hideaway, formerly called **Porterhouse**, recently changed its name. With fine food and service, the comfortable booths are decked out in black-and-white understated elegance. All entrées include a loaf of warm bread and a mixed salad with your choice of homemade dressing. The chef's specialty is a 22-ounce porterhouse, but the filet mignon, prime ribs, double-cut lamb chops, center-cut pork chops, or charbroiled chicken breast are equally good. There's a piano bar, dancing, and free hors d'oeuvres from 10:30PM to 4AM. ♦ Steak house ♦ Daily dinner. Reservations recommended. 6370 Windy St (between Post Rd and W Sunset Rd). 896.1993

51 Boomtown $$ Featuring an Old West mining town theme, this $75-million hotel, casino, and RV resort is located five minutes south of Tropicana Avenue on I-15. The property meanders over 62 acres and includes a 300-room hotel, 460-space deluxe recreational vehicle park, 350-seat buffet and chili bar, two specialty snack bars, 100-seat lounge featuring country-western bands that perform nightly, 600-seat theater, 30 table games, 1,100 slot and video-poker machines, and a sports book. ♦ 3333 Blue Diamond Rd (at I-15). 263.7777, 800/588.7111; fax 896.4925

Bests

Marilyn Ming
Publicity Manager, Four Queens Hotel & Casino

My favorite summer event: The Las Vegas Jazz Society hosts "Jazz in the Park," free evening concerts that are usually held each Saturday in June. Bring a picnic dinner (or a bucket of chicken) and a blanket or chair and sit back and listen to such jazz greats as Carl Fontana, Joe Williams, and Marlena Shaw. The temperature in Las Vegas in June is around 100 degrees, but the evenings cool off to a comfortable 90 degrees. And Las Vegas has no flies, mosquitoes, or other nighttime summer bugs to bother you.

Drive at night to downtown Las Vegas. From **Las Vegas Boulevard** turn west onto **Fremont Street** and just stare in awe at the millions of colorful lights of **Glitter Gulch**. It's no wonder why locals and visitors alike say, "Now *this* is Las Vegas."

When Elvis Presley made his Las Vegas debut at the Frontier Hotel on 23 April 1956, the then-controversial young rocker received third billing in the hotel's Venus Room. By all accounts, he bombed. Presley went on to complete only one week of a scheduled two-week engagement. It would be nearly a decade before the King of Rock 'n' Roll returned to town and began playing to sold-out showrooms.

"Where else in the world could I have worked for Howard Hughes and his Summa Hotel chain of the Desert Inn, Sands, and Frontier for more than 36 weeks a year for 13 years; own my own hotel; and be able to go home and sleep in my own bed each night?"

Wayne Newton

West Las Vegas

From 1905 on, the railroad reigned supreme in Las Vegas for three and a half decades, wielding authority over civic affairs as if this were a company town. In fact, so crucial was the railroad to the city's development that it held a firm grip on the community for several decades *before* the first train actually pulled into the station. Beginning in 1871, when the first stretch of track was laid southwest from Salt Lake City in the direction of Los Angeles, and up to the turn of the century, the ranchers and cowboys of the Las Vegas Valley, along with everyone else familiar with the lay of the southern Nevada desert, were anxiously awaiting the imminent arrival of the iron horse.

Helen Stewart was one of those who were banking on the railroad. Her husband, Archibald Stewart, had foreclosed on the 640-acre Las Vegas Ranch in 1881 after its owner, original valley homesteader O.D. Gass, failed to repay a loan. Shortly thereafter, a neighboring ranch hand shot and killed Stewart, who was defending Helen's honor against gossip that she was morally fast and loose. The widow assumed control of the ranch and managed it so effectively that by the early 1900s she'd amassed an additional 1,160 acres and most of the valley's water rights. For the next 20 years, she speculated that the railroad would eventually roll through. Sure enough, in 1902, the San Pedro, Los Angeles, and Salt Lake Company offered Helen $55,000 for most of her property (little more than $33 an acre, a paltry sum even then). It was the only offer she received, and she readily agreed to the deal.

In 1903 Helen hired J.T. McWilliams to survey the boundaries of the property she planned to sell. During the course of his scrutiny, McWilliams determined that 80 acres west of the ranch were untitled, and he promptly claimed them for himself. He then mapped out a town plan and began selling lots to the first arrivals, people who were either seeking jobs with the railroad or land investors looking to make a profit once the depot opened for business. Though neither McWilliams nor the widow Stewart got wealthy from their speculation, a town was named after McWilliams.

McWilliamsville, popularly known as **Ragtown** (either for its canvas dwellings or wash-strewn clotheslines), sat just west of the train tracks. It grew quickly, and after a year was a burgeoning boomtown with a population of more than a thousand. But the fledgling city was doomed when the railroad conglomerate plotted its own company town to the east. When this "official" Las Vegas was established in 1905, Ragtown's access to running water was deliberately curtailed by the railroad to bring on its demise. Within six months, McWilliamsville was nearly abandoned.

But a small shantytown remained, inhabited by squatters; cut off from Las Vegas by the railroad tracks, it was gradually ghettoized. Over the next 60 years, as the city grew up around it, McWilliams's original town site came to be designated as the **Westside**. Even today, it's still considered the wrong side of the tracks.

In the last 20 years, Las Vegas has spread west, northwest, and southwest on its quest to conquer the entire valley. The Westside is only a tiny pocket of what is now called West Las Vegas. Vacant desert a decade ago, patchy subdivisions and skeletal commercial strips a mere five years ago, today West Las Vegas is a grid of residences and retail centers, a triumph of suburbia. Embryonic planned communities continue to encroach on the sheer limestone and sandstone escarpment of the Spring Mountains, which erupt from the edge of the Las Vegas Valley.

The swelling new subdivisions, however, are merely an advance guard,

comparable to what Ragtown was to downtown in its day. Though they contain thousands of condos and row houses, they're dwarfed by the scale of the crowning real estate achievement of western Las Vegas: **Summerlin**, a 22,000-acre planned community.

A drive to Summerlin answers the oft-posed question "People actually live in Las Vegas?" Close to one million do. A territorial breed, West Las Vegans venture onto the Strip and into downtown infrequently, rarely even going to the east side of the city. They shop at the corner supermarket and the **Meadows Mall**, eat at the many neighborhood restaurants, and play in off-Strip casinos, such as **Arizona Charlie's, Gold Coast, Palace Station, Rio**, and **Santa Fe**, all of which are among the most popular and profitable in town.

Other than the casinos, parks, and museums, the **Southern Nevada Zoological Park**, the YESCO neon sign company, and the largest dance floor in town, at the **Gold Coast Hotel**, the primary reason to explore West Las Vegas is for the good local restaurants, bars, and shops. Even if you don't make a special trip here, certainly stop on the way to Red Rock Canyon—the heart of the Spring Mountains. The lofty and rugged Springs, southern Nevada's preeminent pinnacles, are perhaps the only barrier that can halt as inexorable a manifest destiny as that of Las Vegas.

1 Santa Fe Hotel and Casino $$ As the name suggests, each of the 200 rooms in this hotel is decorated in soothing Southwestern style. Amenities include three restaurants, a 24-hour coffee shop, the **Lone Mountain Buffet**, a fully equipped casino with sports and race book, over 300 slot machines, keno, and bingo; a state-of-the art 60-lane bowling center; and the public ice skating rink (see "Child's Play," page 21) where Olympic champions Oksana Baiul and Southern Nevada resident Viktor Petrenko practice when they are in town. ♦ 4949 N Rancho Dr (between Lone Mountain Rd and I-95). 658.4900, 800/872.6823

Within the Santa Fe Hotel and Casino:

Ti Amo ★★★$$ An airy courtyard setting and open kitchen make this an appealing place to relax and watch your dinner being prepared. Favorites on the innovative menu include pineapple pizza (with oven-dried pineapple and sun-dried cherries) and *française* trio (crab leg, veal, and chicken in a light wine sauce). Among the pasta specialties are *cappellini pomodoro* (thin pasta with basil and tomato sauce) and tortellini pesto. On Saturday and Sunday, there's an all-you-can-eat jazz and champagne brunch. ♦ Italian ♦ M-F lunch and dinner; Sa-Su brunch and dinner. Reservations recommended. 658.4900

Suzette's ★★★★$$$$ A perfect special occasion spot, this elegant restaurant seats only 50 guests. The formal French provincial decor is enhanced by sparkling crystal chandeliers, which are hung from a trompe l'oeil blue-sky ceiling. White-gloved waiters in formal attire serve such classic French presentations as capon à la Suzette (stuffed with wild mushrooms and spinach), tournedos of beef with truffles, scampi flambéed in a brandy cream sauce, and salmon poached in a Champagne sauce with smoked scallions. The extensive wine list includes Château Latour and Mondavi Opus One. ♦ French ♦ Tu-Sa dinner. Reservations recommended. 658.4900

Kodiak Lodge ★★★$$ Resembling a rustic hunting lodge, this charming room features rockscapes, redwood decor, and a 13-foot hand-carved bear at its entrance. Thick steaks and chops are prepared over a mesquite grill in the open kitchen. Seafood from the Pacific Northwest, including salmon, swordfish, and rainbow trout, is also featured. Chicken, pork loin, prime ribs, and baby back ribs are prepared to perfection on a rotisserie. Try the "shell and shore"—smoked scallop brochette and beef kabob. ♦ Steak house ♦ Daily dinner. Reservations recommended. 658.4900

2 Southern Nevada Zoological Park From the outside, this funky little zoo doesn't look like much. Once inside, that impression is often confirmed. But the big cats, chattering apes and monkeys, warbling tropical birds, Ronald the talking raven (he squawks "Hello!"), and other small animals are certainly worth a look, especially if you have kids in tow. There's also a petting zoo with six pygmy goats; full grown, they stand two feet tall. ♦ Admission. Daily. 1775 N Rancho Dr (at Melody La). 648.5995

3 Siegfried & Roy House Tucked away behind a high white fence and a gate guarded by lions (the statuary type), this mission-style mansion topped by a gilt dome sprawls over half a city block. The luxuriant landscape provides a suitably exotic hideaway for the two German-born magicians who shoot tigers from a cannon—and then bring them home for a dip in the pool. Siegfried & Roy are now at the top of their game: Their $57.5-million deal with **The Mirage** is, according to Guinness, the largest live entertainment contract ever signed. They sell out the 1,500 most expensive seats in Las Vegas every night. (Tickets to their show are double the price of the second most expensive one in town.) This is your opportunity to gawk at a Hollywood-type home in Las Vegas, but remember, it's private property. ♦ 4200 Vegas Dr (at Valley Dr)

4 Lorenzi Park David Lorenzi's **Twin Lakes Resort,** a ritzy hideaway for locals, stood on this site in the 1920s. The five-acre pond is still a popular place for small boating, duck feeding, and lazing on sunny afternoons, although the once-famous bandstand is now gone. In various far-flung corners of the park are the **Nevada State Museum and Historical Society,** the **Las Vegas Art Museum,** a 20-year-old rose garden, numerous tennis courts, soccer and base-ball fields, a play-ground, and picnic tables. Wide-open grassy areas are abundant in the center of the park and are ideal for Frisbee tossing. ♦ 3300 W Washington Ave (at Twin Lakes Dr). 229.6358

Within Lorenzi Park:

Las Vegas Art Museum With a nod to the city's indigenous industry, this 1930s-era relic from the **Twin Lakes Resort** is constructed of railroad ties. Inside, a trio of galleries displays the works of local modern artists; a public reception for the exhibitors is held on the first Sunday of each month. The museum also houses a permanent collection of 200 pieces of western American art, which are rotated frequently. ♦ Donation requested. M-Sa 10AM-3PM; Su noon-3PM. 3333 W Washington Ave (at Twin Lakes Dr). 647.4300

5 Nevada State Museum and Historical Society The exhibits at this state-run museum give visitors a surprisingly in-depth overview of the history, anthropology, and archaeology of the region. One room is devoted to natural history, where the various environmental zones of southern Nevada are presented in compelling dioramas of bighorn sheep, cougars, and a variety of snakes, cholla and cactus, and insects. Another section focuses on the historical events that shaped the state, from the era of the Pueblo and Paiute Indians through the ranching, railroad, and mining days to modern times (a parti-cularly poignant exhibit covers the nearby Nevada Test Site and its atmospheric and underground nuclear explosions; the photos of soldiers purposefully exposed to shock waves and fallout are quite graphic). A third gallery hosts changing historic and photo-graphic exhibits. In the lobby, a gift shop sells books, cards, jewelry, and souvenirs. History buffs can consult the on-site research center for help in answering questions. ♦ Admission. Daily. 700 Twin Lakes Dr (at W Washington Ave). 486.5205

6 Meadows Mall Four major department stores anchor this sprawling, two-level enclosed shopping center. Besides the usual jewelry, apparel, home furnishings, book, and toy stores, there's a merry-go-round in the mall—a great diversion for the kids. ♦ M-F 10AM-9PM; Sa-Su 10AM-6PM. 4300 Meadows La (between Valley View and N Decatur Blvds). 878.4849

7 Summerlin Smitten with Las Vegas, billionaire Howard Hughes began investing in the city in the early 1950s. One deal involved purchasing 25,000 acres of desert from the Southern Pacific Railroad for $62,500. Hughes then engineered a trade for an extremely valuable 22,000-acre tract between the town and the Spring Mountains, using reasons of "national security" (in the guise of his defense contracts with the Pentagon) to steamroll over the objections of locals, who were shocked that the federal government would make such a blatantly bad exchange. For the next three decades, the 39-square-mile parcel was known as Husite.

Today, the property is being developed by Hughes's Summa Corporation and is named Summerlin, after Howard's grandmother. Summerlin ranks as the fastest-growing community in the fastest-growing city in the country. Fifteen minutes from downtown and 20 minutes from the Strip, it is Las Vegas's largest bedroom community. Its slight elevation affords beautiful views of the whole valley, which looks especially spectacular when the sun sets over the Spring Mountains, providing a natural light show to rival the neon display of downtown.

The community is so vast that it won't be finished until the year 2020, when it will be nearly as large as Las Vegas was in the 1980s. Eighty thousand houses will be spread over 30 neighborhoods, which are slated to be 60 percent residential, 25 percent parkland and greenbelt, and 15 percent retail and roads. Three of seven villages in the 6,000-acre first phase are currently under construction, including Del Webb's 2,000-acre Sun City, an adult (50 and over) community rising frantically to handle the huge demand of the many migrating retirees. ◆ Take Hwy 95 north 4 miles to Summerlin Pkwy; make a left onto the parkway, which will lead to the information center

8 West Charleston Library Bookies of a different sort will appreciate this 1993 work of the local architectural firm **Welles-Pugsley.** The interior is spacious and comfortable, with ample windows conducive to curling up with a classic. A high, vaulted ceiling runs down the main axis of the library, directing visitors to the reference and circulation desks. Within the 40,000-square-foot building are 160,000 volumes, a 280-seat lecture hall, conference rooms, an art gallery, a health-science library, and a young people's library complete with the **High-Flying Theater,** where storytelling programs are held. The landscaping is an artful example of Xeriscaping, which employs drought-resistant plants. ◆ M-Th 9AM-9PM; F-Sa 9AM-5PM; Su noon-5PM. 6301 W Charleston Blvd (at Torrey Pines Dr). 878.3682

9 Arizona Charlie's
The Southwestern flair of this neighborhood casino attracts a local patronage; it's usually jammed with video-poker players, paycheck cashers, and West Las Vegans out for a few drinks in the popular lounge. And it has a well-deserved reputation as a hot spot for video poker; look for the quarter video-poker machines that pay a thousand dollars for four aces as well as a royal and give you a 2.5 percent edge over the house. There's a hard-count room with windows where you can watch casino personnel count and process a river of quarters. ◆ Daily 24 hours. 740 S Decatur Blvd (at Evergreen Ave). 258.5200, 800/342.2695

Within Arizona Charlie's:

Coffee Shop $ Breakfast for four bits? You bet! Choose from eggs and bacon, pancakes and sausage, or biscuits and gravy, for just 49¢. Take a friend and spring for the bill: $1.06. ◆ Coffee shop ◆ Daily 24 hours; closed Monday 2-7AM. 258.5200

Chin's ★★★$$$ This intimate 64-seat jewel is decorated with framed antique Asian embroideries and portraits of royalty from the Qing and Tang dynasties. A mural of an old Chinese house on one wall is complemented by one of a garden on another; a dragon and phoenix medallion hangs inside the entrance for good luck. A stream of water (which symbolizes money and luck, according to Chinese tradition) flows through the restaurant; there are even miniature bridges across it. A pagoda in the center of the cozy room encloses the traditional round table for 10, and Chinese lanterns hung overhead create a romantic glow.

The menu duplicates that of Tola Chin's other popular, eponymous eatery on the Strip. Appetizers include *moo shu* pork (shredded pork and vegetables rolled in pancakes), steamed scallops on the half shell, and hot-and-sour and *war won ton* soups. Among the best main dishes are wok-cooked vegetables with chicken, sea-food, or beef; lobster with mushrooms; spicy chicken; crispy duck; and sweet-and-sour pork. For dessert, choose the lychees and cherries jubilee, flamed at tableside. ◆ Chinese ◆ Tu-Su dinner. Reservations recommended. 258.5173. Also at: 3200 Las Vegas Blvd S (at Spring Mountain Rd). 733.8899

10 Aristocrat ★★$$$$ One of a handful of independent gourmet restaurants, this cozy hideaway with English touches reflects its British owner's heritage. It's a favorite among well-heeled locals, who come to partake of such house specialties as mussels vinaigrette, osso buco, beef Wellington, and chicken Oscar (chicken topped with crabmeat, asparagus, and béarnaise sauce). ◆ Continental ◆ M-F lunch and dinner; Sa-Su dinner. Reservations recommended. 850 S Rancho Dr (between W Charleston Blvd and Alta Dr). 870.1977

11 Amber Unicorn
Las Vegas isn't exactly known for its literary traditions. Most of the used-book stores in the city are of the 50¢ paperback variety, which is why this shop is such a standout. Stocking thousands of titles in every conceivable category, they have paperbacks, hardcovers, leatherbound volumes, and first editions and author-signed copies. It's as well organized and neat as a library (except for the children's section, which is supposed to be untidy). Best of all, a big sign on the door proclaims "Ice Cream Welcome," encouraging cone-carrying customers from the next-door **Baskin-Robbins** to come in and look while they lick. ◆ Daily. 2202 W Charleston Blvd (at S Rancho Dr). 384.5838

12 Poppa Gar's ★$$ Poppa Garland Miner is without a doubt the oldest restaurateur in these parts, having started his culinary career in a Fremont Street coffee shop in the early 1940s. The walls here are peppered with autographed photos of celebrities and politicians, deer and moose trophies, and mounted fish. Poppa serves unadulterated diner-style food, with a few oddities thrown in, such as buffalo burgers, quail omelettes, pan-fried trout, and grape-nut custard. ♦ American ♦ M-F breakfast, lunch, and dinner; Sa breakfast and lunch. 1624 W Oakey Blvd (at Western St). 384.4513

13 Palace Station Hotel $$ This tiny bingo parlor opened in the late 1970s. Since then, it's grown into one of the premier off-Strip hotels. The 12-story tower was built in 1991 and the well-maintained rooms still feel new, with firm beds and comfortable chairs; they have good views of the city too. Including the older garden rooms, which are low-rise, motel style, there are 1,030 rooms. The lounge has entertainment nightly, and a free shuttle bus runs every hour to and from the Strip. ♦ 2411 W Sahara Ave (at Rancho Dr). 367.2411, 800/634.3101; fax 367.6138

Within the Palace Station Hotel:

Palace Station Casino The hotel sports a railroad motif, and the main casino pit offers a brief lesson in Nevada's railway heritage: Depot-type awnings advertise the Union Pacific, Las Vegas & Tonopah; Tonopah & Tidewater; and Virginia & Truckee lines. The 550-seat bingo room is one of the busiest around, and the 200-seat race and sports book has 42 TV screens. ♦ Daily 24 hours. 367.2411

Fisherman's Broiler ★★$$$ An amazing meal deal is the main draw here. From Sunday through Thursday, the one-pound Alaskan king crab-leg dinner, served with bread, salad, potato, and vegetables, is half price. The fat foot-long legs are cooked to steaming perfection and piled high on the plate. The food is not only first-rate, it's also reliable, appearing on the *Las Vegas Advisor*'s "Top 10 Values" list for years. Other dishes include trout, orange roughy, scallops, shrimp tempura, and the catch of the day. ♦ Seafood ♦ Daily lunch and dinner. Reservations recommended for dinner. 367.2411

Guadalajara Bar and Grill ★$ Stop first at the bar outside the restaurant and grab a 16-ounce margarita for the price of a straight keno ticket. Then sit down at a booth inside and savor the excellent burritos, *chile verde*, *típico del mar* (seafood platter), the Humunga Chunga (a one-and-a-half-pound chimi-changa), or *chimijitas* (grilled marinated steak with onions, green peppers, guacamole, and sour cream, wrapped in a tortilla and deep-fried). ♦ Mexican ♦ Daily lunch and dinner. Reservations recommended for dinner. 367.2411

Feast Buffet ★$ The feast proffered here is worthy of its moniker and good reputation. Short-order cooks prepare eggs, waffles, burgers, and sandwiches and slice huge slabs of lamb, beef, and pork before your eyes. Salads and desserts are plentiful. ♦ Buffet ♦ Daily breakfast, lunch, and dinner. 367.2411

14 Cafe Michelle West ★★★$$$ Romeo's has closed down, and in its place in **The Plaza**—a strip shopping center on one of the busiest drags in Las Vegas—is this newly opened replica of East Las Vegas's popular **Cafe Michelle.** Lush landscaping creates a secluded, even bucolic setting. A footbridge spans two ponds with spurting Roman fountains and leads to two courtyards that are ideal for alfresco dining. The front patio is shielded from the parking lot by thick, high shrubbery; the sheltered side piazza is shaded by ivy-covered trellises. Inside, choose between two very chic dining rooms. The menu is just as diverse as at its East Side cousin, and the Monique and Normandie crepes are just as good. ♦ Continental ♦ Daily lunch and dinner. Reservations recommended for four or more. 2800 W Sahara Ave (at Paseo del Prado). 873.5400

Many locals still refer to the predominantly African-American Las Vegas neighborhoods just west of Interstate 15 and the Union Pacific railroad tracks as the Westside, although geographically the area is now closer to the middle of town. The name, now considered politically incorrect by many of Las Vegas's black leaders, dates back to the city's early days, when poor and minority residents settled on the side of the railroad tracks opposite downtown.

14 Coffee Pub ★★$$ This charming, friendly gathering spot featuring patio dining is popular with local movers and shakers. The menu includes imaginative salads, sandwiches, pastries, espresso, cappuccino, and *caffè latte.* ♦ American ♦ Daily breakfast and lunch. 2800 W Sahara Ave (at Paseo del Prado). 367.1913

15 In-N-Out Burger ★$ An institution in southern California since 1948, this Las Vegas location, opened in 1992, is the chain's first venture outside the Golden State. Quick to cop top honors in the *Las Vegas Review-Journal's* "Best of Las Vegas" readers' poll, its popularity derives from its use of fresh ingredients. Management claims that no restaurant in the entire chain has ever owned a freezer. The french fries are peeled, cut, and fried to order, and the lemonade is freshly squeezed. The Double-Double is the specialty: two quarter-pound burgers and two slices of cheese. If you're hankering for a real cholesterol fest, order a Three-by-Three or a Four-by-Four, even though those options aren't on the menu. The building is so white and brightly lit that it's impossible to miss; just look for the dozen or so cars lined up at the drive-through window. ♦ Burgers ♦ Daily lunch and dinner. 2900 W Sahara Ave (at Paseo del Prado). No phone

16 Port Tack ★$$$ This popular restaurant has something for every appetite at almost any hour of the day or night. In addition to one of the town's few oyster bars, there's the usual rib-sticking repertoire of burgers, hot sandwiches, ribs, steak, and chicken. But the fish dishes are really the stars here. An ocean of choices—shark, ono, ahi, sea bass, trout, king crab, live Maine lobster, and seafood kabobs—comes with bread, linguine with clam sauce, and one trip to the salad bar. A record 1,150-pound blue marlin is fixed mid-leap on one wall, and east-facing window seats enjoy a panoramic view of downtown. ♦ American ♦ Daily lunch, dinner, and late-night snacks 10AM-6AM. 3190 W Sahara Ave (at Spanish Oaks Dr). 873.3345

The next time people talk about "Sin City," throw this statistic at them: There are more churches per capita in Las Vegas than in any other city in America. Locals representing 63 religious faiths attend services in almost 500 places of worship.

17 The Venetian Ristorante ★★★$$$ Bearing a trompe l'oeil mural worthy of early Disney (or late **Circus Circus**), the structure in which this restaurant is housed has been a local landmark for almost four decades. The painter's touch continues inside, with a *Mona Lisa* replica and cityscapes of Venice adorning the walls. The menu is a work of art as well, with pages of pasta, veal, chicken, seafood, and wine selections. The pork neckbones marinated and simmered in a vinegar, caper, and wine sauce are humble but succulent. From 4PM to 6PM, a less pricey early-bird menu features *bruschetta* (toasted garlic bread) with roasted peppers, basil, and parmesan; Caesar salad; pizzas; and the famous Venetian greens on a bed of pasta. ♦ Italian ♦ Daily dinner. 3713 W Sahara Ave (at Valley View Blvd). 876.4190

18 Saigon Restaurant ★★ $ This intimate 12-table restaurant is the best place in Las Vegas for Vietnamese food. Anyone who tastes the imperial rolls will never accept mere egg rolls again. Other light eats are the Vietnamese pizza appetizer, sour soups, or spicy lemon-beef salad. Fifteen *pho* (noodle) dishes and a couple of clay-pot (hearty soup) selections are available. The Vietnamese version of beef fondue and several other authentic entrées are cooked right at the table. Ask for the special coconut-curry sauce to spice things up. ♦ Vietnamese ♦ Daily lunch and dinner. 4251 W Sahara Ave (at Arville St). 362.9978

19 Philip's Supper House ★★$$$$ Between the Strip's **Golden Steer** and this place, upward of 2,000 steak dinners can be served on Sahara Avenue on a busy night. This rambling building is divided into a number of small dining rooms; those looking for tête-à-tête tables can reserve one of several *very* private booths. Going beyond beef, there's blackened or crab-stuffed scampi, sand dabs (small fish from the West Coast served sautéed or fried), halibut *picanti* (with hot chilies), and daily fresh fish specials. Veal, chicken, and lamb chops round out the menu. All meals come with soup or salad, potato or vegetable, and hot, fresh-baked bread. A mannequin sits at the player piano in the bar, and a sign makes the management's sentiments on unruly children perfectly clear. ♦ American/Italian ♦ Daily dinner. Reservations recommended. 4545 W Sahara Ave (between Arville St and S Decatur Blvd). 873.5222

20 Chiasso Cafe ★★★$$ This bright, cheerful restaurant serves good, light Italian fare. The salads—with grilled chicken, salmon, or shrimp and unusual vinaigrette dressings—are topped only by the gourmet pizzas. For something a little heartier, look for the creative recipes developed by owner Giovanni Vancheri's late father, Salvatore. Family tradition lives on in such culinary legacies as eggplant Angelina (named for Giovanni's mother, it has three cheeses, boiled egg, and tomato sauce) and veal scallopini Salvatore (sautéed in white wine and baked with eggplant, mozzarella, and marinara sauce). Particularly tasty is the angel hair *gamberetti* (with shrimp in a lemon-pepper sauce). ♦ Italian ♦ Daily lunch and dinner. Reservations recommended. 4712 W Sahara Ave (at S Decatur Blvd). 877.2870

20 Mayflower Cuisinier ★★★$$$ Hong Kong–born chef-owner Ming See Woo and her daughter Theresa offer their well-heeled clientele (many of whom are Chinese) a unique fusion of Asian and French cuisines. Fashioning their menu after the likes of LA superchefs Wolfgang Puck and Tommy Tang, the mother-daughter team's cross-cultural recipes include roast duck salad with plum vinaigrette, grilled tenderloin of beef with Mongolian sauce, shrimp in pineapple-apricot sauce with scallion noodles, and the ginger chicken ravioli with scallion-Szechuan sauce. The decor is sleek and modern, with Asian etchings on the walls. There's a mezzanine that seats about 30 and a patio for alfresco dining; it's heated in the winter and cooled in the summer. ♦ Asian/French ♦ M-F lunch and dinner; Sa dinner. Reservations recommended. 4750 W Sahara Ave (at Decatur Blvd). 870.8432

Locals like to brag that Las Vegas has only about 10 rainy days a year. But in 1992 the National Weather Service measured 9.88 inches of rain in the Las Vegas Valley, or more than double the city's annual average of 4.2 inches. That made 1992 the second wettest year in the valley since 1907.

Howard Hughes's Las Vegas purchases between 1966 and 1970 included six casinos, several office buildings, hundreds of pieces of property, an airport, airline, TV station, and mining claims. The total bill: $300 million.

---

20 Cafe Nicolle ★★★$$$ Featuring an eclectic menu of Greek, American, and Italian cuisine, this place serves spinach pie side by side with osso buco and Atlantic salmon cakes. You can also choose from a variety of pastas, egg and crepe dishes, salads (the garlicky Caesar is very popular), and seafood or chicken preparations. The outdoor patio is comfortable for alfresco dining year-round. It's heated in the winter and—more important in the desert—cooled with an overhead misting system in the summer. After dinner, move to the lounge to hear the singer–piano player perform a set combining rock, jazz, and contemporary music. Scrumptious desserts —apricot crepes, tiramisù, or *tartufos* (ice-cream balls covered with chocolate, white chocolate, or macadamia nuts)—are served here, as are cappuccino, espresso, and *caffè latte*. ♦ Continental ♦ M-F lunch and dinner; Sa dinner. Reservations recommended for dinner. 4760 Sahara Ave (at Decatur Blvd). 870.7675

21 Cul-tur-ati ★★$$ Though at first glance this place looks like a coffee house (there are magazines and newspapers for diners' perusal), it's a bona fide restaurant. The cheerful, young wait staff serves everything from homemade muffins and pastries and a variety of imaginative salads, soups, and sandwiches to full-course meals. Appetizers such as turkey cakes, fried calamari, and focaccia are followed by pizzas or such whimsically named entrées as Sam 'n' Luigi (fettuccine with smoked salmon, cream, and chives), Foo C. Lee (pasta with grilled chicken, broccoli, garlic, and extra virgin olive oil), Urban Cowperson (grilled rib-eye steak and mashed potatoes), and Big Bird on the Barbie (grilled turkey breast on fettuccine with artichokes, olives, mushrooms, and capers). ♦ American ♦ M-Th lunch and dinner; F-Sa breakfast, lunch, and dinner; Su brunch and dinner. Reservations recommended. 2570 S Decatur Blvd (at W Sahara Ave). 227.8080. Also at: 3801 N Rainbow Blvd (between Cheyenne Ave and Lake Mead Blvd). 655.8800

22 North Beach Cafe ★★★$$ At this casual bistro, named for an Italian neighborhood in San Francisco, you can almost feel the breeze off the bay. The walls are decorated with customers' tablecloth crayon drawings and Impressionist paintings. Though owner Osvaldo Montano was born in Spain and grew up in Argentina, his father was born in Italy, as was the family of his wife and co-owner, Judy. The cuisine is mainly Northern Italian, reminiscent of the foods of Genoa, where seafood cooked in a light tomato sauce is prevalent. Among the specialties are *linguine pesto alla Genovese* (with extra virgin olive oil, fresh basil, garlic, and parmesan cheese), *agnolotti alla crema* (pasta with cream sauce) or *pomodoro* (with basil and tomato sauce), *linguine pescatore* (pasta with shellfish) with red or white sauce, and *chicken piccata* (with capers, white wine, and lemon). ♦ Northern Italian. ♦ M-F lunch and dinner; Sa dinner. Reservations recommended. 2605 S Decatur Blvd (at W Sahara Ave). 247.9530

22 Shalimar Fine Indian Cuisine ★★$$ A culinary-savvy clientele of Indian nationals and vegetarians raves about this place. Start with a vegetable or lamb *samosa* (deep-fried pastry) or the chicken *biryani* (basmati rice cooked with mildly spiced boneless chicken), then order some bread (seasoned to complement your menu choice) baked in the tandoori oven. The curries are spiced to your preference: mild, medium, hot, or incendiary. Veggie plates include eggplant stew, potato and cauliflower curry, and *chana masala* (chickpeas cooked in the traditional Punjabi style). ♦ Indian ♦ M-F lunch and dinner; Sa-Su dinner. 2605 S Decatur Blvd (at W Sahara Ave). 252.8320

23 Chinese Garden Restaurant ★$$ This giant pagodaesque restaurant (pictured above) seats nearly 400 and has a similarly expansive menu of fresh and healthy Cantonese and Szechuan food. Stir-fry, noodle, and rice dishes abound, and there's also dim sum for lunch, *kung pao* and *moo shu* entrées, and live lobster and crab. Chef's specialties include pressed almond duck with taro, walnut shrimp, and steak *kew* (sliced tenderloin with a tangy sauce, bell peppers, onions, and pineapple). ♦ Chinese ♦ Daily lunch and dinner. 5485 W Sahara Ave (between S Decatur and Jones Blvds). 876.5432

Nevada ranks 49th out of 50 states for the adverse impact of lifestyle factors on health, according to studies by the Nevada State Medical Association. The death rate from smoking is 22 percent higher than the national average, and deaths from chronic liver disease (caused by alcohol) are 62 percent above the national average.

Restaurants/Clubs: Red   **Hotels:** Blue
Shops/🍴 Outdoors: Green   **Sights/Culture:** Black

24 Big Dog's Cafe & Casino ★★$$ The 15-foot-tall mural of a whiskey-toting Saint Bernard on the facade is a sign of things to come inside. All manner of doggie decor fills the bar: Dogs play pool and poker, pups have a picnic, hounds howl at the moon. Posters of poodles, puppies, and pugs cover the walls. The restaurant serves American, Mexican, and Italian food. Of course, there's a row of video-poker machines. On your way out, pick up a T-shirt with the slogan "If you can't run with the big dogs, then just stay on the porch." ♦ American/Mexican/Italian ♦ Daily 24 hours. 6390 W Sahara Ave (at Torrey Pines Dr). 786.3647

25 Ferraro's Cafe ★★★$$$ The combined aromas of bread baking and sauces simmering enhance the Old World atmosphere in this traditional Southern Italian restaurant. Originally a combination grocery store, deli, and sandwich shop, it now offers a classic Roman-style setting, with white walls, columns, and recessed lighting; there's also a 60-seat banquet room, a full bar, and dancing and live entertainment in the evening.

The most popular appetizer is the *ripieno di carciofo* (artichoke stuffed with bread crumbs, fresh garlic, romano cheese, and black olives in a light wine sauce). Owner Gino Ferraro, who doubles as chef and assists his wife Rosalba in the dining room, creates imaginative pasta and seafood dishes. Osso buco is Gino's specialty, and Rosalba makes the tiramisù. ♦ Italian ♦ Daily dinner. Reservations recommended. 5900 W Flamingo Rd (at S Jones Blvd). 364.5300

26 Traveling Books & Maps Whether you're bound for foreign soil, looking for local info, or are an enthusiastic armchair traveler, you'll find a good selection of all kinds of guides here. Maps and atlases, a few travel accessories, globes, "Wearing the World" windbreakers, and language aids are also stocked. There's an extensive section on the Southwest, including, of course, guides and maps to Las Vegas and its environs. ♦ M-Sa. 4001 S Decatur Blvd (at W Flamingo Rd). 871.8082

27 Garlic Cafe ★★$$ A theme restaurant, its menu includes the largest variety of dishes made with the fragrant rose that you can imagine. Meals begin with garlic bagel chips accompanied by garlic dip. Pungent entrées include fettuccine Ginalollabroccoli (pasta with sautéed garlic, chicken, and broccoli in a creamy alfredo sauce), Jamaican Me Crazy chicken (charbroiled chicken with a tangy jerk sauce of peppers, black pepper, and allspice), Veal Burt & Ernie, Because Oscar's A Grouch (veal scallopini sautéed with garlic and topped with crab, shrimp, and béarnaise sauce), all served with sliced red potatoes baked in olive oil and spices. You'd think they couldn't carry the clove theme to the dessert course, but adventurous customers order the garlic ice cream every time. Of course, if you are not planning on meeting any vampires for a postprandial stroll, you can request a lesser degree of garlic in any of the dishes.
♦ Continental ♦ M-F lunch and dinner; Sa-Su dinner. Reservations recommended. 3650 S Decatur Blvd (at Twain Ave). 221.0266

28 Bamboo Garden ★★★$$ The city's sleeper restaurant of the decade, its unique and imaginative menu is known only to the most informed West Las Vegans. The cream of seafood soup is thick with crab, shrimp, and scallops. A fiery sesame sauce douses deep-fried Hunan eggplant. Other favorites include clams *dou chi* (sautéed in a hot black-bean sauce with ginger, scallions, and sherry) and *kung pao* frogs' legs served with red peppers and peanuts. The room is very comfortable, although the decor is a bit sparse—all the flourishes are found in the food. Because it's hidden away in a common corner shopping center, the restaurant is rarely crowded. The service is superb. ♦ Chinese ♦ M-Sa lunch and dinner; Su dinner. 4850 W Flamingo Rd (at S Decatur Blvd). 871.3262

29 Hometown News Anywhere else in the country, this funky and bare shop might lead you to suspect the presence of a back-room gambling den. But this newsstand carries all the major American Sunday papers, from the *Anchorage Daily News* to the *Tampa Tribune,* from the *Boston Globe* to the *San Diego Union.* They also stock about 20 foreign newspapers, hundreds of national and international magazines, and tons of paperbacks. Even so, the racks and stands hardly make a dent in the vast storefront space. ♦ Daily. 4557 W Flamingo Rd (at Cameron St). 364.0052

30 Terrible Herbst's Detail Plus In the freewheeling 1930s, Old Man Herbst was such a ferocious competitor in the midwestern oil business that he earned the nickname "Terrible." His company later moved to Las Vegas and now has a couple of dozen gasoline stations, car washes, and detail centers around town. This one will give your auto a total interior-exterior scrubbing, which includes everything from shampooing the carpets to cleaning out the heater vents and fender wells, plus a hand wash and wax. The name is something of an in-joke among residents, with a meaning more or less synonymous with a hangover or headache. (You might hear someone say, "I was at **Big Dog's** till the wee hours yesterday and I have a Terrible Herbst" or "If you don't stop bugging me, you're gonna give me a Terrible Herbst.") ♦ Daily. 4310 W Flamingo Rd (at Arville St). 876.9105

31 Gold Coast Hotel $$ If ever a hotel-casino tried to be all things to all people, this one did. Besides the 700 reasonably priced rooms, there are two lounges showcasing live entertainment nightly. Happy hoofers fill the largest dance floor in Las Vegas, and two movie theaters screen first-run flicks. The second floor hosts a 72-lane bowling alley and a cavernous bingo hall. A big buffet, coffee shop, and snack bar serve tons of food daily. There's also a steak house, a Mediterranean restaurant, an ice-cream parlor, a liquor store, a gift shop, and slot-club redemption center (members play slots with a type of credit card and accrue points that they cash in for prizes). Drive on over—thousands of cars can park here. And the consensus is that the best prizes in town are offered to those who cash their paychecks here—some lucky winners get a turn in the money-grabbing booth. You could stay in this hotel for weeks on end and never run out of things to do. ♦ 4000 W Flamingo Rd (at Valley View Blvd). 367.7111, 800/331.5334; fax 367.8575

YESCO (Young Electric Sign Company) has installed 3.5 million light bulbs in Las Vegas; if laid end to end, they would stretch 15,000

Reels of Fortune: Vegas Goes to Hollywood

The gaudy rhinestone Las Vegas skyline has long provided a visually irresistible backdrop for movies, advertisements, rock videos, and TV series.

The following list stars the most significant movies filmed in Las Vegas, plus a few that were supposedly set here but were actually shot elsewhere.

Las Vegas Story (1952) Gambler Vincent Price takes his wife (Jane Russell) to Las Vegas, where she runs into her former-lover-turned-detective (Victor Mature). Howard Hughes produced this melodrama more than a decade before he moved to Vegas and ushered the city into the corporate world.

Meet Me in Las Vegas (1956) Cyd Charisse is a French ballerina lured to the showrooms of Las Vegas and romanced by Dan Dailey in this MGM musical. Showroom stars Lena Horne and Frankie Laine make guest appearances.

The Amazing Colossal Man (1957) This laughably camp thriller offers amazing footage of **the Strip** when the title character—an Army officer turned into a giant by a nuclear explosion—decides to go for a stroll. The final showdown takes place at **Hoover Dam.** See it back-to-back with *Honey, I Blew Up the Kid.*

Ocean's Eleven (1960) Frank Sinatra, Sammy Davis Jr., Dean Martin, and Peter Lawford lead a group of war buddies planning to rob five casinos at once on New Year's Eve.

Viva Las Vegas (1964) One of the best Elvis movies, thanks to costar Ann-Margret and a title tune that gave the city an anthem.

Diamonds Are Forever (1971) For James Bond fans, there's skulduggery in **Circus Circus,** a car chase on **Fremont Street,** and agent 007's (Sean Connery) ascent to the villain's headquarters on top of "The Whyte House."

The Gauntlet (1977) Clint Eastwood plays a dimwitted cop sent to Las Vegas to bring back a hooker (Sondra Locke) to testify against corrupt police officers.

The Electric Horseman (1979) The romantic pairing of Robert Redford and Jane Fonda when both were at the height of their appeal was a hit. Redford's the fallen rodeo champ who saves a racehorse from corporate evildoers by riding it through **Caesars Palace** and down the Strip into the nearby mountains.

Melvin and Howard (1980) Perennial loser Melvin Dummar (Paul Le Mat) gives scruffy hitchhiker (Jason Robards) a ride to Las Vegas. He later produces a will supposedly written by Howard Hughes, a.k.a. the hitcher, that leaves him $156 million.

One From the Heart (1982) The film that sent Francis Ford Coppola into bankruptcy eschews the real **Glitter Gulch** for a stylized soundstage mock-up that's the way people wish downtown could be.

Oh God! You Devil (1984) Portraying both God and the Devil, George Burns works his old **Caesars Palace** haunts (Burns himself has been a Vegas showroom performer for five decades) in this pleasant but forgettable comedy.

Starman (1984) A road-flick/science-fiction romance pairs a stranded alien (Jeff Bridges) with an earthling companion (Karen Allen). The couple taps some slots in Las Vegas during their quest to get him home.

Lost In America (1985) The **Desert Inn** is the unfortunate first stop for a yuppie couple who decide to drop out of the rat race and travel across America by motor home. This cult classic directed by Albert Brooks includes a hilarious marital argument at Hoover Dam.

Rocky IV (1985) Props from the *Jubilee!* show at **Bally's** turn up in James Brown's "Living in America" musical number in this Sylvester Stallone boxing film. Stallone returned to Las Vegas for an arm-wrestling tournament in the equally silly *Over the Top* (1987).

Heat (1987) Burt Reynolds is a Las Vegas bodyguard with a compulsive gambling problem.

Kill Me Again (1988) A private eye (Val Kilmer) follows a mysterious woman (Joanne Whalley) from Reno to Las Vegas, **Lake Mead,** and the **Valley of Fire,** all of which are shown to good effect amid the violent plot twists.

Rain Man (1988) A hostile young man (Tom Cruise) gets to know his long-separated autistic brother (Dustin Hoffman) on a cross-country road trip in this Oscar-winning drama. **Caesars Palace** looks dazzling as the site of their triumph at the card table. Nearby Nevada locations were used to shoot scenes of rural America.

Bugsy (1991) The riveting story of charismatic gangster Benjamin "Bugsy" Siegel (Warren Beatty) and his vision of Las Vegas could not be filmed here—except for a closing shot of the **Flamingo Hotel**—simply because nothing in Las Vegas looks as it did in 1946.

Cool World (1992) A Las Vegas comic book artist (Gabriel Byrne) and his fantasy-girl-come-to-life (Kim Basinger) share adventures in this combination live-action and animation film created by Ralph Bakshi (*Fritz the Cat*).

Honey, I Blew Up the Kid (1992) Disney's comic sequel to *Honey, I Shrunk the Kids* revisits the climax to *The Amazing Colossal Man*, setting a giant baby loose on Fremont Street.

Honeymoon In Vegas (1992) A charming sleaze ball (James Caan) tries to woo away the fiancée (Sarah Jessica Parker) of a commitment-shy detective (Nicolas Cage). The memorable climax features a team of Elvis impersonators parachuting into the **Bally's** parking lot.

Indecent Proposal (1993) Robert Redford is the smooth gambler who comes between a young couple (Demi Moore and Woody Harrelson) by offering the wife $1 million to spend the night with him. Locations include the **Las Vegas Hilton.**

City Slickers II (1994) The sequel starring Billy Crystal and Jack Palance continues the story of male bonding out West. Although Palance expired in the original, the Oscar winner comes back as his own brother.

Sister Act II (1994) Whoopi Goldberg, a nightclub performer, hides from the "bad guys" in a convent.

Star Trek: Generations (1994) Shot in the colorful Valley of Fire, this time-travel story pairs retired Starship *Enterprise* Captain Kirk (William Shatner) with the future's Captain Picard (Patrick Stewart) to save a planet from destruction.

When a player wins a jackpot of more than $1,200, the casino is required to check ID and to file the IRS's Form W-2G. The winner must provide identification and sign the form, and then has to report the winnings to the IRS as income; gambling losses may be deducted against winnings, but only with proof of loss, which is difficult to substantiate.

Within the Gold Coast Hotel:

Gold Coast Casino A large pit dominates the main room, and the din of hundreds of video-poker machines fills another chamber. The casino boasts more than 2,000 slots and video-poker machines. The bingo parlor is a 750-seater, and of the 32 blackjack tables, more than half have one-, two-, or three-dollar minimum bets. ◆ Daily 24 hours. 367.7111

32 Rio Suite Hotel $$$ Since this hotel opened in 1990, it's been a continuous hit; its stunning neon sign immediately supplanted the **Stardust**'s as the town's most popular. Locals like the off-Strip location, easily accessible from Interstate 15, and visitors appreciate the festive atmosphere and luxurious accommodations. Each of the 1,410 rooms is a 600-square-foot suite, with a mini-refrigerator, a wet bar, and unobstructed views of the Strip to one side and West Las Vegas to the other. Everyone raves about the food; the restaurants are excellent. Delicious breads are baked for the hotel's eateries and sold to the public at the **Toscano Deli & Market**. At lunch, the **Beach Cafe** and the **All American Bar & Grille** are popular contenders for the best grilled chicken sandwiches in town. A sandy manmade beach leads to the shallow end of the swimming pool. ◆ 3700 W Flamingo Rd (at I-15). 252.7777, 800/752.9746; fax 252.7670

Within the Rio Suite Hotel:

Rio Suite Casino An unusual feature in this casino has players seeing double: video-poker machines topped with small TVs. You can catch a football game, your favorite soap opera, or an "I Love Lucy" rerun while you try to beat the odds. ◆ Daily 24 hours. 252.7777

Celebrities who call Las Vegas home (at least for tax purposes) include Wayne Newton, Siegfried & Roy, Paul Anka, Jerry Lewis, Debbie Reynolds, Robert Goulet, Rip Taylor, Gladys Knight, jazz singer Joe Williams, and the rock band Slaughter (singer Mark Slaughter is a native).

Opened in February 1991, the Santa Fe Hotel and Casino is the most recent Nevada addition to the Sahara Gaming Corporation, which is now listed on the American Stock Exchange.

Antonio's ★★★$$$ Few Las Vegas restaurants can match the quality, setting, and service found here. The elegant dining room is a mélange of marble and glass crowned with a domed trompe l'oeil ceiling. Veal is the specialty; try the osso buco, veal scallops in a mushroom-wine sauce, or veal piccata. Chicken preparations include parmesan, Marsala, or *melanzana ai pomodori* (with layers of eggplant, provolone, and tomato sauce). And the chef isn't afraid to experiment—pasta with baby artichoke hearts, fresh garlic, and black olives and veal ravioli in a black-walnut cream sauce are just two of his interesting concoctions. Top off your meal with a selection from the extensive wine list. ◆ Italian ◆ Daily dinner. Reservations recommended. 252.7777

Fiore ★★★★$$$$ This unique dining room sports a gleaming brass-colored open kitchen and such nice touches as an embroidered footstool at each table for purses or briefcases. The restaurant's master sommelier has an extensive background in wine and has created a list that includes some rare bottles priced in the four figures. Rotisseried steaks, chicken, and seafood are the signature dishes. Grilled scallops topped with lemongrass vinaigrette, herbed risotto, braised striped bass with fennel, and spit-roasted, garlic-studded lamb are among the selections that might appear on the seasonally changing menu. ◆ Continental ◆ Daily dinner. Reservations recommended. 252.7702

Buzios ★★★$$$ The ceiling is draped with striped Roman shades, the floor is marble with wood planks, the massive chandeliers provide a warm glow, and the tall windows offer a view of the hotel's pool and sandy beach. Steamers, chowders, seafood pastas, cioppino, and bouillabaisse are among the many can't-go-wrong choices. The kitchen emphasizes freshness: Chowders are created in steam pots while you wait and fish choices change with the seasons. ◆ Seafood ◆ Daily lunch and dinner. Reservations recommended. 252.7697

Carnival World Buffet ★★★$ The new generation of mass-quantity mess halls has arrived. Convivial and chaotic, this lively room seats 900 diners, and the volume and the variety of food are overwhelming. For lunch and dinner, mini-buffets offer Italian, Mexican, Chinese, and American dishes, along with salads, soups, breads, and luscious desserts. The jewel of the buffet, however, is the Mongolian grill, where you spoon vegetables and spices into a bowl and hand it to a cook, who adds chicken, beef, pork, or veal and stir-fries it on a grill. Astoundingly inexpensive, it's far cheaper than the average Las Vegas buffet. And it doesn't close between meals, so you can drop in at any time. During peak hours the room can get extremely crowded; the best bet is to go early for breakfast and dinner and late for lunch. ◆ International ◆ Daily breakfast, lunch, and dinner. 252.7777

Copacabana Showroom This magnificent 430-seat circular showroom is decked out with a dozen high-tech video screens overhead that display constantly changing images depicting everything from exotic scenes of Rio, tropical rain forests, picturesque beaches, to the chefs in the kitchen preparing your dinner. Tuesday through Saturday, the lively *Copacabana* revue is better than most (see "A Review of Revues," page 50); and Thursday through Sunday after 11PM, the disco beat begins. ◆ Revue: admission. Disco: cover. Revue: Tu-Sa 6PM, 8:30PM. Disco: Th-Sa 11PM-4AM; Su 10PM-4AM. Collared shirt or jacket required. 252.7776

33 King 8 Hotel & Gambling Hall $$ For what it's worth, truck drivers swear by this hotel, which is adjacent to the Tropicana Avenue exit off Interstate 15 and surrounded by huge parking lots. The 300 rooms are small and utilitarian, yet comfortable and cool, and are often available at excellent rates, especially at the height of the summer and winter seasons. As for the casino, it's a no-surprise grind joint, with low-minimum blackjack and crap tables and 5¢ video-poker machines. The coffee shop is renowned for its 99¢ breakfast, cheap snow crab–leg dinner, and excellent coffee. ◆ 3330 W Tropicana Ave (at Industrial Rd). 736.8988

34 El Paso Kitchens ★★$ Since it opened a few years ago, this eatery's been such a smashing success that about a dozen branches are now scattered throughout the residential areas of the city. Bench-pressing the hefty burritos provides a pretty good workout. Open around the clock, this is the place if you're craving chips and guacamole or a tasty chorizo-and-bean burrito at 3AM.

Lines can get long during the peak lunch and dinner hours. ◆ Mexican ◆ Daily 24 hours. 3720 W Tropicana Ave (at Valley View Blvd). 891.0222

35 Young Electric Sign Company (YESCO) In the late 1920s Thomas Young came to Las Vegas from Ogden, Utah, and had a vision. As he looked at the budding businesses of Fremont Street, a light bulb went off—literally. Neon, the new European sign fad, had recently arrived in the States. Within a few years, most of the major clubs on Fremont (and Virginia Street in Reno) had dazzling technicolor displays in their windows, and Young's company had established itself as the premier sign maker in the state. More than 60 years later, the signs continue to get bigger and brighter. A new technology, whereby cheaper digital message marquees are illuminated by thousands of computer-programmable bulbs, is now taking the industry by storm, and the company has kept up with the pace, its primacy still intact. The neon graveyard in back of the building contains old casino signs and letters, uniquely preserving the city's history. There are no tours of the factory, and visitors aren't allowed to wander around the junkyard, but peeking through the fence will give you a sense of the long and brilliant love affair between YESCO and Las Vegas. ◆ 5119 Cameron St (at W Tropicana Ave). 876.8080

> I first came to Las Vegas in November 1968 to open at the Flamingo Hotel for the brilliant singer-composer Charles Aznavour. I was so naive about the city that when I heard 'desert,' I arrived in mid-November with a wardrobe consisting only of shorts, bathing suits, and cotton dresses. I remember shivering and running back and forth each evening to the stage entrance where the stage manager waited with a hot cup of coffee."
>
> Joan Rivers

Restaurants/Clubs: Red   **Hotels:** Blue
Shops/ 🌳 Outdoors: Green   **Sights/Culture:** Black

Bests

Larry Grossman
Columnist/Photojournalist/National Radio Talk Show Host, American Sports Network

Great Caesar salads at **Cafe Michelle.** When the temperature reaches 100 degrees, eat outside, where a gentle mist keeps you cool and refreshed. Lunch and dinner are very good.

Feel the Old West at **Binion's Horseshoe.** If you like to play craps, the **Horseshoe** offers 10 times odds. If you happen to be there in the late evening, take advantage of the best deal in town: a complete steak dinner for two dollars between 10PM and 5:45AM.

The **Forum Shops at Caesars** must be seen to be believed. The architecture transports you to old Rome. Statues move and entertain. The sky subtly and realistically fades from day to night. **Spago** and **The Palm** also have restaurants in the mall.

For people with a big appetite, the buffet at the **Rio Suite Hotel** will fill your stomach with a wide variety of foods, without draining your wallet.

The lights on the **Strip** and downtown at night.

The **Mirage** when the volcano erupts.

New Year's Eve.

The action never stops in Las Vegas, so you won't miss anything if you take a short drive out of town to **Mount Charleston** for fresh air and blue skies. Have a drink at the lodge or enjoy lunch with a view.

A ride in the desert when the cactus flowers are blooming.

The sports books, where you can legally put your money where your mouth is.

The pool scene at any of the major hotels is people watching at its best.

A heavyweight championship fight.

Watching the Kentucky Derby in a race book.

The World Series of Poker.

Erik Joseph
Associate Director, Motion Picture Division of the State of Nevada Commission on Economic Development

Certain sights and sounds in Las Vegas can't be missed, including downtown's **Glitter Gulch,** a corridor of neon. Any major casino sports book provides sensory overload. The boxing scene is Runyonesque. Shopping or dining at **Caesars' Forum Shops** indulges certain decadences, while playing video poker at **Silver City** is simple and relaxing small-time entertainment.

For fun, take the *Desert Princess* Sunday brunch riverboat cruise on **Lake Mead.** For an eerie chill, go on a tour of "Ground Zero" at the **Mercury Test Site,** about a two-hour drive northwest of town. This is where all those bizarre late '50s and early '60s atomic bomb survival and testing films were made. Blasted structures still stand.

Lobster pizza at **Spago.** *Ravioli fra diavolo* at the **Palace Station**'s **Pasta Palace.** Sunday brunch at the **Tropicana**'s **Rhapsody Room,** for those who can't get enough caviar. The apple dumpling dessert at the **California Hotel**'s **Pasta Pirate.**

Steve "Biscuit" Walker
Rapper/Actor

One day, one of the New Kids on the Block asked me, "Hey, Biscuit, where do you live?" I quickly responded, "Las Vegas." On my next day off I flew into Vegas and got a place.

Why? For the peace and quiet (I *really* needed it). And I love the desert and its beauty, probably because I grew up in a major city. I also love **McCarran International Airport;** I can fly just about anywhere nonstop (for cheap fares) when I gotta get out and get loose. Sometimes the people here are a little slow, but I like slow.

My other favorites:

Gates & Sons Bar-B-Q—St. Louis Q in the desert.

Mad Dogs and Englishmen—I'm not English, but this pub is unique.

Rio—for once, a friendly casino where I even win sometimes.

Hoover Dam—may make you dizzy.

Green Valley—like living with the Brady Bunch.

Matthew Q. Callister
Nevada State Senator

Breakfast: **Coffee Pub**—suburb coffee and fresh-squeezed orange juice year-round, and lots of early morning sunlight to bask in.

Brunch: **Desert Inn Coffee Shop**—I recommend the lox and bagels. The "DI" combines the best of old Las Vegas's charm with immense picture windows overlooking seminaked sunbathers poolside.

Lunch: **Doña Maria's** tamale shop—you know you're in Mexican food heaven when most of the waiters barely understand your order and the tamales are still homemade daily.

Dinner: **Cafe Nicolle**—fine food and beautiful people. The outdoor air-conditioning assures cool summer nights.

Pub: **Mad Dogs and Englishmen**—especially on Friday night when local yuppie lawyers clash with alternative/student angst.

Venue: **The Huntridge**—owner Richard Lentz has parlayed his 20 years of professional lighting and sound expertise into the city's only noncasino club venue in this 50-year-old Art Deco landmark. From Jesus and Mary Chain to Ice-T, it's a great change from the ordinary Vegas evening.

Outdoor recreation: **Red Rock Canyon**— 15 minutes west of Las Vegas is the Ayers Rock of the Southwest. It is awe-inspiring.

Louis A. Shore
Longtime Las Vegas Resident

The **Forum Shops at Caesars,** where the indoor painted sky turns from sunrise to sunset in a span of three hours. Statues at the Bacchus fountain come to life and talk every hour on the hour. Chic shops à la Rodeo Drive.

The **Rio Suite**'s **Carnival World Buffet.** Spectacular foods from around the world in one huge room.

Ham steak and eggs at **Binion's Horseshoe Hotel and Casino.**

The erupting volcano in **The Mirage** at night, the fish aquarium behind the registration desk, and the white tigers at play.

Anthony Curtis
Publisher, *Las Vegas Advisor*

I love the competition. With 70-plus casinos, Las Vegas is the perfect microcosm of a capitalistic society. The consumer is king.

John Earl Williams
Host of "Cruisin' for a Bluesin' "/DJ, KKLZ 96.3FM

Lied Discovery Children's Museum—many interesting displays and activities for the whole family.

All of the libraries for the wealth of knowledge they hold for everyone in our community at no cost to the visitor.

The city and county parks for the wonderful facilities and the wide scope of programs and activities they provide for the entire populace.

Red Rock Canyon—a well-kept park and nature area that is appreciated and enjoyed by all who witness its splendor and majestic beauty.

The many wonderful people who live and work in our ethnically rich and diverse community.

Ed Kane
Chef

Palace Court restaurant—the gourmet room of **Caesars Palace**. . . and Las Vegas. Truly the ultimate in epicurean food, beverage, and service. The Grand Marnier soufflé is a must.

Folies Bergere—the **Tropicana Hotel**'s production show offers all the glitz and glamour of Las Vegas. If you only see one show while in Las Vegas, make it the *Folies Bergere.*

Green Valley—a short distance from the Strip you'll find this beautiful master-planned community that proves people really do live in Las Vegas.

California Pizza Kitchen—located in the **Golden Nugget Hotel,** they serve the finest pizza, baked in a wood-burning oven. My favorite is the blend of duck sausage, spinach, and sun-dried tomatoes.

The pool at **The Mirage**—if you consider the swimming pool an important hotel amenity, then this will be your choice. Be sure to visit the dolphins while you're there.

Lenny Frome
Author of Video-Poker Books

You haven't lived until you've played video poker in Las Vegas.

Sam's Town—world's best (most liberal) deuces wild games.

Binion's Horseshoe and the **Palace Station**—world's best sequential and reversible royal games.

El Cortez and the **Plaza**—world's best joker's wild games.

Circus Circus—world's best "aces & eights" games.

Always remember to play *with* your head—not over it. Translation: Read a book before you invest.

Craig Kunitz
Promotions Supervisor, Fitzgeralds Casino/Hotel

The late great columnist Forrest Duke pegged Las Vegas TBCOTA! (The Best City of Them All!), and how true it is. . . .

Watch the lights of the **Strip** and downtown trip fantastic.

True joy: Sit in on a live poker game. Forget the time and the day and play for eternity. Remember, you are in Las Vegas, "The City that Never Sleeps!"

Go out after 11PM and have the terrific complete steak dinner at the **Horseshoe** for the price of a tip.

Mesmerize yourself at the volcano at **The Mirage** or by the ambience at the **Forum Shops at Caesars.**

Be sure to see the other side of Las Vegas, a quality community in which to raise a family.

Take a walk around the beautiful campus of the **University of Nevada, Las Vegas.**

Witness the phenomenal growth in all directions on the outskirts of town.

Take a scenic drive to cool **Mount Charleston** and visit the lodge or have a picnic.

Go to **Lake Mead** and sail aboard the *Desert Princess,* a beautiful paddle wheeler.

The cocktail waitresses at the **Rio Suite Hotel & Casino.**

The ice rink at the **Santa Fe Hotel & Casino.**

Read the marquees for where the stars are playing and what fantastic food specials are offered.

Enjoy our main industry (casino gaming and tourism) and marvel at the fastest-growing city in the US. Almost one million people now call Las Vegas home.

Frank Marino
Female Impersonator/Star of *An Evening at La Cage*

Lunch at **Cafe Nicolle** on Decatur and Sahara.

Skiing at **Mount Charleston.**

Shopping at the **Forum Shops at Caesars** and lunch at **Spago.**

Watching the lights downtown at **Glitter Gulch.**

East Las Vegas

You won't see theme parks or artificial volcanoes on the "Eastside," as locals call the area east of the Las Vegas Strip. But you will visit an eclectic mix of attractions and some middle-class, residential communities (a refreshing reprieve from the gambling palaces on Las Vegas Boulevard).

For the most part low-key and suburban, the Eastside still has enough idiosyncrasy to escape blandness. Las Vegas's only **Hard Rock Cafe** is located in this area, as is the garish **Liberace Museum**, a monument to the late entertainer's love of excess, where his flamboyant cars, furs, rings, and pianos are on display. Visitors in search of some of the city's beautiful people will spot them soaking up the desert sun at **Cafe Michelle**, a trendy lunch spot known for its cellular phone–carrying clientele and its patio dining. From there, it's just a short drive down **Maryland Parkway** to the **University of Nevada, Las Vegas**, home to the town's beloved **Runnin' Rebels** basketball team, winners of the 1990 **NCAA** championship. And

Nellis Air Force Base, a major Eastside employer, is the site of the **Thunderbird Museum,** which is chock-full of aeronautical memorabilia.

The Eastside is also the site of **Sunrise Mountain,** home of the **Las Vegas Mormon Temple,** a towering white structure built by the Church of Jesus Christ of Latter-day Saints. The peak is still a favorite of residents: Each year readers of the *Las Vegas Review-Journal* newspaper vote the mountain the best place to view the nocturnal light show of Las Vegas.

While they lack the flashy facades that pulsate on the Strip, a few good-size casinos in East Las Vegas draw plenty of business from both locals (a combination of military families, retirees, blue-collar workers, and middle-class residents) and tourists. The oldest and tallest, the **Showboat,** is one of the first casinos that chose to cater to locals, with a combination of decent food, low prices, and a convenient location. **Boulder Station,** which opened in August 1994, has duplicated the success of its long-popular older brother, **Palace Station,** on West Sahara. One local rival, **Sam's Town Hotel & Gambling Hall,** is popular with Eastsiders who crowd its western dance hall and bowling complex. Adjacent to **Sam's Town** on the **Boulder Highway** is **Nevada Palace,** an overgrown motel and casino that has carved out a niche for itself with low-rolling locals and folks who prefer to avoid the crowds next door at **Sam's Town.**

The Eastside also supports a number of offbeat mom-and-pop businesses. You'll find some of the more interesting places clustered around the intersection of **Fremont Street** and **Charleston Boulevard,** such as the funky **Green Shack,** a saloon and supper club where cholesterol counters plead temporary amnesia when ordering the house specialty, crusty fried chicken. The restaurant sits in the shadow of the **Showboat** in a building considered historic by Las Vegas standards, dating back to at least 1932. Just down the street, the weathered and slightly rough-looking **Silver Dollar Saloon** caters to country music lovers who two-stepped to the Nashville sound long before Billy Ray what's-his-name shook his way to the top of the charts. The bar and dance hall offer live honky-tonk seven nights a week and even maintain two 21 tables for those who want to squeeze in still more gambling. A great escape from the Strip, East Las Vegas is where you'll meet Las Vegans and see how the residents live.

1 Alexis Park Resort $$$$ If you're tired of walking by clanging slot machines to get to your room, this understated and elegant hotel might be your kind of place. It's a first-rate resort and there's not a slot machine or a table game in sight. While each of the resort's 500 rooms is a suite, the property also offers a spate of amenities: a gourmet restaurant, spacious meeting rooms, three pools, a health spa, a beauty salon, a nine-hole putting green, two lighted tennis courts, and all the usual perks found at fine hotels. It's also within walking distance of two of the Strip's brightest intersections. Without a casino to subsidize the hotel, the room and meal prices here are high by Las Vegas standards, but then so is the quality. The rooms, built around a sprawling courtyard, are designed with the business traveler in mind; each includes a desk, and the decor is more sedate than that found at most Las Vegas hotels. Ten two-bedroom suites are also on the property. ♦ 375 E Harmon Ave (between Paradise Rd and Koval La). 796.3300, 800/453.8000; fax 796.0766

Within the Alexis Park Resort:

Pegasus Gourmet Room ★★★$$$$
Fine cuisine is served in a quiet and subtly decorated dining room with a waterfall view. Frequent patrons rave about the oysters Rockefeller and the pasta, which is made on the premises. ♦ Continental ♦ Daily dinner. Reservations recommended for dinner; jacket and tie requested. 796.3300

2 Hard Rock Cafe ★$ The ever-expanding restaurant chain known for its trendy T-shirts and rock 'n' roll memorabilia built one of its most unique branches here in 1990. The swanky structure, with a flashy white and gold color scheme reminiscent of downtown's **Golden Nugget**, is pure Vegas, even if the cuisine is classic California. Boasting one of the city's most striking neon signs, an 82-foot replica of a classic Gibson guitar—billed as the biggest instrument of its type in the world—has strings that move, as if being strummed by a giant hand. Inside, hundreds of music mementos are on display. They range from a gorgeous 1968 Harley Davidson Electraglide motorcycle once owned by the late Roy Orbison to an autographed album cover from the Irish rock band U2. Of course, the King's presence is felt throughout: Busts of Elvis ring the ceiling; a guitar broken by his Highness is enshrined here; and imitation Graceland gates stand under the "Viva Las Vegas" sign. Tourists pack the place on weekends, crowding a bar that's already a bit small. Few are elders, since the nonstop rock music tends to drive off anyone whose heyday predates the 1960s. But the food's not bad—if you're lucky enough to get a table. ♦ American ♦ Daily lunch and dinner. 4475 Paradise Rd (at E Harmon Ave). 733.8400

3 Hard Rock Hotel $$$ This progeny of the world-famous cafe offers 339 rooms and suites, a European-style concierge, 24-hour room service—and, of course, a multi-million-dollar collection of rock 'n' roll memorabilia. In addition to the cafe next door, there are two restaurants to choose from within the hotel: An Italian eatery, **Mortoni's**, features pizza and huge salads, served either indoors or on the garden patio overlooking the pool; and **Mr. Lucky's 24/7** is a coffee shop that is open round the clock. The **Hard Rock Beach Club**, exclusively for guests and included in the price of a room, features whirlpools, spas, luxury cabanas, and even a sandy beach. The **Athletic Club**, available to guests for a fee, provides an exercise room and personal trainer, outdoor pool, and a 2,000-square-foot clothing, personal electronics, and collectibles store.♦ 4455 Paradise Rd (at E Harmon Ave). 693.5000, 800/473.7625; fax 693.5010

Las Vegas has hosted every type of performer imaginable, but the largest audience in the city's history (for a single event) goes to one of the more unlikely acts: the venerable hippie band the Grateful Dead. Nearly 40,000 people packed the Sam Boyd Silver Bowl football stadium for the Dead's debut at the bowl in 1991.

Basketball great Kareem Abdul-Jabbar broke the National Basketball Association record for earning the most points in a career during a game in Las Vegas. The Los Angeles Lakers were playing the Utah Jazz on 5 April 1984 at the Thomas & Mack Center at the University of Nevada, Las Vegas campus, when Jabbar swished a long sky hook over Utah center Mark Eaton. The basket gave the legendary Lakers' center 31,421 points for his career, breaking Wilt Chamberlain's record of 31,419.

Restaurants/Clubs: Red	**Hotels:** Blue
Shops/ ♥ Outdoors: Green	**Sights/Culture:** Black

4 Continental Hotel $$ This unassuming hotel anchors the corner of Flamingo and Paradise Roads, too far from the Strip to attract foot traffic and too close to the big hotels (and the seedy **Crazy Horse Saloon** strip club across the street) to lure many locals. The three-story, 400-room facility, which is not much more than a motor inn with a sizable casino attached, was built in 1981 and is gearing up for a proposed expansion and face-lift. The current accommodations are basic but adequate. Each room comes with either one king-size or two queen-size beds. The **Renaissance Room** coffee shop serves Vegas staples such as midnight breakfast for less than a buck and cheap prime ribs and is open 24 hours a day. At the basic Las Vegas-style **Buffet** you can chow down on standard fare such as baked ham, barbecued ribs, and fried chicken, or feast on all the snow crab you can stomach for supper. And there's no cover charge to see live bands like Cook E. Jarr and the Krumbs tear up the **Continental Lounge** late into the night. The hotel also operates free shuttle service to the Strip. ♦ 4100 Paradise Rd (at E Flamingo Rd). 737.5555, 800/634.6641; fax 369.8776

Within the Continental Hotel:

Continental Casino The hotel's unremarkable and cramped casino offers all the usual games of chance, plus Indian-style bingo. It's smokier than most and is crammed with slots, but the minimum bets are low and the folks fairly friendly. ♦ Daily 24 hours. 737.5555

5 La Strada ★★★$$$ Old World charm —an intimate dining room with a balcony, mirrored walls, and soft chandelier lighting— is the setting for elegant service and classic Italian fare. Among the sumptuous antipasti are chicken-liver pâté, marinated mussels on the half shell, buffalo mozzarella with basil and sliced tomato, marinated mushrooms, calamari salad, and roasted zucchini. Delectable entrées include calamari provençal (with garlic, oregano, wine, and tomato sauce), chicken *Dama Bianco* (with mushrooms, wine, and cream), veal *boscaiola* (with sautéed mushrooms and wine), veal *Strada* (with ham, cheese, and eggplant in wine and tomato sauce) and *spaghettini Vesuvio* (with chicken, capers, olives, garlic, wine, and tomato sauce). ♦ Italian ♦ Daily dinner. Reservations recommended. 4640 Paradise Rd (at Naples Dr). 735.0150

6 University of Nevada, Las Vegas (UNLV) Traffic from nearby **McCarran International**

Airport runs right into the southern tip of the campus, site of the massive **Thomas & Mack Center,** home of the school's **Runnin' Rebels** basketball team and the **International Hockey League's Las Vegas Thunder.** Most visitors to the campus only see the 18,776-seat, all-purpose arena, which is fitting since many sports fans across the country still think of **UNLV** as a basketball team with a school attached. The controversial **Rebels** have drawn quite a lot of bad press, as well as two **NCAA** probations for recruiting violations by a former coach. The team, with its outlaw reputation, epitomizes to some all that is wrong with college athletics. That's an image that university administrators would like to change. They're fond of pointing out that nearly 20,000 students now attend the school and that *U.S. News and World Report* has named it one of the West's up-and-coming regional universities.

Founded in 1957, the university's new and mostly unremarkable buildings fill the 335-acre campus. One of the most interesting places to visit is the **Marjorie Barrick Museum of Natural History,** which showcases traveling exhibits from the Smithsonian (M-F 8AM-4:45PM, Sa 9AM-2PM). Aside from the **Thomas & Mack,** the other big campus landmark is the huge black-metal *Flashlight* sculpture that points skyward from the plaza at the **Performing Arts Center,** where most of the school's cultural events are held. Not far from the big basketball arena, and just outside the **Harry Reid Center for Environmental Studies,** visitors can stroll through an almost-hidden desert garden that symbolizes the school's recent blossoming. But beware: Campus parking can be a problem as it is at most urban universities. Luckily, the new **Citizens Area Transit** bus system runs right along Maryland Parkway, stopping several times an hour in front of the school. ♦ 4505 S Maryland Pkwy (bounded by E Flamingo Rd and E Tropicana Ave, and Swenson St and S Maryland Pkwy). 895.3011; basketball tickets 895.3900

7 Mamounia ★★★$$$ Romance abounds at this exotic Moroccan restaurant. There are richly decorated pillows to lean back on; a traditional hand-washing ceremony to prepare you for eating with your fingers; a multicourse feast of *harira* (lentil) soup (drunk from a bowl), Middle Eastern salads, kabobs speared into a whole pineapple, couscous, Cornish hen, *pastilla* (chicken pie), and mint tea; and a belly dancer. An à la carte menu is also offered. ♦ Moroccan ♦ Daily dinner. Reservations recommended. 4632 S Maryland Pkwy (between E Harmon and E Tropicana Aves). 597.0092

Regulation 6-A of the National Banking Laws specifies that casino cash transactions exceeding $10,000 must be reported to the Nevada Gaming Control Board.

8 The Liberace Museum If ever an entertainer belonged in Vegas, Liberace did. Before he died in 1987, Mr. Showmanship spent much of his career living and performing in Las Vegas and trying to top his own outrageous costumes and audience-pleasing acts. Despite his exaggerated on-stage image, the Wisconsin native born Wladziu Valentino Liberace was actually down-to-earth, often seen grocery shopping in supermarkets near his home, just a mile or so west of this glitzy museum. Lee, as his friends called him, founded the museum in 1979, and it has since been expanded into an entire complex containing three exhibit areas, a gift shop, and **Carluccio's** restaurant.

The museum has taken over most of **Liberace Plaza** shopping center. The main building houses the many customized cars and pianos Liberace collected during his lifetime. His favorite piano, a Baldwin grand covered with thousands of mirrored tiles, revolves on a stage in the middle of the room. Nearby, his red, white, and blue Rolls-Royce convertible draws big crowds. Some of his wild costumes and gaudy jewelry are on display in the rear of the complex. One highlight is a piano-shaped ring topped with 260 diamonds, a gift from the Hilton Hotel baron Barron Hilton. A third exhibit area includes a library containing Liberace's miniature piano collection, musical arrangements, and family photos. The museum is hard to miss. Just look for the showmeister's oversize signature on the sign out front, the gold lettering on the buildings, and the tour buses lined up in the parking lot. Tickets are tax-deductible; proceeds benefit the Liberace Foundation for the Performing and Creative Arts. ♦ Admission. Daily. Liberace Plaza, 1775 E Tropicana Ave (at Spencer St). 798.5595

8 Carluccio's ★ ★$$ When this place was known as **Liberace's Tivoli Gardens,** it was a frequent hangout of Lee himself. Although it is no longer affiliated with the museum, the restaurant has retained the original decadent design, along with one of Liberace's showpiece mirrored pianos, which anchors the bar. Less formal than in the past and frequented by more locals than ever before, the kitchen still serves Italian preparations of chicken, veal, steak, and pasta. Two highly recommended specialties are the crab-stuffed shrimp and the veal florentine. ♦ Italian ♦ Tu-Su dinner. Reservations recommended for eight or more. Liberace Plaza, 1775 E Tropicana Ave (at Spencer St). 795.3236

9 Bootlegger Ristorante ★ ★ ★$$$ One of the oldest restaurants in town (since 1949) and still run by the same family, its hearty portions and consistent quality make this a popular local dining spot. Turn-of-the-century decor and Italian family portraits provide an attractive setting in which to enjoy complimentary homemade *panettis* (small bread puffs) tossed with garlic, oregano, and oil served with tomato-basil sauce; *mostaccioli* (two-inch-long macaroni tubes), one of the most popular dishes; and eggplant parmesan. Entrées named respectively for the husband-and-wife owners—veal saltimbocca à la Blackie (with prosciutto and wine) and veal Lorraine (with fresh mushrooms in a wine and cream sauce)—are also first-rate. For the health-conscious, there are such "Project Lean" selections as angel hair *pomodoro* (with fresh tomato and basil sauce) and linguine with clams, shrimp, or calamari. ♦ Italian ♦ Tu-Sa lunch and dinner; Su dinner. Reservations recommended. 5025 Eastern Ave (at Tropicana Ave). 736.4939

10 Cafe Michelle ★ ★$$$ During lunchtime, local movers and shakers come here to graze and soak up some sun. Although cellular phones aren't a prerequisite for getting a seat on the patio overlooking the parking lot, setting one on your table will help you fit in. The menu, diverse and chic, is a bit pricey by Las Vegas standards. Then again, that's part of the attraction, as is the casual yet trendy dress code. Specialties include such standards as fettuccine alfredo and broiled halibut steak; a garlic-laced Caesar salad served with garlic toast; spinach pie; and luscious desserts. ♦ Continental ♦ Daily lunch and dinner. Reservations recommended for four or more. Mission Center, 1350 E Flamingo Rd (at S Maryland Pkwy). 735.8686

Las Vegas has about 85,000 hotel and motel rooms (with more continually being built) and a citywide hotel occupancy rate of more than 85 percent. Remember that the next time you think about blowing into town for an unplanned, spontaneous vacation on a holiday weekend.

11 Pasta Mia ★★★$$ Founded by popular chef Piero Broglia and run by his wife and daughter, this casual, friendly restaurant is known for the scent of garlic and the sounds of Sinatra (on tape). The homemade anti-pasto features roasted peppers, marinated eggplant, and stuffed artichokes. Extra-large portions (doggie bags are de rigueur here) are preceded by superb garlic bread and *pasta e fagiole* (pasta and bean soup) or a hearty romaine salad with garlic vinaigrette. Specialties include *tortellini bolognese* (meat sauce), penne with broccoli and spinach, chicken *angelo* (with artichoke hearts and white wine sauce), orange roughy, and roasted chicken with peppers and onions. ♦ Italian ♦ M-F lunch and dinner; Sa-Su dinner. No credit cards accepted. 2585 E Flamingo Rd (between Eastern Ave and McLeod Dr). 733.0091

12 Cipriani ★★★★$$$ Outside, a three-story lighthouse complete with beacon sets the mood: French doors with pale salmon-colored drapes, crystal chandeliers, and hanging plants decorate the interior of the elegant dining room. A prime Las Vegas destination for lovers of fine Italian fare, it presents classic cuisine in equally classic surroundings. Among the house specialties prepared in the open kitchen are escargots; steamed clams in herbs, shallots, and garlic; a superb *pasta e fagioli* (pasta and bean soup); *veal scallopini boscaiola* (with wild mushrooms); fettuccine with fresh salmon, caviar, and a light cream sauce; cioppino (fish and shellfish in a hearty tomato sauce); and such scrumptious desserts as tiramisù, crème caramel, and chocolate mousse. ♦ Italian ♦ M-F lunch and dinner; Sa dinner. Reserva-tions recommended. 2790 E Flamingo Rd (between Topaz St and McLeod Dr). 369.6711

13 Las Vegas Hilton Country Club One of only two public golf courses east of Paradise Road, this lush country club is tucked away in one of the area's finer neighborhoods, its borders defined by Eastern Avenue to the east and Desert Inn Road to the north. The course traces its history back to 1961, when it was the **Stardust Country Club.** Until 1967, it hosted the **PGA**'s Tournament of Champions, and from 1969 to 1976 was the site of the Sahara Invitational, won by such golfers as Jack Nicklaus (in 1969) and Lee Trevino (in 1971). The course record of 62 is shared by David Graham and Tom Kite. With 71 bunkers and five lakes, the course is considered challenging by local golfers, but the greens fees are a bit steep. Amenities include two putting greens, one chipping green, a lighted driving range, and a beverage cart. There's also a pro shop, the **Country Club Restaurant** , where breakfast and lunch are served, and a bar. Proper golf attire is required. Due to heavy demand, the management suggests calling or faxing up to three weeks in advance to reserve a tee time. ♦ Admission. Daily 5:30AM-6PM (driving range until 8PM). 1911 E Desert Inn Rd (between S Maryland Pkwy and Eastern Ave). 796.0016; fax 796.0015

The **Boulevard**

14 The Boulevard Mall The largest shopping center in Nevada, it boasts 1.25 million square feet of shopping space; 5,825 parking spaces; and 140 stores spread out over 77 acres along Maryland Parkway. The newest specialty stores in the mall include the Bay Area–based **Nature Company** and the **Sesame Street General Store,** both of which have caught on with kids. The oldest of the city's four major malls, it's a good distance from the local freeway system. But it has a reputation for being less touristy than the Strip's **Forum Shops at Caesars** and **Fashion Show Mall,** and less crowded than the rival **Meadows Mall** on the other side of town. ♦ Daily. 3528 S Maryland Pkwy (at E Desert Inn Rd). 735.8268

15 Gates & Sons Bar-B-Q ★★$ Greeting customers with a hearty "Hi, may I help you?" has been a tradition at this family-owned chain since 1946, when George W. Gates I founded it in Kansas City, Missouri. The Las Vegas location, one of seven in the country and the only branch in Nevada, is run by a third-generation Gates, who can frequently be found in the kitchen. If you like moist, tangy barbecued pork ribs and chicken, you'll love this place. They'll even ship jars of their patented sauce to your home. ♦ Barbecue ♦ Daily lunch and dinner. 2710 E Desert Inn Rd (between Eastern Ave and Pecos Rd/MacLeod Dr). 369.8010; fax 796.0992

All that Glitters is Neon

ART BY M. BLUM

Think of Las Vegas and chances are a dazzlingly bright blur of neon comes to mind. In this veritable museum of neon culture, huge glittering signs front the hotel-casinos, serving the dual role of heraldry and billboard: Above is an image, identifiable from a distance and at cruising speed; below is a marquee that announces entertainment, gambling, and dining options. The overall effect works best after darkness

transforms the **Strip** and downtown into a magic garden of exotic and brilliant blooms, which tint the air, dematerialize the architecture, and render the night into a frenzied crazy-quilt of color.

The most concentrated and startling light show in town is the four-block stretch of **Fremont Street** downtown between Main and Fourth Streets. The stars are the neon cowboy and cowgirl: "Vegas Vic" atop the **Pioneer Club** (waving and welcoming since 1951) and "Vegas Vickie" atop the **Girls of Glitter Gulch.** The **Horseshoe** and **Fremont** hotel-casinos are fronted entirely by neon; if all the tubing were laid end to end, it would stretch more than 10 miles.

On the Strip, the **Sahara** sign is the tallest, at nearly 23 stories. The **Stardust** sign has the most animation, with 26 lighting sequences. "Lucky the Clown" at **Circus Circus** is the heaviest, weighing in at 120 tons. The **Flamingo Hilton**'s is especially stunning, with a rush of pink-petaled blooms up a single long stem, spilling out at the top in an explosion of color. And the impressive, multicolored sign at the **Rio** (emblazoned with the casino's logo and a pair of maracas) now wins the "Best of Las Vegas" poll every year.

Neon, a rare atmospheric gas, was first isolated in 1898. By the early 1900s electricity pioneers had discovered that if they filled a glass tube with neon and zapped it with high voltage, it would produce a brilliant red light. French sign maker Georges Claude installed the first neon sign, a red- and white-striped barber pole, on a Parisian barber shop in 1910. It caused such a sensation on the street that within a few years Claude Neon had become a million-dollar business. By 1930, some 300 sparkling, elegant neon creations lit up Times Square, and in the mid-1940s, considered the Golden Age of Neon, 2,000 neon-sign manufacturers employed nearly 10,000 craftspeople in America alone.

At that time, neon was highly regarded among sign makers, advertisers, architects, and artists. The flexibility of glass tubing and variety of color provided a limitless potential for conveying complex images and ideas through fluid lines, animated shapes, and abstract designs, as well as illuminating brand names, logos, and trademarks so that they appeared to spring from the flat surface of the nighttime sky. Neon transcended the mere sign to become part of the dramatic landscape of the city.

The evolution of neon as a symbol of popular American culture in the mid-1900s was closely related to the country's emerging passion for automobile travel and its influence on roadside architecture and advertising. Las Vegas was perfectly suited to large-scale displays of neon graphics. The flat topography, clear air, and dark desert nights lent themselves to neon's pizzazz, and Las Vegas's location on the highway to and from Los Angeles proved ideal for drawing attention to commercial establishments, especially through the windshield of a fast-moving car. But most of all, Nevada's lax sign regulations and the casinos' large advertising budgets, not to mention their intense desire to outdo each other, provided the perfect canvas for neon sign makers to practice their craft. Las Vegas attracted the cream of the industry—designers, glassblowers, electrical and structural engineers—who literally overran the town with neon, some say depreciating the effect so much by the mid-1960s that neon fell out of favor for three decades. Today, neon is enjoying a resurgence elsewhere in the US, especially as a highlighting element for both internal and external architecture.

The technology used to fabricate neon light has changed little from the early days of the industry. Every piece of a neon sign must be produced by hand. First, the design is drawn on paper, then transferred onto an asbestos sheet. Varying lengths of glass tubing are heated over Bunsen burners and bent, while soft, to correspond to the design; the glassworker blows through the tube while bending it to keep it from flattening out. Herein lies the true art of neon sign making: achieving the complexity of curves while maintaining the integrity of the glass.

Next, electrodes are melted into either end of the tube and the joints are blacked out with paint or tape. All the air is vacuumed from the tube through a tiny vent and the impurities are eliminated by shocking the tube with up to 30,000 volts. At this point, the neon (argon is sometimes used, combined with a little mercury) is injected, and then the vent is sealed. A transformer attached to the electrodes introduces 15,000 volts to fire up the neon, after which it steps down the current to provide a maintenance level of electricity. In a clear tube, neon glows orange-red, while argon with mercury emits an intense blue. The entire spectrum (approximately 150 colors) can be achieved from neon and argon by using colored glass, coating the

interior of the tubes with phosphor powder, or painting them with durable enamels.

A well-made tube can glow brightly for 30 years or more, though the elements, bird nests, and vandalism usually take their toll sooner, as the junkyard for defunct Las Vegas signs at the Young Electric Sign Company (see page 71) attests. Peek into this neon cemetery to see these ghosts of Vegas's past, but never fear—the lights of Glitter Gulch and the Strip will illuminate the sky for years to come.

In Spanish, Las Vegas means "The Meadows," a name the town earned as an oasis of springs, creeks, grasses, and cottonwoods amid the fiercely hot and dry Mojave Desert. Several comedians have come up with new twists on the name: "The Veggies" was coined by Joe E. Lewis, and "Lost Wages" was made famous by Milton Berle.

Restaurants/Clubs: Red   **Hotels:** Blue
Shops/ Outdoors: Green   **Sights/Culture:** Black

16 Huntridge Performing Arts Theater

On the corner of Charleston Boulevard and Maryland Parkway, this Las Vegas landmark (ca. 1944) was the city's main movie house for years. Once owned by actress Irene Dunne and frequented by star-studded audiences (including Frank Sinatra and Marlene Dietrich), the movie theater fell on hard times during the 1980s, and the Art Deco building, with its 75-foot-tall tower, eventually closed. Current owner Richard Lenz reopened it in 1992 as a 725-seat concert venue. Since then, it has hosted everything from classic films to a performance by rapper Ice T and has become one of the city's best concert halls. With such an eclectic mix of entertainment, the best bet is to call ahead for information. Parking is limited, and because the lot is poorly policed, there have been numerous instances of cars being broken into. You might be better off taking a cab. ♦ Box office Tu-Sa noon-5:30PM. 1208 E Charleston Blvd (at S Maryland Pkwy). 477.0242

17 Bill Ladd's Silver Dollar Saloon

No watered-down country music here. This is a real cowboy bar, with country-and-western bands playing seven nights a week. It dates back to 1931, when it was the **Black Cat** (later the **Saddle Club**). Over the years, the saloon has survived several waves of new nightclub competition and the rise, fall, and rise in country music's popularity. Owner Bill Ladd's loyal, almost exclusively blue-collar crowd sports Wrangler jeans, boots, and cowboy hats. Thanks to an old gaming license, it's still the only bar in town with blackjack tables. It also has plenty of video-poker machines built into the bar, a crude snack bar, and three pool tables in a separate room to the side of the stage. Every Wednesday is ladies' night, when women drink free from 8PM to 10PM. ♦ Cover charge Friday and Saturday nights. Daily 24 hours. 2501 E Charleston Blvd (at Fremont St). 382.6921

18 The Green Shack

★$$ One of the oldest saloons and supper clubs in town, it opened back in 1932, when workers bound for Hoover Dam would stop to wet their whistle here before the long drive down dusty Boulder Highway. Up to a decade later, regulars from town were still riding up on horseback for some hot grub and a cold beer. Current proprietors Jim and Barb McCormick are distant relatives of the club's founder, Jimmie Jones. Despite the fact that the little wooden

building is painted green and garlanded with tiny white Christmas lights, its location—next door to the towering **Showboat**—makes it hard to spot. Locals like the Old Vegas atmosphere and famous fried chicken. They hang out, get a peek into the city's past, and enjoy plenty of homespun hospitality. ♦ American ♦ Tu-Sa dinner. 2504 E Fremont St (between E Charleston and E Oakey Blvds). 383.0007

19 The Oklahoma Kitchen

★$ Since 1978, locals have feasted on hearty home cooking at this bare-bones restaurant. The kitchen whips up chicken-fried steak and homemade Mexican food, among other specialties. Pictures of western figures such as John Wayne and Willie Nelson grace the dining room walls. ♦ American/Mexican ♦ Daily breakfast, lunch, and dinner. 23 N Mojave Rd (at Charleston Blvd). 382.2651

20 Showboat Hotel

$$ A longtime favorite of Eastside slot players, the **'Boat,** with its big electronic marquee, boasts two specialty restaurants, a buffet, a bingo hall, a poker room, the New Orleans Square courtyard with an old-fashioned ice-cream shop, and a six-story parking garage. Despite its recent face-lift, the 495-room hotel has retained its famous riverboat facade and is still known as a locals' joint with friendly employees, decent food, and fast service. It's also famous for its 106-lane bowling center, the largest in the US. ♦ 2800 Fremont St (between E Charleston and E Oakey Blvds). 385.9123, 800/826.2800; fax 385.9154

Within the Showboat Hotel:

Showboat Casino While not as crowded as most popular locals' casinos, this one seems to have picked up steam after treading water for a while in the 1980s. The place feels roomier after the 1990 expansion, which widened the aisles between the rows of slot machines that dominate the sprawling complex. ♦ Daily 24 hours. First floor. 385.9123

Bowling Center

This cavernous bowling palace founded in 1959 has its own snack bar and a lounge that sports plenty of TVs and bowling memorabilia. The 106-lane center is also the oldest stop on the Pro Bowlers Tour and home of the High Roller Bowling Tournament. Daily 24 hours. First floor. 385.9123

Captain's Buffet $

One of the more popular feasts in town, the buffet features fair food at better than fair prices. On any day the generous spread could include ham, shrimp, cooked-to-order omelettes, barbecued chicken, crab legs, and corned-beef hash. ♦ American ♦ Daily lunch and dinner. Second floor. 385.9123

Coffee Shop $

Around the clock, the hotel's coffee shop serves traditional and inexpensive specials such as steak and eggs. ♦ American ♦ Daily 24 hours. First floor. 385.9123

Di Napoli ★$$

The **Showboat** seems an unlikely place to find fine cuisine from southern Italy, but the hotel made a valiant effort when it built this restaurant. The setting includes Roman columns, statues, a domed, trompe l'oeil ceiling painted to look like the sky, and a fountain in the center. Vintages from the ample wine list suit the refined menu of pasta, veal, chicken, and beef dishes. The veal parmesan and the eggplant rollatini are highly recommended, as is the family-style feast offered from 2PM to 10PM Sunday. ♦ Italian ♦ M-Sa dinner; Su brunch and dinner. Reservations recommended. First floor. 385.9123

Plantation ★$$

Next door to **Di Napoli,** the room features a Southern plantation decor, but you won't find corn bread and grits here. Specialties include mesquite-grilled steaks and fresh seafood flown in daily. The lobster tails are Australian and reasonably priced. ♦ American ♦ Daily dinner. Reservations recommended. First floor. 385.9123

21 Boulder Station $$ Looking much like its older, West Las Vegas sibling, **Palace**

Station, this 15-story hotel opened in August 1993 with 300 rooms and five full-service restaurants. The casino offers more than 2,000 slot machines, 40 gaming tables, a 70-seat keno lounge, 10 poker tables, and a 240-seat race and sports book. Among the restaurants are the 24-hour **Iron Horse Cafe;** the "Feast," featuring an all-you-can-eat buffet; a steak and seafood restaurant called **The Broiler;** the **Pasta Palace;** and the **Guadalajara Bar & Grill,** all patterned after the **Palace Station**'s restaurants. ♦ 4111 Boulder Hwy (at Lamb Blvd). 432.7777, 800/683.7777; fax 432.7744

22 Sam's Town Hotel & Gambling Hall $$
Ever since Boyd Group founder Sam Boyd built this place in 1979, it has been booming. Long a favorite with locals, it's a bit off the tourist track, but its location, about six miles east of the Strip, is convenient for most Eastsiders; it's where Las Vegans take visitors. All 650 rooms and 33 suites are decorated in Old West style. In addition to the three-floor casino, the hotel's attractions include two RV parks, **Calamity Jane's Ice Cream Shop and Coca-Cola Museum,** and a 56-lane bowling center with a playroom for the kids. There's also a spectacular 25,000-square-foot atrium and indoor park complete with trees, waterfalls, footpaths, and a mountain. The atrium features a variety of shops, including a western attire shop called **Cowboy Christmas** (open year-round) and a general store. Of the 10 restaurants, two—the Italian **Papamios** and the steak house **Billy Bob's**—as well as the international food court, have recently been added.

Lucky gamblers can blow their take at the **Western Emporium,** which carries a wide selection of western wear, art, jewelry, candy, and other souvenirs. Parking is available (though sometimes scarce) at various locations within the 58-acre property or in the five-story parking barn. ♦ 5111 Boulder Hwy (at Nellis Blvd). 456.7777, 800/634.6371; fax 454.8060

Las Vegas celebrity weddings in the 1950s and 1960s included Joan Crawford and Alfred Steel at the Flamingo in 1955; Paul Newman and Joanne Woodward at the El Rancho in 1958; Jane Fonda and Roger Vadim at the Dunes in 1965; Xavier Cugat and Charo at Caesars Palace in 1966; Elvis Presley and Priscilla Beaulieu at the Aladdin in 1967; and Ann-Margret and Roger Smith at the Riviera in 1967.

"I came to Las Vegas in a $28,000 Cadillac and left in a $280,000 Greyhound bus."

Milton Berle

Within Sam's Town Hotel & Gambling Hall:

Sam's Town Casino The bustling, three-story casino covers 58,000 square feet and is crammed with slot machines. Most of the high-stakes action takes place on the ground floor, where gamblers play to the sounds of live country music blaring from **Roxy's Saloon,** an action-filled lounge located between the coffee shop and the race and sports book. There are more than 30 hand-dealt blackjack tables, a busy poker room, and a 590-seat bingo parlor. After dining and gambling, aspiring two-steppers can take free lessons offered nightly in the western-style dance hall on the second floor. ♦ Daily 24 hours. 456.7777

Diamond Lil's ★★$$$ Mesquite-grilled steak and seafood are served in plentiful portions here, and the quiet atmosphere is Old West elegance at its best. Try the 18-ounce porterhouse or the stuffed lobster special, or—even better—the champagne brunch on Sunday. The staff is efficient and polite. ♦ American ♦ W-Sa dinner; Su brunch and dinner. Reservations recommended. First floor. 454.8009

Mary's Diner ★$ Fans of the 1950s come to this Art Deco diner to feast on bacon and eggs and burgers. Breakfast is served around the clock Thursday through Saturday. Service can be slow, but the thick malts and milk shakes amply reward your patience. ♦ American ♦ Daily breakfast, lunch, and dinner. Second floor. 456.7777

Smokey Joe's Cafe & Market $ A country market atmosphere greets hungry gamblers within earshot of the action in the main casino. The coffee shop is always busy. The midnight breakfast and prime rib specials are among the best bargains in town. ♦ American ♦ Daily 24 hours; closed 11PM Thursday to 6AM Friday. First floor. 456.7777

Uptown Buffet $ Brunch and dinner are served daily at this large (526 seats), popular buffet. Basically, what that means is you can get as much breakfast or lunch as you would like at any hour of the day up until dinnertime. Seafood gets star billing on Tuesday and Friday nights; Italian food take center stage Wednesday; and Asian heads the culinary carte on Thursday. ♦ Buffet ♦ Daily brunch and dinner. Second floor. 456.7777

Crime Story

The tale of organized crime syndicates' involvement in Las Vegas reads like an epic parable in which the evil villains eventually meet their nemesis: justice.

By the time 37-year-old Benjamin "Bugsy" Siegel first set foot in Las Vegas in 1942, he'd been a gangster and a ranking member of New York's criminal underworld for more than 20 years. In the early 1920s, after Prohibition—the constitutional amendment that declared the production, distribution, and possession of alcohol illegal—Bugsy and his mob partners helped unite the nation's criminal syndicates, masterminding the large-scale illegal production of liquor. Smugglers, boot-leggers, and urban street gangs, protected by corrupt police and politicians, supplied 300,000 speakeasies nationwide with the demon drink.

The underground liquor business funneled enormous sums of untaxed dollars to a new class of gangster millionaires, including Siegel, Cleveland's Morris "Moe" Dalitz, and Chicago's Al Capone. When federal legislators finally repealed Prohibition in 1933, the well-organized and well-capitalized underground networks run by these mobsters were ready to exploit other criminal vices, such as drugs, prostitution, loan-sharking, and gambling.

Gambling proved especially profitable. It had nearly as large a customer base as bootlegged booze, and it was highly portable: Games such as craps and blackjack could be set up almost anywhere and taken down in a moment's notice. Gaming was also subject to a widely varying laws enforced by local police, who could be easily

"persuaded" with bribes. However, gambling was often a target of moralistic crusaders who periodically mounted successful political campaigns to shut down the back-room games.

Despite the efforts of self-righteous lobbyists to eradicate betting, gamblers gained one safe haven in the country in 1931, when Nevada legislators legalized casino gambling in the state. Suddenly, men who would have been arrested and jailed for operating games of chance or betting joints elsewhere in the nation had only to cross the Nevada line to become legitimate entrepreneurs.

It took a decade for underworld gambling-hall operators to recognize that Nevada, and Las Vegas in particular, could be the promised land. When Siegel made his fateful trip to Vegas in the early 1940s, as chronicled in the 1991 film *Bugsy,* **Fremont Street** consisted of a motley collection of saloons with Wild West facades, sawdust floors, cigars, whiskey, and poker. Their small-time owners (unlike the powerful operators working in Reno at the time, including Bill Harrah, Raymond "Pappy" Smith, and several well-established ranching families) proved no match for the notorious East Coast gangster, who quickly muscled into the downtown joints, then helped himself to pieces of fledgling businesses on the seminal Las Vegas **Strip.**

Then came Bugsy's ill-fated obsession: the fabulous **Flamingo.** Although he invested $1 million of his own money in building his grandiose casino-resort, he eventually needed $6 million to finish the project. Some think that Bugsy's mobster partners believed he was skimming funds borrowed from them for construction and decided to stop him—permanently. Another hypothesis has it that Siegel's Las Vegas mob associates had him eliminated out of fear that his notorious hysteric outbursts—he wasn't known as Bugsy for nothing—might give gambling a bad reputation. Whatever the reason, in 1947 Bugsy Siegel's body was found in a Beverly Hills mansion with two bullets in the head (an unwritten mob code held that no one was to be eliminated in Las Vegas). Once Siegel was conveniently out of the picture, the mob emerged with a trophy, its first wholly owned Las Vegas casino.

Moe Dalitz, old-time bootlegger and gambling boss in Ohio and Kentucky, opened the **Desert Inn** in 1950. Over the next eight years, underworld cash supplied by mobsters from New England, New York, New Orleans, Miami, Chicago, Dallas, and the West Coast financed seven major Las Vegas hotel-casinos. By 1958, the mob controlled a dozen of the 15 major casinos on the Strip and downtown.

By all accounts, the 1950s were the mob's heyday in Las Vegas, an era that arouses nostalgia among many old-timers. Frank Sinatra, who owned a piece of the **Sands,** performed there regularly; his friends in the "Rat Pack" (Dean Martin, Joey Bishop, Peter Lawford, and Sammy Davis Jr.) held court all over town, sometimes stealing the stage from lesser-known lounge performers to give impromptu shows. Tourists shot craps with visiting mobsters. A little "juice" (in other words, knowing the right people) ensured complimentary food, rooms, shows, and even chips for visitors with influential connections. Floating crap games (literally played in the pool), cheating gamblers buried unceremoniously in the desert, and couriers transporting paper bags stuffed full of cash were a few of the mythic highlights that occurred during the mob's zenith.

Throughout most of the 1950s the Nevada Tax Commission, headquartered in Carson City, 400 miles from Las Vegas, oversaw the casino industry. Individual licenses were granted by city and county officials, who could be relied on to turn a blind eye toward criminal records and associations. Since gambling wasn't a crime in Nevada, the locals preferred to let these mobsters-turned-executives—the only people who had the money, muscle, and experience to control gaming—handle the volatile business.

By the early 1960s, the state Gaming Control Board had been established to batten down the licensing hatches and police casinos. Robert Kennedy, the new attorney general, fired up the federal heat on the Las Vegas underworld. In addition to this pressure, the price of opening a casino was skyrocketing. Hotels that cost $3 million, $6 million, even $10 million to build in the mid-1950s now ran $20 to $30 million, too much for even a gangster syndicate to afford. Because banks and other conventional sources of capital refused to finance gambling, which they considered a pariah industry, the only source of adequate funding for mob-owned Las Vegas casinos between 1958 and 1966 was the Midwest Pension Fund of the Teamsters Union, controlled by Jimmy Hoffa. The union used the pensions of thousands of truck drivers to float tens of millions of dollars in unsecured loans to mobsters to operate and expand properties, and build new ones.

When **Caesars Palace** opened in 1966 (financed primarily by Hoffa), Las Vegas casino owners, with or without underworld associations, were sweating under state, federal, and media pressure. Almost daily, officials and reporters denounced Las Vegas as the most mob-infested, crime-ridden city in the country.

That's when Lancelot, otherwise known as the billionaire Howard Hughes, snuck into town on a private midnight train. Hughes, who had decided to transform Las Vegas into the western gateway for the supersonic jets that he predicted would soon be flying all over the world, took over an entire floor of the **Desert Inn.** Moe Dalitz, owner of the hotel, saw the perfect opportunity to escape increasing police surveillance and make a tidy profit in the bargain. He sold the **Desert Inn** to Hughes, who then purchased a total of eight casinos, an airport, a TV station, and millions of dollars worth of undeveloped Las Vegas property. Hughes bought out a number of mobsters, replacing them with his own corporate executives. The reclusive billionaire's four-year presence in Las Vegas, along with the $300 million he invested, helped legitimize the gambling industry in the eyes of big business. The media, along with local officials, tagged him a savior, and soon thereafter, Hilton Hotels became the first major legitimate corporation to license a hotel-casino. Holiday Inn quickly followed suit.

Meanwhile, the FBI, IRS, and the Gaming Control Board, along with other agencies, were engineering a massive, nationwide purge of organized crime. In 1978, Nevada auditors uncovered a large-scale slot-machine–skimming operation at the **Stardust** and the **Fremont** (the unreported cash making its way to mob bosses in Chicago, Kansas City, and St. Louis), and hidden underworld ownership of the **Dunes** and the **Aladdin.** Even as recently as the mid-1980s, the Midwest mob's continuing interest in Las Vegas was overseen by Tony "the Ant" Spilotro, a well-known and ruthless local figure. But internal power struggles, along with informers, wiretaps, and dogged pursuit by police, weakened the mob's ability to siphon off undeclared cash from casinos. Spilotro turned up in a shallow grave in Indiana in 1985 after a failed coup against his Chicago bosses, who themselves were subsequently either murdered or imprisoned. By the late 1980s, the last vestigial traces of the underworld were gone, ending organized crime's 45-year relationship with Las Vegas.

Willy & Jose's Mexican Cantina ★★$$
Diners here can wash down authentic Mexican food with massive margaritas in this casual cantina. They have all the standard dishes, including tacos, burritos, and enchiladas. You can eat for free on your birthday. ♦ Mexican ♦ Daily dinner. Reservations recommended. First floor. 454.8044

23 Las Vegas Super 8 Motel $$ This 150-room, bare-bones motel recently added the **Longhorn Casino & Restaurant.** The casino boasts a handful of blackjack tables and **Leroy's Sports Book.** There's also a small bar and the modest **Chuck Wagon** coffee shop. ♦ 5288 Boulder Hwy (at Harmon Ave). 435.8888, 800/825.0880

24 Nevada Palace Hotel-Casino $$
Founded in 1981, this overgrown motel and casino clings to its massive neighbor (**Sam's Town**), luring locals, truckers, and overflow crowds with a combination of cheap food, reasonable rooms, and low-cost gaming options. Like **Sam's Town,** it offers live country music and free dance lessons Tuesday through Saturday nights in its **Silverado Saloon & Dance Hall.** The 200 rooms, though of the typical roadside motor-lodge variety, are clean and quiet. The hotel is less than four miles north of the **Sam Boyd Stadium,** site of **UNLV** football games and the occasional rock concert. ♦ 5255 Boulder Hwy (at Harmon Ave). 458.8810, 800/634.6283

Within the Nevada Palace Hotel-Casino:

Nevada Palace Casino A good place to gamble when your bankroll isn't as big as you'd like, there's two-dollar blackjack, one-dollar roulette, and 50¢ keno here. All the basic casino games are offered, as well as bingo and giveaways, such as a $1-million drawing in which contestants guess which numbers will come up in the California lottery. ♦ Daily 24 hours. 458.8810

Boulder Cafe ★$ The hotel's inexpensive 24-hour coffee shop serves the basic sandwiches and burgers, plus such full-course meals as a steak and snow crab special, and grilled beef liver with bacon strips and onions. For the amount most places charge for a muffin and coffee, diners can choose one of seven copious breakfast specials on Monday through Friday mornings; night owls can enjoy the same breakfast bargains any Sunday through Thursday night. ♦ American ♦ Daily 24 hours. 458.8810

The world outdoor Frisbee-throwing record of 551 feet was set in Las Vegas in 1984.

La Bella Pasta ★$$ Although primarily Italian cuisine is served in a country-and-western setting here, on Sunday night this is the site of a $5.95 Bavarian buffet, which features roast baron of beef (two loins of sirloin joined at the backbone and carved to order—very popular in Las Vegas), veal loaf, baked *leberkäse* (liver sausage), and bratwurst. On Monday night, there's a western buffet for the same price. ♦Continental/ Western ♦ Daily dinner. 458.8810

25 Desert Rose Golf Course Although this modest, 147-acre course isn't the most scenic in town, it is one of the cheapest and it does overlook nearby Sunrise Mountain. But the view is blocked by an unsightly power plant to the east of the links. Some golfers steer clear of this course because it's watered in part with treated wastewater. Still, it's crowded all year long, especially from February to June, when golfers should call a week in advance to reserve a tee time. Amenities include a pro shop, a clubhouse, a driving range, a small restaurant, and a bar. ♦ Fee. Daily sunrise to sunset. 5483 Clubhouse Dr (entrance between Sahara Ave and Vegas Valley Dr). 431.4653; fax 431.7910

26 Las Vegas Mormon Temple The 60,000-square-foot temple, surrounded by an iron fence, sits on 12 well-manicured acres at the base of Sunrise Mountain, which forms the eastern boundary of the Las Vegas Valley. Since it was built in 1989 by the Church of Jesus Christ of Latter-Day Saints, the $18-million structure has become one of the area's most recognizable pieces of architecture. The public is allowed to tour the grounds, but cannot enter the temple. Even many Mormons have to content themselves with viewing the stately exterior, which features a copper roof and six cast-stone towers. The tallest tower rises 125 feet above the east entrance and is topped by a 10-foot-tall, gold-leaf statue of Moroni, the angel Mormons believe helped the prophet Joseph Smith to "usher in the restoration of the gospel of Jesus Christ." The Eastside landmark is especially striking at night, when it's illuminated with soft lights. Unlike the dozens of Mormon churches in Vegas, this temple is, according to church leaders, "a special place where couples are married for eternity, where families are joined together forever, and where members receive sacred instruction." To many locals, including some 100,000 Mormons in Nevada and portions of Arizona and California, the temple is also a symbol of the historical importance and political power the church holds in the state. ♦ Call to find out when the grounds are open. 827 Temple View Dr (end of E Bonanza Rd, just east of Hollywood Blvd). 452.5011

26 Nellis Air Force Base The largest and busiest base in the Air Combat command covers about 12,000 square miles of airspace and approximately three million acres of land northeast of Las Vegas. More than 7,000 military and civilian employees work at the base, which was established in 1941 as the Las Vegas Gunnery Range. While the base is not open to the public, the hangar that houses the famed Thunderbirds air demonstration squadron is usually open for free 90-minute guided tours on Tuesday, Wednesday, and Thursday. The tour begins at 2PM and includes a brief lecture on the history of the team and a 13-minute film showing the red, white, and blue jets in action. It concludes with a walk through the **Thunderbird Museum,** which also is open only for tours. The museum thrills aeronautics buffs with its collection of photos and memorabilia of the T-Birds and the pilots who have flown them.

If you're lucky and the Nellis-based daredevils aren't performing somewhere, you'll get a close-up view of one of the team's F-16 jets. Unfortunately, air shows are not part of the package. To take the tour, visitors must check in at the **Nellis Visitors' Center** between 1:30 and 1:45PM to receive a vehicle pass and directions to the hangar. Groups of 20 or more can request their own tour by calling the Thunderbird Public Affairs Office at least a month in advance. ♦ Free. Tu-Th 2PM. Enter through main gate at Las Vegas Blvd N and Craig Rd. 652.4018

Las Vegas is the cellular phone capital of the nation, according to Sprint Central Telephone–Nevada, the company that serves southern Nevada. The city not only boasts the nation's highest percentage of cellular-phone owners, but Las Vegans also use their portable phones more often than people in other cities.

Suburban Las Vegas has come to resemble the stucco-and-tile residential sprawl of southern California for a reason. A substantial number of southern Californians relocated here. Of all the out-of-state driver's licenses collected by the Department of Motor Vehicles, about 36 percent belong to transplanted Californians.

"I've performed in Las Vegas for 20 years. One night, in the middle of a tender ballad, I heard discordant tones emanate from the string section. After at first ignoring them, I angrily turned to glare at the offenders, only to find Wayne Newton, sitting with the musicians, looking at me with an expression that said, 'What's the matter with you?'"

Robert Goulet

Bests

Arnold Snyder
Author/Editor/Publisher, *Blackjack Forum* magazine

Dinner with my wife, Alison, at the **Golden Nugget**'s **Lillie Langtry's** restaurant, where the after-dinner close-up magic artistry of resident house magician Michael Skinner never ceases to charm and amaze.

Also downtown, dinner after 10PM at **Binion's Horseshoe,** where two dollars buys a complete New York strip steak meal prepared to order.

Rubbing shoulders with the gambling cognoscenti at **Gambler's Book Club.** Hang out here for any length of time, and you'll hear tall tales of incredible schemes and scams. The store has an amazing inventory—thousands of books on gambling, horses, billiards, chess, magic, con artists. . . . Book collectors will go nuts in their used-book room. Be sure to pick up a copy of the *Las Vegas Advisor,* a monthly "Consumer Reports" on the best bargains and deals in a dealing town.

Head east on Charleston to about the 2000 block and you'll find a cluster of antiques shops. Alison and I have found treasures here, and browsers are welcomed.

Back on the **Strip,** try the **Tropicana**'s swim-up blackjack table. Hit me dealer, and pass the towel.

Walk through **Caesars Palace** to reach the **Forum Shops,** where a Roman street scene is re-created under a marvelous false sky and the stone statues come alive every half hour or so.

Slip next door to **The Mirage** and walk through their indoor jungle. Don't miss the enormous aquariums behind the registration desk—they are beautiful and hypnotic. Outside watch the volcano erupt, except if there's a wind, when it will only fizzle.

Drive or walk down the **Strip (Las Vegas Boulevard)** at night and marvel at the lights, the nonstop energy, and the amount of money that's spent here. There's nothing else like it in the world.

Lynne Foster
Stage Producer, Dick Foster Productions, Inc.

Las Vegas **Strip** hotels—free valet parking; nominal tip paid at departure.

The **Forum Shops at Caesars**—don't miss the great statue show.

Green Valley—a super suburb.

Spellbound—a fantastic magic production show at **Harrah's** on the Strip.

Kabuki Japanese Restaurant—excellent sushi at good prices.

Boulder City's *Art in the Park,* held the first weekend in October, is an outstanding arts and crafts display.

Gambling

Gambling is as old as civilization itself. Even before the advent of written records, a Neanderthal carved the first dice from ankle bones of sheep. Later, another of our ancestors devised one of the first practical applications for paper: the playing card. Gambling myths are common in most ancient religions. Indeed, gambling can be considered a theological by-product, if you subscribe to the idea that divine authority controls luck, fate, and destiny. And though mass public gambling has evolved into its current sanitized manifestation—a high-volume, corporate-profit assembly line, euphemistically known as gaming—it's still mono-theistic. Nowadays, though, the Higher Power, the Great Pit Boss in the Sky, is represented by a simple mathematical concept: the house advantage.

Let's face it. Every game in every casino in the world yields the advantage to the house. The house advantage is an invisible, automatic, and efficient system that ensures that the casino reaps a commission from every dollar the players win. All the pennies, nickels, dimes, and quarters that the casino "rakes" (takes off the top) from all winning wagers eventually grind bettors' bankrolls into dust. This process, in gambling lingo, is known as a "long-term negative expectation." In layman's terms, it's called "going broke."

Players can make nearly a hundred types of wagers in a casino. (Craps alone accounts for a couple of dozen.) The house advantage for each of these bets is calculated as a percentage, the difference between the true odds of a winning wager (what the wager would pay if the casino were not deducting a profit) and what the casino actually pays. For example, since a roulette wheel has 38 numbers, the odds of choosing the correct number are 37 to 1. Therefore, the true odds would call for a $37 payoff for a one dollar bet on a winning number. However, the casino only pays $35. This two dollar difference between the true odds and the actual payoff amounts to a house advantage of 5.26 percent. The house recoups a little more than a nickel commission from every dollar it pays out.

The house percentage ranges from zero—with perfect play at blackjack (when the player makes no mistakes) and on some video-poker machines—up to a whopping 30 percent on a typical keno wager. This averages out to a casino "hold," or pre-tax profit margin, of 20 percent (holds vary only slightly since most casinos operate under similar game rules). This opulent hold is evident throughout Las Vegas. It pays the massive hotel-casino overhead and subsidizes bargain room rates, rock-bottom food prices, and "comps" (complimentary accommodations, meals, and drinks). It helped finance the construction of megaresorts such as **The Mirage, Excalibur, Luxor, Treasure Island,** and the **MGM Grand**—and still continues to bankroll newer and bigger monuments to the almighty house advantage.

Betting Smart

Sticking to bets that yield the lowest percentage to the house gives you an advantage over less discriminating gamblers. If you win, you contribute a smaller portion of your winnings to the casino's 20 percent profit margin. Listed below (in order) are the five best and five worst casino wagers from a bettor's perspective. Refer to the sections on each individual game (beginning on page 90) for further explanation.

Five Best Bets

- any cash wager augmented with a casino coupon (which supplements your return if you win)
- single-deck blackjack using perfect basic strategy
- maximum-coin bet on a 9/6 video-poker machine with a $4,000 royal flush jackpot
- placing a bet on either player or banker at baccarat
- making line bets with full odds at craps

Five Worst Bets

- any bet at keno
- any bet on the money wheel
- proposition bets at craps
- nickel reel slots
- tie at baccarat

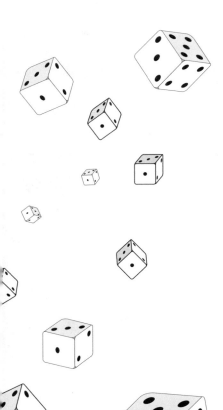

Mastering the Basics

The best way to increase your chances of winning is to learn the rules, odds, and etiquette of casino games before you attempt to play. You can choose from countless books covering all aspects of gaming, from probability theory and how to play slots to shuffle variations at blackjack and professional tournament strategy. **Gambler's Book Club** (630 S 11th St, at Charleston Blvd, Las Vegas, NV 89101; 382.7555) has the most complete selection of titles on gambling in the US and will send books by mail. Call to order their free catalog of titles.

Interactive computer software that simulates blackjack, craps, or video poker can help develop strong gambling skills. You can purchase a range of gambling software from **Huntington Press** (5280 S Valley View Blvd, at Hacienda Ave, Las Vegas, NV 89118; 597.1884).

Most of the large casinos provide free gambling lessons during slack periods in the day. Here you can gain some experience and insight on how to play. Show up early so that you're close to the "layout" (the playing area of the table games) to take full advantage of this free service.

In the Casino

Always begin gambling, especially at the live table games (those with a dealer), with all of your powers of observation on alert. There are many customs and rules of etiquette, and until you master them, you're an obvious novice. From the outset, don't be shy about asking questions of dealers or pit personnel. It's perfectly acceptable to ask a crap dealer what the odds are on a particular bet, or a blackjack dealer what the basic strategy is for a certain hand. Dealers should be polite and helpful. If they're not, leave.

A friendly dealer can help provide an enjoyable, and sometimes unforgettable, gambling experience. An occasional "toke" (tip) or bet for the dealer will quickly loosen up a mechanical and impersonal game. Dealers earn little more than minimum wage and depend on tokes for a large portion of their income. You can either give the dealer a chip by placing it on the layout (never hand it over directly), or make a side bet for the dealer. If the player hand wins, the dealer takes the wager and winning payoff; if the dealer hand wins, the house gets the wager.

Remember, the whole idea of a trip to the casino is to have fun (at least for nonprofessionals). If you consider gambling recreation, you'll be willing to spend money for the enjoyment of it, just as you would pay for the pleasure of a meal or a concert. Be patient and courteous with the people around you. Remain friendly and gracious even when you're losing.

Here are some examples of Las Vegas-speak: A "george" is a player who tokes (tips) the dealer; a "stiff" doesn't tip. A "grind" is a one-dollar or two-dollar bettor. A "plunger" or "screamer" increases his bets when he loses. And a "turkey" is an unpleasant player.

BACCARAT

Named after an Italian word meaning zero, baccarat (*bah*-kah-rah) made its way from Italy to France, where, in the late 15th century, it evolved into chemin de fer, a game enjoyed primarily by the French nobility. In the late 1950s, Las Vegas casinos imported chemin de fer and adopted the original name. Today, baccarat is one of the simplest, and at the same time most exclusive, casino table games. It's easy to learn and play, and is as thick in tradition, glamour, and exclusivity as it is thin in substance and nuance. And while the house advantage is minor (a little more than one percent), the minimum bet (usually $20 to $25) is major. Thus, neither the casino nor the players take baccarat lightly. Though it offers excellent odds and takes little skill, it requires a large investment.

How to Play

The object of baccarat is to come as close as possible, with two or three cards, to a hand that

totals nine. Picture cards, 10s, and cards that together total 10 are treated as zero. Ten is subtracted from a hand that totals more than 10. Aces count as one. Therefore, a three and a four add up to seven; eight and seven add up to five; a king and ace together count as one; a jack, a five, and a nine add up to four. A hand totaling eight or nine is called a natural.

Baccarat involves obscure ritual, orchestrated by the "caller," one of the four casino employees who run the game. Two dealers handle the betting, the caller oversees the dealing, and a ladderman handles the dealers (he supervises the game and has the final word if any questions or disputes arise). Eight decks of cards are shuffled by a dealer, and the cards are placed in a "shoe" (card-holding device). The cards are dealt from the shoe by the players themselves, who, when they're dealing, are known as the bank. The caller instructs the players as to the proper sequences of the dealing ritual. The simplicity of the game lies in the fact that there are only three bets to baccarat: player, bank, and tie. The whole idea is to

Hands counting 0

Hands counting 5

Naturals

bet on which hand, bank or player, will come closest to nine. The player bet has a house edge of 1.36 percent, the bank 1.17 percent; the casino collects a five percent commission on winning bank wagers. The tie has a 14 percent edge, which means you'll lose your money 14 times faster than if you stick to player or bank bets.

Two cards are dealt to each hand (usually face down, but some casinos deal them face up). Depending on their totals, it may be necessary for one or both hands to draw a third card, governed by a specific set of rules. If both hands total eight or nine, no cards are drawn and the nine beats the eight; in a tie, the hands are redealt. The winning hand is paid off at even money (ties are paid at eight to one).

Player's Rules

Hand	Action
1, 2, 3, 4, 5, 10	draw a third card
6, 7	stand (hand stands as dealt)
8, 9	natural (wins or ties)

Bank's Rules

Hand	Draw if third card is:	Stand if third card is:
3	1, 2, 3, 4, 5, 6, 7, 9, 10	8
4	2, 3, 4, 5, 6, 7	1, 8, 9, 10
5	4, 5, 6, 7	1, 2, 3, 8, 9, 10
6	6, 7	1, 2, 3, 4, 5, 8, 9, 10
7	stand	
8, 9	natural (wins or ties)	

Mini-baccarat

While baccarat is played in its own ritual-laden pit with a table minimum of $20 to $25, mini-baccarat (see below) takes place in the main blackjack pit, with none of the ritual and a two- to five-dollar table minimum. One dealer handles dealing the cards, taking the bets, and receiving the commissions; the rules and house advantage are the same as with baccarat. It's a faster game and much more casual— a good training ground for anyone who aspires to play at the big table.

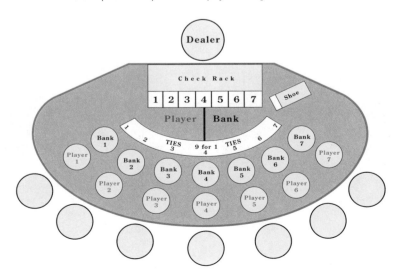

BLACKJACK

On one hand, blackjack is an easy game. You play at least two cards to come as close to 21 as you can without "busting" (going over). You always have four choices for playing your cards: stand, hit, double down, or split (see "Blackjack Glossary," on page 94). You may have a fifth option of surrendering immediately after the deal and losing half your bet. And sometimes you have the option of buying insurance if the dealer is showing an ace. On the other hand, strategies for playing blackjack can be as complicated as a pro football offense, and the action can be nearly as intense.

Here's a typical scenario for a round of blackjack. Several players sit around a blackjack table facing the dealer, who deals two cards to each person, including herself. The players' cards are dealt face down, but one of the dealer's cards is face up; it's an 8. The players look at their hands to see how close their two cards have brought them to the magic number: 21. (Cards are tallied at face value, except for face cards, which count as 10, and aces, which can be worth either one or 11.) The player with two jacks stands. The player whose hand totals 16 hits (asks the dealer for a card), receives a king, and busts; he throws his two other cards toward the dealer, who collects the cards and the bet. The guy who holds two fours hits, receives a 10, and stands on 18. The woman with 11 doubles down and receives a single card, face down.

Now the dealer turns up his or her hole card (unexposed card) and shows a queen, for a total of 18. The dealer pays even money to the player with a 20. To the player with 18, the dealer says "Push," meaning a tie, and no money changes hands. The dealer turns over the card that's face down for the player who doubled down: It's a three, for 14, and the dealer collects the bet. The dealer quickly places all the used cards in the discard tray and starts dealing another hand. The whole round takes less than a minute.

Natural

Ever since Dr. Edward O. Thorp wrote and published *Beat The Dealer* (Vintage Books) in 1960, in which he described a system for "counting" the cards that have been dealt and determining if the remaining cards are advantageous or detrimental to the player, the blackjack table has been the fiercest battleground in the casino, with players facing off against dealers and pit bosses. Knowledgeable players have invented, tested, and refined strategies to the point that they can sometimes reduce the house advantage to mere fractions of a percentage, even it out, or in some cases turn it in their favor.

Because a player who counts cards can achieve a long-term advantage, however slight, over the house, professional gamblers play blackjack; people actually earn a fair living doing a daily shift at the 21 table. Of course, establishing a career as a card counter can require up to a year of advanced study and practice, a substantial financial stake, and facing risk every minute on the job. In short, it's not for everyone. Luckily, you can learn a less demanding blackjack strategy in a day, which can tilt the odds in your favor so that you're in the rare position of being on a level playing ground in the casino.

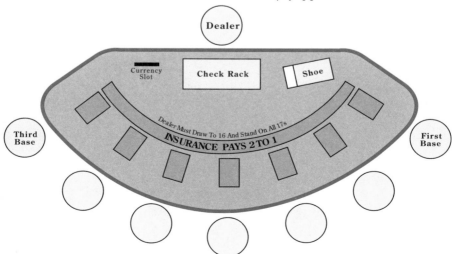

| H — Hit | S — Stand | D — Double Down | P — Split |

The Dealer's Up Card

Your Hand	2	3	4	5	6	7	8	9	10	A
8	H	H	H	H	H	H	H	H	H	H
9	H	D	D	D	D	H	H	H	H	H
10	D	D	D	D	D	D	D	D	H	H
11	D	D	D	D	D	D	D	D	D	H
12	H	H	S	S	S	H	H	H	H	H
13	S	S	S	S	S	H	H	H	H	H
14	S	S	S	S	S	H	H	H	H	H
15	S	S	S	S	S	H	H	H	H	H
16	S	S	S	S	S	H	H	H	H	H
17	S	S	S	S	S	S	S	S	S	S
A,2	H	H	H	D	D	H	H	H	H	H
A,3	H	H	H	D	D	H	H	H	H	H
A,4	H	H	D	D	D	H	H	H	H	H
A,5	H	H	D	D	D	H	H	H	H	H
A,6	H	D	D	D	D	H	H	H	H	H
A,7	S	D	D	D	D	S	S	H	H	H
A,8	S	S	S	S	S	S	S	S	S	S
A,9	S	S	S	S	S	S	S	S	S	S
A,A	P	P	P	P	P	P	P	P	P	P
2,2	H	H	P	P	P	P	H	H	H	H
3,3	H	H	P	P	P	P	H	H	H	H
4,4	H	H	H	H	H	H	H	H	H	H
6,6	H	P	P	P	P	H	H	H	H	H
7,7	P	P	P	P	P	P	H	H	H	H
8,8	P	P	P	P	P	P	P	P	P	P
9,9	P	P	P	P	P	S	P	P	S	S
10,10	S	S	S	S	S	S	S	S	S	S

Basic Strategy

This system for blackjack was developed by mathematicians and statisticians using high-speed computers to run simulations of hundreds of millions of blackjack hands. They've analyzed every possible combination of cards you might wind up holding against every possible dealer's up card and have come up with the strategy for each play that optimizes your chances of winning the round. The chart above shows the proper play for the cards in your hand against the dealer's up card. Memorize the entire chart and practice with cards, then review the chart periodically until you play optimum blackjack automatically.

Hard Hand

Six Basic Rules

What if you're reading this in your Las Vegas hotel room, about to go down to the casino to play a little blackjack, and you don't have time to memorize the chart? Take the chart with you; casinos allow gamblers to consult basic strategy while playing. Another option is to memorize the following rules, which will see you through all but the most advanced doubling and splitting situations.

- When you hold 12 to 16 and the dealer's up card is 2 to 6: stand.
- When you hold 12 to 16 and the dealer's up card is 7, 8, 9, 10, or ace: hit.
- Stand on 17 to 21.
- Double down on 10 and 11 against the dealer's up cards 2 to 9.
- Always split aces and 8s.
- Never take insurance (a real sucker bet).

Soft Hand

Bust

If you play perfect basic strategy for eight hours at a $1 blackjack table, your expected loss is about $2.50.

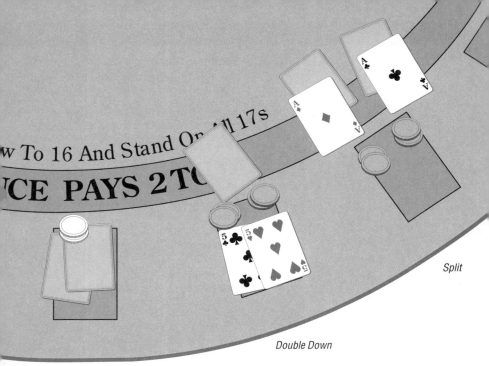

w To 16 And Stand On All 17s

CE PAYS 2 TO

Split

Double Down

Stand

Blackjack Glossary

Burn A ritual in most casinos; the dealer places one or more cards at the bottom of the deck or in the discard tray just after shuffling (to confuse card counters)

Bust Any hand that exceeds 21

Card counting An advanced blackjack strategy that tracks the cards played to determine if the remaining pack is favorable or unfavorable to the player

Double down Doubling the bet on the first two cards of the hand (see above)

Flat bet Betting the same amount each time

Front loading When the dealer inadvertently exposes the hole card to a player

Hard hand A hand totaling 12 or more that includes an ace

Hit Take another card

Hole card The dealer's unexposed card

Insurance This side bet, made when the dealer's up card is an ace, is a wager—half your original bet—that the dealer won't have a natural blackjack

Natural A two-card 21

Push A tie

Round One complete hand, start to finish

Shoe Multiple-deck card holder

Soft hand Any hand containing an ace valued at 11

Split Dividing two like cards into two hands (see above)

Spooking Catching a glimpse of the dealer's hole card

Stand Don't take another card (see above)

Stiff A hand totaling 12, 13, 14, 15, or 16

Surrender Folding a hand after viewing the first two cards

Tells Dealer mannerisms after checking the hole card

Warp Slightly bent card

"For those who are disgusted by gambling in America, only a few consolations can be offered. It is not as destructive as war or as boring as pornography. It is not as immoral as business or as suicidal as watching television. And the percentages are better than religion."

Mario Puzo

Casino managers can control the house advantage at blackjack by varying the rules of the game, the number of decks dealt, the number of rounds dealt, and the type and number of shuffles.

Volumes on Vegas

Perhaps because Las Vegas has such unique visual appeal, the city has appeared more often as the subject of films and TV shows than literary efforts. Still, more than a handful of authors have parlayed their fascination with the neon oasis into works in print.

Fiction

The Desert Rose, by Larry McMurtry (1983; Simon and Schuster). Las Vegas is the perfect place for McMurtry to explore his trademark characters: outcasts and dying breeds who never give up hope even when they know better. The title of the novella refers to Harmony, an aging showgirl in the **Stardust**'s *Lido de Paris* review who's in danger of being replaced by her own daughter.

Fool's Die, by Mario Puzo (1978; Putnam). Las Vegas figures prominently in Puzo's best-seller *The Godfather* (in that book, protagonist Moe Green represents Bugsy Siegel), but *Fool's Die* is the book that truly reveals Puzo's passion for gambling and the gaming capital. He weaves sex, wagering, and corruption into a potboiler. (Puzo also penned *Inside Las Vegas,* which is basically a long essay that accompanies a volume of photos.)

Last Call, by Tim Powers (1992; William Morrow and Company). Poker is the link between the science of randomness and the supernatural in this fantasy set in present-day Las Vegas. Powers creates mythology from carefully researched history and weaves in the true story of Bugsy Siegel. A poker game on **Lake Mead** turns out to have cosmic stakes.

The Stand, by Stephen King (1978; Doubleday). When a deadly strain of flu kills most of the world's population in this apocalyptic epic, many of the survivors are drawn to the most wonderful place on earth (Boulder, Colorado), while the bad guys convene in—you guessed it—Las Vegas.

Vegas: Memoir of a Dark Season, by John Gregory Dunne (1974; Random House). The author of *True Confessions* paints a cynical, memorably seedy portrait of the city and three of its inhabitants—a hooker, a private detective, and a lounge comic—in this semi-autobiographical book.

Nonfiction

Fear and Loathing in Las Vegas, by Hunter S. Thompson (1972; Random House). With the immortal opening sentence "We were somewhere around Barstow on the edge of the desert when the drugs began to take hold. . . ," *Rolling Stone* magazine's infamous gonzo journalist launched a surreal first-person account of one wild weekend. Probably the most popular book ever written about Vegas, to the chagrin of civic leaders.

The Green Felt Jungle, by Ed Reid and Ovid Demaris (1963; Trident Press). The hard-boiled prose of this exposé blasts the lid off the history of organized crime in the casino industry. The book created quite a stir in its day, but now serves mainly as a point of

contrast to the corporate-run **Strip** of today.

The Kandy-Kolored Tangerine Flake Streamline Baby, by Tom Wolfe (1965; Farrar, Straus & Giroux). Wolfe's lead-off essay in this anthology of proto-typical "new journalism" carries the lengthy title "Las Vegas (What?) Las Vegas (Can't hear you! Too noisy) Las Vegas!!!" It offers a manic tour of the Strip in its heyday and a whimsical treatment of a serious theory: that the neon landscape of the Strip in the early 1960s was a monument to the freedom of the postwar lifestyle and that Las Vegas is the only city in America with an indigenous architectural makeup.

Las Vegas: As It Began—As It Grew, by Stanley W. Paher (1971; Nevada Publications). The city's frontier-era history is detailed in this fascinating account.

Las Vegas: The Entertainment Capital, by Don Knepp (1987; Lane Publishing Co.). The Las Vegas News Bureau provided the outside world with some memorable images of the city, including a swim-up crap table and a shot of downtown silhouetted against the backdrop of a nuclear explosion. This coffee-table book filled with photos culled from the bureau's archives focuses on Las Vegas's entertainment history.

Once Before I Go, by Wayne Newton with Dick Maurice (1989; William Morrow and Company). "The Midnight Idol" of Las Vegas showrooms spins his legend in this autobiography. Newton pulls no punches against enemies such as Johnny Carson and tells his side of the story of his famed libel lawsuit against NBC.

Resort City in the Sunbelt: Las Vegas, 1930-1970, by Eugene P. Moehring (1989; University of Nevada Press). This is the definitive, scholarly historical account of the development of Las Vegas and the community's economic and social relationship to casino gambling.

Vegas: Live and In Person, by Jefferson Graham (1989; Cross River Press). This coffee-table book is filled with amusing personality profiles, ranging from those of local movers and shakers to "the little people"—cocktail waitresses, bellmen, and PBX operators. Historical and current photos enliven the thorough, if already dated, overview.

We Only Kill Each Other: The Life and Bad Times of Bugsy Siegel, by Dean Jennings (1967; Prentice-Hall). Though this biography of Las Vegas's most infamous founding father was credited in the movie *Bugsy,* the screenwriters did not follow the true story too closely.

Yes I Can: The Story of Sammy Davis Jr., by Sammy Davis Jr. and Jane and Burt Buyar (1965; Farrar, Straus & Giroux). Davis and Vegas hit their stride at the same time, and their names were forever entwined. But this book is one of few that documents the period when blacks—even well-loved black performers—were barred from casino floors and forced to stay in a ghetto on the city's west side.

CRAPS

Dice! Those magical spotted cubes that have been the cause of exultation and desolation among gamblers since Zeus won the heavens from Hades and Poseidon in an Olympian crap shoot. "Bones" (slang for dice) have been around for thousands of years, and the American game of craps is descended from hazard, a French dice game that evolved from *az-zahr,* an Arabic dice game inspired by *ish-char,* the Sanskrit word for, you guessed it, dice.

The crap table is where the fastest moving and

rowdiest action in the casino takes place. Craps is a complicated game that offers a couple dozen betting options. It's possible to have thousands of dollars—on a score of different wagers—riding on a single roll of the dice. The dealers double as human calculators, the cocktail waitresses keep one eye out for flying objects, and the players lose track of their bets often enough that vociferous arguments over stray chips are not uncommon. Fortunately, you can learn craps in increments and start by playing a satisfying (and low-risk) version when you know only the basic, most common wagers on the layout.

Points	Possible Rolls	Odds
2		1 in 36
3		1 in 18
4		1 in 12
5		1 in 9
6		5 in 36
7		1 in 6
8		5 in 36
9		1 in 9
10		1 in 12
11		1 in 18
12		1 in 36

Don't Pass Bar

PASS LINE

Pass-line bet

Free-odds bet

For the Beginner

Even if you've never played craps before, you can make the simplest bets, which also happen to have the lowest house advantage, by playing the "line." Watch a crap game until you hear the stickman (he who wields the stick that moves the dice) call "seven out" and the dealers sweep up most of the chips on the layout (shown below). The pair of dice then goes to a new shooter (player), whose first roll is called the "come-out" roll. On the come-out, everyone places a bet on either the pass line (betting *with* the shooter) or the don't-pass line (betting *against* the shooter). If the come-out is a seven or 11, those who bet the pass line win. If it comes up "craps" (two, three, or 12), they lose. On the pass line means you think the shooter will roll his point before "sevening out" (rolling a seven, an automatic loser); if you bet on the don't-pass line, you wager that the shooter will seven out before he rolls his point. Both bets are wagered against the house.

- Pass line: Wins even money with a 7 or 11 on the come-out roll; loses on a 2, 3, or 12.

- Don't-pass line: Wins even money if the come-out roll is a 2 or 3, and loses on a 7 or 11; 12 is a tie—no money changes hands.

- Point (4, 5, 6, 8, 9, or 10): If the point is rolled before a 7, a bet on the pass line wins even money.

A bet on the don't-pass line loses. If a 7 is rolled before the point, a pass-line bet loses and a don't-pass-line bet wins. A black-and-white plastic "buck" marks the point on the layout.

- Come: Same as a pass-line bet, except it's made after a point has been established. A 7 or 11 wins; a 2, 3, or 12 loses; and any other number is a second point. If the newly established point is rolled before a 7, you win even money; if a 7 is rolled first, you lose.

- Don't come: The opposite of the come bet. A 7 or 11 loses; 2, 3, and 12 win. If a 7 is rolled before the point, you win even money; if the point is rolled first, you lose.

- Free odds: One of the best bets in a casino is taking the "true odds" on a line bet (many players don't even realize it exists since it's not marked on the table). Any pass/don't pass or come/don't come bettor can make a side bet equal to or greater than his previous bet—after the point has been established—that the shooter will roll his point before sevening out. You "back up" your line bets with odds by placing your chips directly behind the line bet (see above). If the point is rolled, the true odds pay off at 2 to 1 on the 4 and 10; 3 to 2 on the 5 and 9; and 6 to 5 on the 6 and 8 (as opposed to even money). (See page 98 for free odds on the come bet.)

- Field: This bet is won or lost on each roll. A 3, 4, 9, 10, or 11 pay even money; a 2 or 12 pay 2 to 1. You lose on a 5, 6, 7, or 8. (See page 98.)

Dealer

Stickman

Dealer places free-odds bet atop original bet but offset to distinguish from come or don't-come bet

Don't-come and free-odds bet

Come and free-odds bet

Bet	Payoff	House Advantage
Pass line/come	1 to 1	1.4 percent
Don't-pass line/ don't come	1 to 1	1.4 percent
With single odds	true odds	.8 percent
With double odds	true odds	.6 percent
With triple odds	true odds	.4 percent
Field	1 to 1	5.5 percent
Field (on 2 or 12)	2 to 1	5.5 percent

For the Advanced

Once you've played craps a few times and are familiar with the line bets and table etiquette, you can start to place more advanced and complicated wagers. The more money you have down on the table, the harder it is to keep track of it all, which is why you should be quite conversant with the game before you get into "placing" and "buying" points. However, even the most experienced crap shooters occasionally lose track of some of their bets. Fortunately, the dealers almost always have a handle on the layout and will make sure you get the money that's coming to you.

- Place: Similar to a come bet, except that instead of waiting for a point to be rolled, you place a bet directly on any point other than the pass-line point. You win if the place-bet point is rolled before a 7. Winning bets are paid at house odds (as opposed to true odds) of nine to five on the 4 and 10; seven to five on the 5 and 9; and seven to six on the 6 and 8.

- Buy: Similar to a place bet, except the odds paid off are true, and the house charges a five percent commission on winnings.

- Lay: Similar to a buy bet, except that you bet against the shooter. A 7 wins, and the point loses.

Bet	Payoff	House Advantage
Place 6/8	7 to 6	1.5 percent
Place 5/9	7 to 5	4 percent
Place 4/10	9 to 5	6.7 percent
Buy	true odds less 5 percent	4.7 percent
Lay 6/8	5 to 6 less 5 percent	4 percent
Lay 5/9	2 to 3 less 5 percent	3.2 percent
Lay 4/10	1 to 2 less 5 percent	2.4 percent

For the Sucker

"Proposition" bets are those made in the center of the layout, handled by the stickman. They all have a punishing house advantage of at least nine percent and can go nearly as high as 17 percent. A lot of crap players make these sucker proposition bets for excitement and the rare payoff; if you can't resist long-shot odds, join in—but be prepared to lose your money nearly as fast as you can play it.

- Big 6/big 8: Paid off at even money if 6 or 8 are rolled before a 7 (9.09 percent).

- Hardways: When the same number is rolled on each die (two 3s for a hardways 6, two 4s for a hardways 8, etc.). These bets pay 9 to 1 on the 6 and 8 (9.09 percent) and 7 to 1 on the 4 and 10 (11.1 percent). (See illustration below.)

- Any 7: Pays five to one when the next roll is a 7 (16.7 percent).

- Any craps (2, 3, or 12): Pays seven to one when the next roll is a 2, 3, or 12 (11.1 percent).

- 2 or 12: Pays 30 to one when the next roll is either of those numbers (13.9 percent).

- 3 or 11: Pays 15 to one when the next roll is either of those numbers (11.1 percent).

- C and E (craps and 11): Pays three to one on any craps; seven to one on 11 (11.1 percent).

KENO

A variation on an ancient Chinese form of bingo, keno was imported to the US by Chinese immigrants in the mid-1800s. Americanized, it's now played with 80 numbered Ping-Pong balls contained in a round plastic bowl (sometimes a wire mesh cage) called a "goose." A "blower" (powerful electric fan) mixes the balls and forces them, one at a time, into two long plastic tubes that hold 10 balls each. A caller announces the numbers, which are also illuminated on electronic keno boards throughout the casino.

It's hard to believe, but the house advantage for keno is even higher than it is for the money wheel: an astronomical 25 to 35 percent! You can expect to throw away roughly 30¢ for every dollar that you bet. On the other hand, it's a slow game. The action is protracted, so your dollar tends to go farther. Thus keno is convenient if you want to relax and drink in the keno lounge or add some excitement to a meal in the coffee shop. Also, keno offers substantial jackpots, often $50,000. If you can't resist a long shot or you're hoping total dumb luck will strike, this may be your game.

How to Play

- Get a keno ticket and, using one of the black crayons provided, mark your lucky numbers. You can mark any number of "spots" from 1 to 15, and sometimes 20, but the lowest house advantage is on the 8-spot wager. You can use a straight, split, way, or combination betting scheme. (See next page)

- Make the appropriate notations in the right-hand margin, depending on the type of ticket you play. Then write the amount of your wager in the box in the upper right-hand corner. The average minimum bet is $1.

- Present your ticket and bet to a keno runner (circulating throughout the casino) or at the keno counter. You'll receive a duplicate ticket with the date, game number, and serial number.

- As soon as you've placed your bet, watch any keno board for the numbers drawn and match them with the spots you've selected. Payoffs are listed in booklets displayed near the tickets and crayons. If enough of the casino's numbers match yours (depending on how many spots you've played), collect your payoff immediately. The numbers from the current game remain on the board for approximately five minutes; as soon as they're erased in preparation for a new game, you forfeit any payoff you haven't collected.

blank keno ticket

straight ticket

Ninety percent of visitors to Las Vegas gamble an average of five hours a day. Fifty-one percent play slot machines, 23 percent blackjack, 12 percent video poker, and five percent craps. Ninety percent make minimum bets of five dollars or less. The average gambler's bankroll is $500.

Types of Keno Tickets

- A "straight" ticket is the simplest and most common keno play. You mark from one to 15 numbers (out of a possible 80) and make a single bet on them. (See illustration on the previous page.)

- A "split" ticket contains a number of straight bets on the same ticket. Draw a circle around different combinations of numbers and place a bet on each combination. By circling, for example, four sets of three numbers and marking 4/3 in the margin, you are making four three-spot straight bets, the same as if you used four different tickets and marked one three-spot bet on each. At one dollar each, your total action would be four dollars (shown at right).

- The "way" ticket is a complicated and fancy way to lose money. You circle three or more equal groups of numbers and then play them by betting on all the different ways that the numbers can come up. For example, if you circled three groups of three numbers each, you'd make a notation of 3/6 in the margin, meaning the three ways to make a six spot, or the three ways that six different numbers could be called. With a betting unit of one dollar, your total bet would be three dollars. Large way tickets can get very complex and expensive. (See illustration, right.)

- The "combination" ticket adds another dimension to the way. Using the three-groups-of-three example, you could bet them separately as three spots, in which case you would be making a one dollar bet on each of the three spots, and you'd mark the margin 3/3 (total bet: three dollars). You could also bet them as three six spots, in which case you would be making a one dollar bet on the three different combinations of six numbers, and you'd mark the ticket 3/6 (total bet, now six dollars). Finally, you could also bet one dollar on all the numbers together as one nine spot, and you'd mark the ticket 1/9 (total action on the three different combinations: seven dollars). (See illustration, bottom art.)

- A "replay" ticket is simply a ticket from a prior game that's reused.

split ticket

way ticket

combination ticket

THE MONEY WHEEL

Also known as "big six" or "wheel of fortune," the money wheel is a legacy of carnival midways that has somehow insinuated itself into the casino pit. Anyone who's ever watched Merv Griffin's popular TV game show "Wheel of Fortune," with Pat Sajak and Vanna White, will be instantly familiar with the basics. The big wheel (usually six feet in diameter) is divided into nine sections. Each section is further divided into six monetary denominations from $1 to $20. There are 24 $1 segments, 15 $2 segments, seven $5 segments, four $10 segments, two $20 segments, and two jokers. Posts protruding from the circumference of the wheel separate the segments. The posts click against a leather or wood pointer at the top of the wheel as it spins; when it stops, the pointer indicates the winning denomination.

The layout (the area on the table where you place your bets) displays the same denominations as the wheel. Players place their bets on the $1, $2, $5, $10, $20, or joker options; the denominations also determine the payoff (i.e., a $1 bet on the $2 spot wins $2; a $5 bet on the $20 spot wins $100).

The player disadvantage on the money wheel is so prohibitive (from 11 percent on a $1 spot up to 24 percent on the joker) that most wheels and layouts need a dusting every few days. Still, if you've never been in a casino, are about to make your first bet ever, and don't know how to play any other game, you might consider putting a buck or two on the money wheel.

ROLANDO CORUJO

ROULETTE

The world's oldest wheel game, roulette traces its origins back to France during the Middle Ages. In French, the word roulette means "little wheel." Compared to the money wheel, the roulette wheel is small, measuring three feet across. The wheel spins counterclockwise, while the ball spins clockwise in the "back track" (the upper-level track). The ball descends as it slows, bounces around eight brass barriers, drops into the "bottom track" (which contains 38 numbered cups), and comes to rest in one of the cups. There are two green numbers (0 and 00) and 18 red and black numbers each (1-36).

You can place any one of 11 bets on the roulette layout (the long part of the roulette table next to the wheel that players lay bets on). The house has a 5.26 percent advantage on all but one—expensive, but not among the five worst bets in the casino. Absolutely no skill is involved; the outcome of each spin is completely random. No system can beat the game, though dozens have been invented and attempted over the past 400 years. The best thing about roulette is the hypnotic spell of watching the wheel go round and round.

How to Bet

You can play roulette with regular casino chips, but it's wise to purchase special roulette chips, sold in stacks of 20, from the dealer. Known as "wheel chips," their color identifies the bettor; this helps avoid confusion when chips are strewn all over the layout. When you buy the chips, inform the dealer of the monetary value you wish to assign to them; he or she will place one of your wheel chips on the rim of the wheel with a denomination marker on top of it.

There are two kinds of bets: "inside" and "outside." The six inside bets are made within the main numbered section of the layout, and the five outside bets are made on the periphery of the layout.

Inside Bets

- "Straight-up" bets, or "single-number" bets, placed on a single number, pay 35 to one. (See illustration, top right.)

- "Split" bets, also known as "two-number" bets, placed on the line separating two numbers, pay 17 to one if the ball lands on either of the numbers. (See illustration, middle right.)

- "Street" bets, or "three-number" bets, are wagered on a group of three numbers; lay your chips on the outside line of the three-numbered row. A win pays 11 to one. (See illustration, bottom right.)

- The "five-number" bet is placed only on the 0, 00, 1, 2, or 3. It pays six to one (with a house edge of 7.89 percent). (See illustration, top left.)

- A "line bet" covers six numbers and is placed like a street bet, except that it's between the two rows of three. It pays five to one. (See illustration, middle left.)

- "Corner" bets, also called "four-number," "square," or "quarter" bets, are placed at the point where four numbers meet and pay eight to one. (See illustration, bottom left.)

Outside Bets

- "Column" bets, placed on 12 numbers at the base of the column, pay two to one. (See below.)

- The "dozen" bets are also a 12-number bet, but these numbers are bet to appear consecutively, 1-12, 13-24, or 25-36, and are placed on the first, second, or third group of 12 numbers. Payoff is two to one. (See bottom of page.)

- You can lay a chip on 1 to 18 or 19 to 36; red or black; and even or odd. These bets pay even money, or one to one. (See bottom of page.)

Shaded boxes show which numbers have been bet.

SLOTS

Mechanical "reel" slots, the kind with three, four, or more spinning reels with various symbols on them (fruit, bars, and sevens are most common), were invented and originally used in San Francisco's notorious Barbary Coast neighborhood at the turn of the 20th century. The fruit symbols corresponded to the flavor of the gum that was delivered as the prize.

With the exception of a few minor variations, the original slot-machine design remained unchanged for 65 years. Electric slots were introduced in the mid-1960s, complete with lights and noisemakers. The miracle of electronics revolutionized the slot-machine industry in the mid-1970s, introducing a vast array of sizes, symbols, and payouts, all controlled by microprocessors. For example, nickel video slots (using a screen instead of reels) can feature 24 symbols with a complicated payout based on a variety of symbol patterns. Likewise, Megabucks is a one dollar, four-reel slot that's connected by modem to hundreds of other Megabucks machines throughout Nevada; each time a player inserts a dollar, the giant "progressive" jackpot grows by a nickel. By the time a player lines up all four Megabucks symbols, the jackpot can be in the $4 million or $5 million range. Nickel slots rank as one of the five worst bets in a casino, with a hold of around 25 percent. Dollar slots can be as low as five percent. With such odds, how they manage to earn casinos more money than all table games combined due to heavy play is one of life's biggest mysteries.

Tips on Playing Slots

- One of the great myths of slot machines is that they become "due," or overdue to hit a big jackpot. Slots fall under the "independent event" category of probability theory (as opposed to games like blackjack and poker, where the odds continually change, depending on what cards are in or out of play). Each spin of the reels has absolutely nothing to do with the last spin, nor the next. Don't spend hours on a machine that you think is "ready."

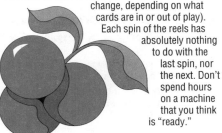

- To be eligible for the highest jackpot, you must play the maximum number of coins that a machine will accept. Megabucks slots, for example, have three paylines, each corresponding to a one dollar bet. To win the three-million-dollar-plus jackpot, you must line up the four Megabucks symbols on the three dollar payline. Imagine yourself lining up the symbols on the three dollar pay-line when you've only played one dollar and winning nothing, instead of millions.

- Dollar slots pay back at a higher percentage than quarters, which pay back at a higher percentage than nickels. Machines with smaller jackpots pay back smaller amounts more frequently than machines with larger jackpots. So you get more action for less money.

- Always join slot clubs, which you can find in most of the large casinos. To join, simply fill out an identification form at the slot club booth, at which time you receive a membership card. You still play with coins, but you insert your card into a digital reader on the machine, which tracks the amount and number of your bets and converts them into points. The more points you accumulate, the more discounts on rooms and food, various comps, gifts, and sometimes even cash are returned to you. Best of all, slot clubs are free.

SPORTS BETTING

The large room, generally off to one side of the casino, with long rows of tables and chairs, banks of TV and video screens on the wall, and a big board covered with team names and hieroglyphic notations is called the sports book. In Nevada, you can bet on all major league baseball, basketball, football, and hockey games, college football and basketball (except for **University of Nevada** teams), as well as boxing matches and horse races from around the country.

Sports books didn't appear in casinos until the mid-1970s, but over the past 15 years or so sports betting has become a billion-dollar adjunct to the casino industry. The **Super Bowl** (professional football) and the **Final Four** (**NCAA** basketball) are the two largest sports betting events of the year; together they generate more than $100 million in action.

The complicated world of sports betting involves handicapping (attempting to predict the winner of a game or race), point spreads (the number of points by which one team beats the other), money lines (the odds of one team beating another), and commissions (the sports book rake). If you don't understand the terminology or procedures, the bookies behind the counter where you place your bets are generally helpful in determining what kind of wager you're trying to place. So don't be afraid to walk up cold and bet on a game that you've been following. The minimum bet is usually five or ten dollars.

The best introductory book on sports betting is *Sports Betting 101*, written by Arne K. Lang and published by Gambler's Book Club.

FDR was the first president to visit Las Vegas; he passed through the city when he dedicated Hoover Dam in 1935. John F. Kennedy was the second president to visit when he made a 90-minute stopover in 1963.

VIDEO POKER

There are only two "bank" games (played against the house, unlike poker, in which you are up against other players) that people play professionally: video poker and blackjack. You can learn, practice, and apply an exact strategy to video poker for optimum results. In addition, unlike reel slots, video-poker machines can be handicapped. In other words, you can tell just by looking at them what the house advantage is. Furthermore, with perfect play (making the correct decision for every hand) on the best machines, you can reduce the house advantage to zero; occasionally, opportunities arise in which you have an edge over the casino.

There is a large, and growing, variety of video-poker machines, including straight draw, joker poker and/or deuces wild, double-down stud, double-down high card, and second chance. They come in penny, nickel, quarter, $1, $5, $25, and even $100 denominations, with "flat-top" (fixed) or progressive jackpots for the royal flush.

Playing Your Cards

For anyone familiar with the nuances of poker, proper play will be nearly automatic on the draw machines (though not on the joker or deuces machines); in other words, you'll keep cards that have the best potential for achieving pairs, three of a kind, straights, flushes, etc. However, the few basic differences in strategy between regular and video poker are important, since mistakes can be costly. The best way to learn video-poker strategy is on your home computer. A program such as *Stanford Wong's Video Poker* simulates draw, joker poker, deuces wild, and joker/deuces; tutors you on correct play; and calculates the house advantage for each hand. After an hour or two with this software, you'll be playing video poker in all its variations on a nearly professional level.

Do's on Playing Video (Draw) Poker

- Always hold any pair, low or high.
- In the absence of a pair, hold a picture card or an ace (or two).
- In the absence of pairs, picture cards, or four-card straights or flushes, draw five new cards.
- Always hold a high pair rather than drawing one card to a straight or flush.

Don'ts on Playing Video (Draw) Poker

- Don't hold a "kicker" (unpaired high card) with a low pair.
- Don't draw to an inside straight (i.e., if you have 2, 3, 5, 6, and 9, don't discard the 9 hoping to get a 4).
- Don't hold three cards to a straight or flush (you probably won't get the two cards needed to complete either hand).
- Never hold two cards to a straight flush.

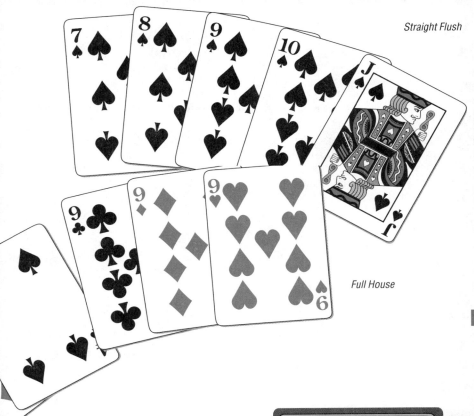

Straight Flush

Full House

Video-Poker Payout Schedules

Playing your cards properly is only half the challenge of video poker. The other, more important half is knowing which machine to play. Surprisingly, you can determine this with complete accuracy in a matter of seconds, by analyzing the payout schedule posted on the machines.

- Make sure the machine pays back your bet on a pair of jacks or better.
- Determine that the maximum wager is five coins.
- Check the payout column for one coin: A full house should return nine coins, and a flush should return six. This is known as a 9/6 machine.
- Determine the payout for a royal flush with five coins played: It should return 4,000 coins.

Full House/Flush Payout (Draw)	Expected Return
10/6	100.7 percent
9/7	100.8 percent
9/6	99.5 percent
8/5	97.3 percent
7/5	96.2 percent
6/5	95.1 percent

Excursions

No one really blames the tourist who still thinks a trip to Las Vegas begins and ends at the Strip. But locals know better, and they're quick to tell you that within an hour's drive of Las Vegas lies. . . well, Nevada: mountains, lakes, and colorful desert landscapes that offer stunning contrasts to the city's famous nightlife.

Face it. You've got to be fairly lucky, ridiculously wealthy, or unhealthily hooked to gamble for more than two or three hours at a stretch. Even experienced players, wise to the rhythms of cards and dice, would agree that it's occasionally necessary to escape the lights and sounds of the casinos. Nerve-soothing getaways can be found just a short drive away in almost any direction.

There's boating and fishing at **Lake Mead**, rock climbing and hiking at **Red Rock Canyon**, and striking natural sculpture at the **Valley of Fire**. And that shrine to human ingenuity—**Hoover Dam**—endures. Many visitors are surprised to learn they can even go skiing on **Mount Charleston** and be back by sundown to answer the siren call of the casinos.

You can easily visit many of these attractions in a day, and you need not make extra arrangements beyond renting a car (or in some cases hopping on bus). But some Las Vegas visionaries are hoping vacationers realize there's more to Nevada than a three-day blowout. As new resorts such as **Treasure Island** and the **MGM Grand Hotel and Theme Park** vie for the family market, count on the city being promoted as home base for an extended tour of the region. **McCarran International** is the closest airport to the **Grand Canyon,** one of the most spectacular natural wonders of North America. And with **Death Valley National Park, Zion National Park, Bryce Canyon,** and the booming river town of **Laughlin** within reach, Las Vegas is no longer simply a so-called "adult Disneyland," but a multifaceted vacation destination to rival any other.

1 Red Rock Canyon National Conservation Area

It's amazing to think that a mere 20 miles from the chaos of Las Vegas there is a serene landscape of giant sandstone formations, rolling desert valleys, craggy hilltops, and—late in the day, when most people have gone—incredible, peaceful silence.

When touring one of Las Vegas's most popular off-Strip tourist attractions, many people begin at the **US Bureau of Land Management Visitors' Center,** located just inside the park entrance. Maps, trail guides, and other information about the park's amenities are available. A short videotape and displays detailing the geology and history of the canyon also whet the newcomer's appetite for what awaits.

Most visitors then hop into their cars for a trip along the 13-mile, one-way scenic roadway that circles the canyon's inside perimeter. The route features several spots where you can leave your car, stretch your legs, perch on a rock, and drink in the sight of thousands of feet of red sandstone jutting into the sky and listen to the eerie sound of the wind whistling through the rocky corridor.

Millions of years ago, everything now visible here was covered by the warm waters of a shallow sea. The multicolored shale and sandstone that form the outcrops, escarpments, cliffs, and caves are products of this era, created as the sea dried up and erosion worked its artistry on the rock faces.

Calico Hills, a series of rust-colored cliffs about a mile past the visitors' center, is the visual centerpiece of the canyon. It's also a favored challenge among rock climbers, who can be seen each day inching up the bluff as sightseers breathlessly chart their progress from a nearby scenic lookout point.

Farther along the picturesque loop are picnic areas, trailheads for several hiking paths, and vistas where drivers can park and bask in the unadorned peace of nature.

Those wanting to enjoy a more intimate experience can take one of the dozen-plus trails within the 83,100-acre conservation area, which range from an easy one-mile trek suitable for children to strenuous hikes that involve a bit of rock scrambling. Checking in at the visitors' center is advisable, since some areas of the canyon are prone to flash flooding and the environment is harsh and unforgiving for unprepared outdoors enthusiasts.

Backpacking is not permitted along the scenic loop drive. Backcountry backpackers must check in at the visitors' center to obtain permits; camping is allowed but restricted. Car campers may use primitive campsites at **Oak Creek,** situated on State Route 159 four miles south of the visitors' center, and **Velvet Canyon,** about 18 miles south.

From March through June, the park becomes a palette of colors, thanks to the red, orange, purple, and yellow wildflowers blossoming throughout. The roster of wildlife includes scorpions, Gila monsters, and three varieties of venomous rattlesnakes.

to Salt Lake City

18 Bryce Canyon National Park

17 Zion National Park
15
Hurricane
89
UTAH
59
St. George
Lake Powell
Fredonia
Marble Canyon
389
89
89
Jacob Lake
89
67
Colorado River
The Grand Canyon 16
64
180
ARIZONA
64
180
40
Flagstaff
17
N
km 50 100
mi 25 50

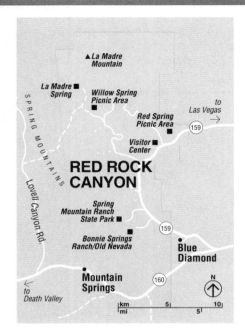

RED ROCK CANYON

But the desert dweller that visitors will most likely see is the friendlier (just slightly) wild burro. About 70 wild burros make their home in the canyon area. Despite their benign appearance and rather endearing tendency to beg from slow-moving vehicles, burros can be mean, ornery, and temperamental critters. Visitors should not feed or play with them, and there is a $25 fine for those caught giving them food. Rangers report that numerous people are bitten each year. ♦ Admission. Visitors' Center daily; scenic loop roadway daily 9AM-sunset.

For information, contact
US Bureau of Land Management
(PO Box 26569, Las Vegas, NV 89126).
From the Strip take I-95 west 20 miles to
Red Rock Canyon (signposted).
363.1921

Within Red Rock Canyon National Conservation Area:

Spring Mountain Ranch State Park
Famed billionaire and eccentric Howard Hughes and German heiress Vera Krupp are two past owners of this historic 520-acre patch of grass and trees.

Thanks to a spring-fed stream, the ranch property spent much of its early days as an encampment for passing wagon trains, horse thieves, outlaws, and various travelers. In the 1880s, it became a working ranch and in the 1940s it was purchased by Chester Lauck, also known as "Lum" of the "Lum & Abner" radio show. The Laucks maintained it as a working cattle ranch and their private vacation retreat until 1955, when they sold it to Vera Krupp, wife of German munitions magnate Alfried Krupp von Bohlen und Halbach.

Krupp lived at her ranch until 1967, when she sold it to Hughes Tool Company. In 1972, two California businessmen purchased the ranch from owner Howard Hughes with plans to build a condominium project. However, after two years of public opposition to their plans, they sold the property to the state.

A picnic area with barbecue pits, grassy spaces, picnic tables, and other amenities takes up a portion of the now public park. Intriguing guided tours of the ranch are offered on weekends and holidays. Visitors can see the main house—preserved as it appeared during the Lauck/Krupp years—the swimming pool added by Krupp, a fish pond, a family cemetery, cabins that date from the mid-1800s, a blacksmith shop, and even a shed once used by a long-ago owner as part of a chinchilla-breeding operation.

During the summer, hundreds of Las Vegans lug blankets and picnic baskets to an outdoor amphitheater on the grounds to watch plays and concerts. Special events such as nature walks, nighttime hikes, lectures, children's activities, and photography and art exhibits are offered on a regular basis. ♦ Per-car entry fee. Daily 8AM-sunset. Guided tours leave from the ranch house on weekends and holidays.

For information, contact
Spring Mountain Ranch
(PO Box 124, Blue Diamond, NV 89004).
Off Hwy 159 (W Charleston Blvd),
signposted.
875.4141

Bonnie Springs Ranch/Old Nevada
These adjacent examples of Old West nostalgia are aimed primarily at visitors, although locals often drop by after an excursion to Red Rock Canyon or **Spring Mountain Ranch**.

Bonnie Springs Ranch, built in 1843, was originally a stopover point for California-bound wagon trains. For more than three decades it's been a tourist attraction, complete with horseback-riding stables, a petting zoo, and a family-style restaurant offering basic meals (breakfast, lunch, and dinner) suitable for kids, but hearty enough for grown-ups.

Old Nevada is a working re-creation of a frontier town, featuring historical exhibits (including a smithy) and more theatrical attractions, such as staged hangings and gunfights. The **Miner Restaurant** proffers the usual snack-joint fare for breakfast, lunch, and dinner—from sandwiches and hot dogs to salads. Separate admission for Bonnie Springs and Old Nevada. Daily. On Bonnie Springs Ranch Rd, 1 mile off Hwy 159 (W Charleston Blvd), signposted. 875.4191

Within Bonnie Springs Ranch/Old Nevada:

Bonnie Springs Motel $$ This clean, basic motor lodge offers family units with kitchens, as well as rooms with one king-size or two double beds. All told there are 50 accommodations. Kids, of course, will like the pool. ♦ 875.4400

2 Floyd Lamb State Park Originally known as **Tule Springs State Park**, this simple, cozy patch offers picnic areas with barbecue grills, easy nature walks, and four lakes suitable for fishing and feeding the resident ducks and geese. ♦ Per-car entry fee. 15 miles from downtown Las Vegas; take US 95 north and follow signs to the park. 486.5413

3 Mount Charleston A 45-minute drive from Las Vegas, Mount Charleston, a small town with 200 or so residents, attracts more than two million

visitors per year. The Mountain—for locals, no additional description is needed—has long been a favorite escape for desert-weary Las Vegans lusting after trees, scenic vistas, and temperatures 20 to 30 degrees cooler than in the city.

Mount Charleston is part of the **Toiyabe National Forest** and is the highest peak in the **Spring Mountain Range,** which comprises the western border of the Las Vegas Valley. During the summer, this is a prime spot for hiking, camping, picnicking, and horseback riding, with skies blessedly free of polluted air. In the winter, organized and impromptu recreational activities include skiing, sledding, and snowball making.

Hikers can explore almost a dozen trails, from one to 10 or more miles in length and ranging in difficulty from sweat-free to strenuous. However, all guarantee excellent views of mountains, wooded areas, and, on the **Mary Jane Falls Trail,** a waterfall.

Be aware, though, that this is serious woodland, and it pays to be prepared for quick weather changes and occasionally tricky terrain. (For weather conditions, call 736.3854.) No sanitary facilities or water are available during the winter months, and rangers recommend cold-weather excursions only for experienced hikers.

Sledding and tubing runs are available at the **Fox Tail Snow Play Area** in Lee Canyon, on

State Highway 156, about one mile south of the **Lee Canyon Ski Area.** The area is open during daylight hours only, and visitors must supply their own modes of downhill transportation.

Now, the downside: The mountain gets incredibly crowded on weekends. Parking is often difficult at the **Mount Charleston Hotel** and the **Mount Charleston Restaurant and Lodge,** the slope's two prime sources of liquid and gustatory refreshment (see below). And, from November to April, the roads can be all but inaccessible to anything but four-wheel-drive vehicles and cars equipped with tire chains. ♦ For trail maps, forest-use regulations, and general information about hiking and recreational activities, contact the Toiyabe National Forest Las Vegas Ranger District (2881 S Valley View Dr, Suite 16, Las Vegas, NV 89102, 873.8800). Approximately 30 miles northwest of Las Vegas; from the Strip, follow I-15 north to US 95 north to Hwy 157 or 156

On Mount Charleston:

Mount Charleston Hotel $$$ Halfway up the mountain, this hotel offers 63 rooms (including suites), a full-service but affordable restaurant, and some of the most breathtaking landscapes in southern Nevada. The best vantage is from the third-floor rooms at the back of the hotel. You'll pay a few bucks more, but the view is well worth the extra tariff. ♦ From US 95 north, turn left onto Hwy 157 and drive 15 miles west to the hotel. 872.5500

Mount Charleston Restaurant and Lodge ★★★ $$ Locals know this woodsy, laid-back establishment simply as "The Lodge." You pass through the lodge to get to the restaurant, but many never make it that far. It's the perfect place to relax in front of a fireplace and enjoy a Mount Charleston coffee—a spirit-lifting mixture of Drambuie, coffee, brandy, and whipped cream. The restaurant serves hearty breakfasts and exotic wild game at dinner. A charming addition, adjacent to the restaurant and lodge, is the cluster of 24 A-frame log cabins built on a terraced hillside with unobstructed views of the forest. There are 20 480-square-foot cabins and four 750-square-foot ones—perfect for a large clan. The cabins feature log furniture—a dining table, chairs, king-size bed, and a sofa bed—plus fireplaces, whirlpool baths, and showers. ♦ Restaurant: daily breakfast, lunch, and dinner. Lodge: daily 24 hours. From US 95 north, turn left onto Hwy 157 and drive 21 miles west through the forest until it ends at the lodge. 386.6899

Restaurants/Clubs: Red **Hotels:** Blue
Shops/♥ Outdoors: Green **Sights/Culture:** Black

Lee Canyon Ski Area For serious downhillers, this small ski operation offers well-groomed slopes (snowmaking machines augment what Mother Nature has supplied), three chair lifts, a lounge, and a gift shop. Ten runs are available for beginning, intermediate, and advanced skiers. Weekend nighttime skiing is scheduled occasionally. ◆ Free shuttle bus service from Las Vegas is available from the Union Plaza Hotel and the Santa Fe Hotel & Casino (reservations required). Call Ski Lee Rentals (646.0008) for general information and shuttle reservations. For ski conditions, call 593.9500. From US 95 north, turn left onto Hwy 156 and drive 18 miles west to the ski area. 872.5462

4 Primadonna Resorts $$ Forty miles south of Las Vegas on both sides of Interstate 15 is an exciting entertainment and hotel complex headlining the $10-million **Desperado** roller coaster, the **Adventure Canyon Water Flume** ride, two motion-simulator theaters, the $130-million **Buffalo Bill's Resort & Casino**, **Whiskey Pete's Hotel-Casino**, and the **Primadonna Resort & Casino.**

Buffalo Bill's is a 16-story, 613-room hotel, which will be adding a tower containing another 650 to 700 rooms this spring. On-site attractions include a 200-seat Victorian-style movie theater and a 6,500-seat special events arena to host rodeos, boxing matches, and concerts. The 777-room **Whiskey Pete's** hotel features the **Silver Spur Steak House** and a 700-seat showroom featuring weekend performances by the likes of Ronnie Milsap, America, and Mickey Gilley. Among **Primadonna**'s highlights are the excellent **Skydiver** steak and seafood restaurant and **Gary's Garage,** a buffet by day and, on weekend evenings, a 750-seat showroom spotlighting such stars as Gordon Lightfoot, Eddie Rabbitt, Patti Page, and Helen Reddy.

On the thrilling **Desperado,** with more than 6,000 feet of track, passengers experience near-zero gravity three times during the two-minute ride. The steel-track coaster has a lift height of 209 feet with a 225-foot drop, the longest coaster drop in the world. Passengers are hurled 80 miles an hour at a maximum gravity force of three Gs (one or two is usual). ◆ 40 miles south of Las Vegas on Interstate

15, at Stateline. Buffalo Bill's 382.1111, Whiskey Pete's 382.1212, Primadonna 382.4388. All three: 800/367.7383; fax 874.1079

5 Ethel M. Chocolate Factory It's a pretty safe bet that at least one-third of the people taking the tour here on any given day are locals sprinting through just to get the free sample each visitor receives when it's all over.

True, that is one of the benefits of making the trip to the nearby town of **Henderson,** where the luscious sweets are made. But it's not the only one, unless you think a table filled with gooey chocolate fudge is a sight that makes Hoover Dam absolutely irrelevant.

Founded by the reclusive Forrest Mars (head of the Mars candy empire) to make strictly gourmet chocolates, the small but well-known company sells its wares nationally via mail order, and in Las Vegas at shops located in casinos, malls, and inside **McCarran International Airport.**

Favorites range from simple milk chocolate coins to foil-wrapped, liqueur-filled morsels. The company prides itself on using only the finest ingredients, thus the expensive price tags for their treats: The special two-pound "Taste of Las Vegas" costs $35.

Tourgoers watch the candymaking process from lip-smacking start to finish through plate glass windows while videos playing on TV monitors along the route explain in delectable detail what is happening.

Work off those newly ingested calories from the free piece of candy by strolling through the two-and-a-half-acre cactus garden just outside the building. More than 350 species of cacti, succulents, and desert plants are artfully arranged along concrete paths. A cactus-themed gift shop is also on the premises. ◆ Free. Daily 8:30AM-7PM. From the Strip, drive east on E Tropicana Ave to Mountain Vista St and turn right. Take Mountain Vista 2 miles to Sunset Way and turn left at the traffic light into Green Valley Business Park, then left onto Cactus Garden Dr. 458.8864

5 Renata's ★★★$$$ On the borderline of Las Vegas and the posh master-planned community of Green Valley in Henderson, this elegant restaurant was created by two former **Caesars Palace** employees—an Asian food and beverage director and a French chef. Families enjoy the options this mix provides—kids can order Chinese while their parents order continental, or vice versa. The pale green and salmon decor, enhanced with plants and soft lighting, cozy booths, and a strolling trio (two violins and a bass) is soothing after a frantic day at the casinos or on the road. Such exquisite appetizers as dumplings filled with pork and water chestnuts, escargots with garlic butter and Pernod in phyllo cups, and lobster ravioli served with gulf prawns make this place worth the trip. Follow one of the above with black-pepper linguine with roasted peppers, mushrooms, sun-dried tomatoes, and light saffron cream, or if you've worked up an appetite pulling slots, choose an entrée. You won't be disappointed with any main dish, but among the favorites are lobster Cantonese served with slivers of green scallions in a fermented black bean sauce, Hong Kong steak (marinated strip sirloin, sliced and served atop a bed of stir-fried vegetables with *hoisin* sauce, a sweet, spicy mixture of garlic, chili peppers, and soybeans), broiled lamb chops with peppery goat cheese and rosemary garlic demi-glace, and seared breast of duckling with huckleberry sauce. Both the Bailey's caramel flan and the truffle chocolate cake are standouts. There is also a lounge and bar open 24 hours a day; in addition to typical bar food, it serves treats like beef teriyaki on a stick, fried wontons, and eggs and waffles all day long. ♦ Continental/Asian ♦ Daily dinner. Reservations recommended. 4451 E Sunset Rd (between Green Valley Pkwy and Mountain Vista St). 435.4000

5 Cranberry World West Ocean Spray Cranberries Inc. opened this 10,000-square-foot visitors' center adjacent to its juice-processing and distribution plant in 1995. Offering an educational, entertaining, and mouth-watering look at an exclusively American fruit, the center includes a theater, exhibit hall, museum, gift shop, and demonstration kitchen. Visitors are shown the cranberry's life cycle from planting through harvesting and quality-control testing. You'll get to taste juice, cranberry pastries, and Craisins (sweetened, dried cranberries)—just three of the surprising array of products into which the berry is made. Free recipes and cups, pens, and key chains with the company's logo are given as souvenirs. ♦ Free. Daily. 1301 American Pacific Dr. From the Strip, drive east on E Flamingo Rd or E Tropicana Ave approximately 4 miles to US 93/95 (I-515). Turn right to go south on 93/95 3 miles to the Sunset Rd exit. Turn right onto Sunset; at the second signal, turn left onto Stephanie Rd. Continue on Stephanie 1.5 miles and turn left onto American Pacific Dr; the plant is directly ahead. 566.7160

6 Railroad Pass Hotel & Casino $ If there is such a thing as a generic hotel-casino, this is it. The bland, institutional white exterior is your first clue that this is by no means a must-see. It's just convenient as the first of many

glorified truck stops common to rural Nevada and benefits from a well-trafficked location near the US 95 turnoff to Laughlin. The serviceable complex on the outskirts of Henderson boasts no themes or gimmicks beyond 120 low-priced rooms and several restaurants. There's a steak house, a buffet, and a 24-hour coffee shop. ♦ 2800 S Boulder Hwy (I-95), 2.5 miles south of Henderson. 294.5000, 800/654.0877

7 Boulder City This lakeside community of 13,000 sprang to life in 1931 as an instant city to house the men who built Hoover Dam. Nowadays, it has the distinction of being the only city in southern Nevada where gaming is *not* legal. Instead, the city lures tourists with antiques and gift shops and a major art festival held outdoors every September. ♦ On US 93, 23 miles southeast of Las Vegas

Within Boulder City:

Boulder Dam Hotel $$ The focal point of the town square is this hotel, built in 1933 to accommodate dignitaries—including US presidents Hoover and Roosevelt—visiting Hoover Dam. The hotel has expanded twice since it opened and now has 61 rooms, a pool, and a gift shop. At press time, the restaurant had been sold and was closed for remodeling. ♦ 1305 Arizona St (between Nevada Hwy and Colorado St). 293.3510

8 Gold Strike Inn & Casino $ Despite its half-hearted attempt to affect the 1890s bordello look (red-velvet wallpaper and hardwood trim) and a display of antique slot machines and cash registers, the real attractions here are the 155 inexpensive rooms and bargain food prices. You can choose from the standard Las Vegas dining options: buffet (lunch and dinner), coffee shop (daily 24 hours), and steak house (dinner). There's also a snack bar near the front door to take care of those in a hurry. The hotel can be described best as a functional way station for Lake Mead recreationists and those headed to or from Hoover Dam. ♦ US Hwy 93 (7 miles east of Boulder City). 293.5000, 800/245.6380

The US Army exploded the first atomic bomb at the Nevada Test Site, 70 miles northwest of Las Vegas, in 1951. Over the next 11 years, 121 nuclear devices were detonated in the state. Since 1962, nearly 500 more tests have been conducted underground.

Big-name entertainment came to the nearby town of Laughlin in November 1987 when the Riverside Casino opened its 900-seat Celebrity Theatre, which has hosted the likes of the Gatlin Brothers, Conway Twitty, and Eddie Arnold. Comedian Sam Kinison was killed in an automobile collision near Laughlin when he was headed there to perform in April 1992.

9 Hoover Dam While the casinos try to keep your attention with white tigers, artificial volcanoes, and Roman centurions, a water and power plant 30 miles from Las Vegas is still Nevada's No. 1 tourist attraction. This 726-foot concrete monolith remains a civil engineering marvel undiminished by the high-tech revolution.

Guided tours of the dam draw about 750,000 people per year, and since 1936, more than 29 million have seen its sights. Each day, hundreds of visitors line up along the US 93 bridge to plunk down two dollars for a 45-minute tour that offers a spectacular view or two and a painless briefing on the principles of engineering. A 44-story elevator inside the dam takes you and two dozen of your closest friends to the base, where you see some of the administration area (which looks as though it's straight out of a 1930s movie) and a few of the massive electrical generators. Then you step outside for a neck-craning, awe-inspiring, one-of-a-kind perspective from below.

The trip back to the top includes a stop at the tunnel that diverted the river while the dam was under construction. Of course, the escort is making your head spin with statistics the entire time: The dam contains 6,600,000 tons of concrete, enough to pave a two-lane road from New York to San Francisco. And no tour passes without the guide fielding two morbid questions: How many people were killed during construction? (96). And how many of those bodies are entombed inside the concrete? (None, they insist.) The dam was dedicated in 1935 after four-and-a-half years of construction by a labor force that peaked at 5,250 workers. Its chief purpose was to control the flood-prone Colorado River, thus ending cycles of drought and flooding in southern California farmland. Electricity was considered a mere by-product of the project, but it proved lucrative in its own right; power sales recouped the original $175 million expenditure with interest.

Nearly all of the tourist facilities at the dam are being rebuilt. Most of the old industrial charm might be lost by the time the new visitors' center opens (slated to open at press time), with new parking, souvenir stands, and snack areas. The $54-million renovation project includes a 420-car garage on the Nevada side, with a walkway leading under the highway bridge to the visitors' center (in the past, to see both sides of the dam people had to cross the road and dodge Arizona-bound traffic, a precarious situation to say the least). A new 530-foot elevator shaft through the Nevada wall of **Black Canyon** (to the side of the dam) has been completed. Two 50-passenger elevators will replace the lifts in the dam, doubling their capacity. Remember that while construction is going on, traffic can back up and parking is often an adventure.

Two-thirds of the dam's visitors come on bus tours from Las Vegas hotels. The excursions are heavily advertised on the Strip and average in price from $16 to $30, depending on whether they include other stops such as the **Ethel M. Chocolate Factory.** If you have six people in your party willing to share the bill (or one magnanimous benefactor), consider renting a limousine; not only do the rates compare favorably to the buses, but you won't have to conform to their schedules; the chauffeur is at your disposal. ◆ Admission. Daily.

For information, contact
Hoover Dam Visitors Services
(PO Box 60400,
Boulder City, NV 89006-0400).
8 miles east of Boulder City on US 93.
293.8367

10 Lake Mead Although Hoover Dam was built for a no-nonsense purpose—to control drought and flooding in California's farmlands—it also created one of southern Nevada's most cherished playgrounds when it backed up the Colorado River into this massive lake, with its 550 miles of shoreline. Most of that is accessible year-round, albeit only by boat. Dozens of coves enable houseboats to dock overnight in virtual seclusion.

Landlubbers aren't completely out of luck, however, since the lake has nine developed areas. Amenities vary, but the majority offer picnic sites, marinas, camping, and swimming. Most commercial activity—boat and scuba rentals and lake excursions—is centered around Boulder City and the Visitors' Center, four miles northeast of Boulder City on Highway 93. Attendants at the Center can direct you to the remote regions of the lake, which extend as far north as the Valley of Fire and as far east as the edge of Grand Canyon National Park.

For information, contact
Lake Mead National Recreation Area,
601 Nevada Hwy,
Boulder City, NV 89005.
293.8907

The Mars family of Las Vegas, owner of the Ethel M. Chocolate Factory and the Mars chocolate company, is listed in *Forbes* magazine as one of the five richest families in the country.

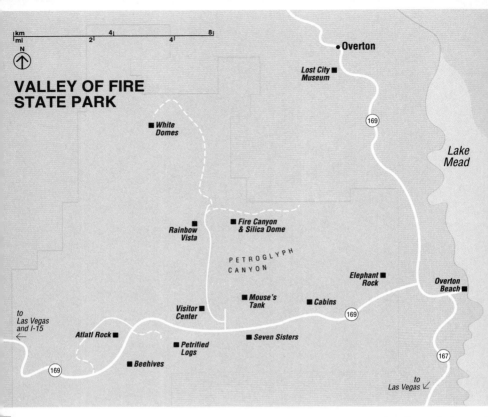

VALLEY OF FIRE STATE PARK

km / mi — N

White Domes

Lost City Museum

• Overton

169

Lake Mead

Rainbow Vista

Fire Canyon & Silica Dome

PETROGLYPH CANYON

Elephant Rock

Overton Beach

Mouse's Tank

Cabins

Visitor Center

169

to Las Vegas and I-15 ←

Atlatl Rock

Seven Sisters

Petrified Logs

Beehives

169

167

to Las Vegas ↙

11 Valley of Fire State Park Centuries of erosion carved this sculptural valley of stunning red sandstone named for the glowing crimson hues at sunset (not the temperature).

Nevada's oldest state park, established in 1935, encompasses 56,000 acres of unusual rock formations both enormous and minuscule, from chunks of petrified wood to Swiss-cheese-like boulders tailor-made for climbing. Visitors approach via a nondescript desert road into an environment that gradually descends into an immense and slightly surreal garden of stones. The otherworldly effect is heightened by the drop in elevation, which varies by 1,500 feet from one end of the park to the other, sometimes obscuring the horizon.

About 300,000 visitors come to the park each year, most of them between March and May and October and November. The valley is open from sunrise to sunset; overnight campers are allowed to remain after dark only at designated campsites, which are available on a first-come, first-served basis.

Almost everyone strolls **Petroglyph Canyon Trail,** a quarter-mile sandy path that offers the most colorful geology in the park as well

as its highest concentration of petroglyphs— symbols left on the rock by prehistoric Indians from the **Lost City,** a pueblo village now submerged in Lake Mead. The trail ends at **Mouse's Tank,** a watering hole in the truest sense: The secluded basin was frequented by a renegade Paiute Indian dubbed "Mouse," who eluded authorities at the turn of the century.

For those making a full day of it, there's no need to backtrack upon leaving the park. Keep going on Highway 169 out the Lake Mead side of the park and cool off at the swimming beach at the **Overton Beach** marina four miles east, or head back to Interstate 15 via Logandale and Overton, with a stop at the **Lost City Museum** (see page 117). ♦ Free. Daily sunrise-sunset. Visitors' Center Sa-Su 8:30AM-4:30PM. Located 35 miles northeast of Las Vegas; take I-15 to the Hwy 169 exit, then go east 18 miles on the two-lane road, signposted. 397.2088

Boulder City, a quaint little town about 30 miles southeast of Las Vegas, is the only city in Nevada where gambling is illegal.

12 Lost City Museum While Hoover Dam was being built, a team of archaeologists excavated a Pueblo ruin; after the dam created Lake Mead, the site was submerged. Artifacts salvaged from the **Pueblo Grande de Nevada** (popularly known as the "Lost City") are preserved in this modest museum in **Overton.** Exhibits are devoted to the dig itself as well as a reconstruc-tion of the village and displays of pottery and hunting tools. ♦ Admission. Sa-Su 8:30AM-4:30PM. 721 S Hwy 169, Overton. 397.2193

13 Mesquite Even in the middle of the desert the exact location of the Nevada state line is usually obvious, because the first casino or slot machine haven usually looms no more than a few yards away. This highway hamlet of 2,400 residents offers the first taste of Nevada gaming for those coming in from Utah or the last chance for Nevadans on the way north. The two major hotel-casino complexes in this otherwise sleepy burg—**Si Redd's Oasis** and the **Virgin River Hotel/Casino/Bingo** (see below)—are usually booked solid on Friday and Saturday. On weekends the **Oasis**—the last outpost of swanky Vegas-style civilization for miles around—is as busy as Grand Central Station. Those who don't plan far enough ahead to land a room at either of these two hotels can take a cruise down the business loop, which has a few small motels—the sight of which may inspire you to have a cup of coffee and hit the road—and a couple of conventional restaurants. ♦ From Las Vegas, take I-15 north 80 miles to the Mesquite exit

Within Mesquite:

Si Redd's Oasis $$$ This popular weekend getaway for native Las Vegans also serves as a launching point for excursions to southern Utah destinations such as **Zion** and **Bryce Canyon National Parks.** The resort (with 728 rooms and 10 suites) prides itself on its golf course, six swimming pools, health club, and three restaurants. The grounds are lush and immaculately groomed, living up to the resort's public image of a desert oasis. The interior decor, however, seems a bit dated, with a 1970s design scheme heavy on chrome and disco lighting. ♦ 897 Mesquite Blvd (at I-15). 346.5232, 800/621.0187

Within Si Redd's Oasis:

The Coffee Shop $ A glade of leafy artificial trees and strategically placed mirrors give this crowded casino coffee shop the surprising feel of a relaxing hideaway. The prime rib and steak plates are the featured attractions. Don't be misled by the lack of a line outside. During busy times, patrons put their names on a waiting list and go off to gamble until they're paged. ♦ American ♦ Daily 24 hours. 346.5232, 800/621.0187

The Redd Room Steak House ★★$$$ The bustling atmosphere slows down inside this dinner-only restaurant, complete with uniformed waiters proffering a respectable wine list. The wait is usually short since the bargain-minded favor the specials at the coffee shop. Even by non-casino standards, the price tag is hardly extravagant. In addition to variations on its namesake, the menu includes lemon chicken (at the low end of the price range) and veal Oscar (sautéed veal medaillons topped with crabmeat, asparagus, and béarnaise sauce) and saltimbocca (at the high end). ♦ Steak house ♦ M-Sa dinner; Su brunch. 346.5232, 800/621.0187

The Paradise Buffet & Grill ★★$$ The masking fake foliage of the coffee shop is also found in this buffet, giving the room a less institutional feel than many of its counterparts and much better food. ♦ Buffet ♦ Daily breakfast, lunch, and dinner. 346.5232, 800/621.0187

VIRGIN RIVER

Virgin River Hotel/Casino/Bingo $ While Si Redd's tries to sport an uptown Las Vegas look, this 400-room, bland, vanilla-colored complex stays true to the more modest country trappings of rural Nevada. The owners let their better-known neighbor do all the advertising, then they catch the overflow customers, as well as those seeking lower room rates.

There's no golf course or health spa here. The guest rooms, in several adjacent buildings surrounding a large pool, are modern, clean, and well maintained. They're nicer than what you might expect after visiting the relatively tiny casino, which packs in as many tables and slot machines as the laws of physics allow. Non-smokers will be chagrined to find their clothes saturated with cigarette smoke soon after walking through the door. The minuscule lounge seems to be almost an afterthought, but the round-the-clock restaurant is roomier and more comfortable, trimmed with wooden beams and decorated with modern Western art. Diners can choose between a buffet and a regular menu. ♦ N Mesquite Blvd and I-15. 800/346.7721

Restaurants/Clubs: Red   **Hotels:** Blue
Shops/ 🌳 **Outdoors:** Green   **Sights/Culture:** Black

14 Death Valley National Park In the summer, visitors swarm over the **Grand Canyon**, but winter is the peak season here. With average winter temperatures between 52 and 59 degrees and summer days routinely topping 110 degrees, the mercury readings tell the tale.

Before approaching the valley, make sure your car is in trustworthy condition for covering a desert that, at 3,231 square miles, is larger than the state of Delaware. Trail signs and monuments tell the stories of prospectors and miners who came to best the wilderness and sometimes failed—fatally. The stark, silent vistas prove there is beauty in nature even at its cruelest extremes.

If you're visiting from Las Vegas, this monument to the American spirit and to the spirit of pioneers merits at least an overnight stay. It's a long drive from one end of the valley to the other (140 miles), and there's plenty to view along the way, including spectacular sunrises and sunsets.

At the **Furnace Creek Visitors' Center,** you can pick up brochures and maps explaining how to take self-guided auto tours. There are also slide shows, nature exhibits, and other activities run by the rangers.

Death Valley is actually a dry lake bed; crunching along this crystallized white salt flat at twilight is like walking on the moon. There are trails for both casual walkers and hearty hikers. Most people like to visit **Badwater,** officially the lowest point in the US at 282 feet below sea level. The **Harmony Borax Works** is a quarter-mile trail leading to the ruins of a borax mine that dates back to 1883. (Death Valley supplies most of the world's borax, a crystalline compound with industrial uses in washing powders, water softeners, and soaps.) Those up for a more challenging trek can try the five-mile round-trip from **Golden Canyon** to **Zabriskie Point,** a panoramic overlook and photo spot that's especially popular with Europeans, who are more daring than Americans when it comes to summer-time exploration of the valley. Park rangers report many Germans and French visit in mid-summer and don't mind soaking up the full heat of the sun since there is no comparable season on their cool continent. ♦ Nominal per-vehicle entry fee is valid for seven days. From Las Vegas, take US 95 east 86 miles to Lathrop Wells. Then head south 23 miles on Hwy 127 to Death Valley Junction, then go another 18 miles south on Hwy 190 to the entrance closest to the Furnace Creek area.

For information, contact Death Valley National Park (c/o Superintendent, Death Valley, CA 92328) Information 619/786.2331, camping 800/365.2267

Within Death Valley:

Death Valley Junction A unique way station, this "town" has seven full-time residents. It's known mainly as the home of the historic **Armargosa Opera House,** where New York–born ballerina Marta Becket stages one-woman dance and performance-art shows in the hundred-seat theater. Becket recently celebrated a quarter-century at the opera house and averages about 95 productions per year. ♦ 23 miles south of Lathrop Wells on Hwy 127

Scotty's Castle This 25-room Mediterranean-style mansion, formally known as the **Death Valley Ranch,** was built in the 1920s by Albert Johnson, a Chicago insurance investor, who lived there with his

wife, Bessie. It takes its more common name from Walter Scott, a former wild West show cowboy and storyteller who bragged that the house was his. The owners treasured their privacy, so the misnomer was fortuitous.

The castle is near a stream that supplies it with water and hydroelectric power. The interior reveals touches of elaborate craftsmanship, such as ornate tile work, wrought-iron fixtures, and intricate wood carvings. The tours, conducted on the hour year-round, are a "living history" experience given by rangers dressed in period garb. Tour groups are limited to 19 at a time, so there is usually a one- to two-hour wait after purchasing tickets; this gives you time for a self-guided tour of the grounds and castle exterior. ♦ Admission. Daily. 60 miles north of the Furnace Creek on Hwy 190; follow signs to the castle. 619/786.2392

Furnace Creek Ranch $$ An unlikely sister to the oh-so-elegant **Furnace Creek Inn** (below), these rustic, reasonably priced lodgings include 224 motel-type rooms, an 18-hole golf course, horseback riding stables, and a pool. The pool is a gathering spot by day—you'll hear a number of languages spoken around the deck—though the water is already hot by noon during the summer. In the evening there's good company in the **Corkscrew Saloon,** which will toast a mini-pizza for you if you fail to get back before closing time at any of the compound's three restaurants. Or if you feel like grilling your own steak or nibbling on snack food in your room, visit the **General Store,** which carries everything from fresh food to camping gear (open daily 7AM-9PM). ♦ Hwy 190. 619/786.2345

Furnace Creek Inn $$$$ Of the many surprising sights in Death Valley, the most incongruous may well be this exclusive 68-room resort where jackets are required for dinner. With a long-standing reputation for luxury that defies its stark surroundings, the inn gets heavily booked in the winter. Its amenities include tennis, golf, and a gourmet dining room. ♦ Closed mid-May–mid-October. Hwy 190. 619/786.2361

Stovepipe Wells Village $$ Though not centrally located in relation to the better-known sites within Death Valley, this 85-room hotel duplicates most of the services within **Furnace Creek Ranch.** There's a dining room, a pool, a saloon, a general store, and a variety of accommodations. ♦ Hwy 190, 10 miles southwest of the intersection of Hwys 374 and 190. 619/786.2387

15 Laughlin Don Laughlin had a vision. A Minnesotan who operated slot machines in gas stations and Elks clubs until it became a felony in his home state, Laughlin decided to head West in 1952. He ended up on the

Colorado River border between Nevada and Arizona, 120 miles south of Las Vegas, where he opened a roadside rest stop. Laughlin watched the town that bears his name grow into a gaming mecca that drew 4.6 million visitors in 1992. Many compare it to Las Vegas in its 1950s boom days; nearly 5,000 of the city's 8,500-plus rooms have been built since 1988.

Today, Laughlin isn't so much an added attraction for Las Vegas visitors as it is an alternative destination. Nearly 20 percent of its tourists come from Phoenix, 240 miles away; another 33 percent come from the Los Angeles area. Laughlin also has become a winter refuge for snowbirds fleeing cold climates in their recreational vehicles, since there are plenty of RV parks and hookups.

Despite its expanding skyline, Laughlin still draws people who are attracted to its small-town feel, its low prices, and lack of high-roller pretension. You won't find jackets or ties, themes or gimmicks, and there's not much in the way of big-name entertainment. But what really distinguishes Laughlin from Vegas is its scenic river setting. Many of the casinos have picture-window views, something unheard of in Las Vegas. **Harrah's Laughlin** has a recreational beach, and the **Flamingo Hilton** uses the river as a backdrop for a series of outdoor concerts in early and late summer. For those who don't bring their own pleasure craft to cruise the river or nearby **Lake Mohave,** some casinos offer riverboat rides.

As you enter Laughlin from State Route 163, you'll first see Don's place: **The Riverside Resort,** the start of the casino strip. The **Riverside** has the town's only movie theater and celebrity showroom. The rest of the strip includes the **Golden Nugget, Gold River, Ramada Express, Harrah's,** the 2,000-room **Flamingo Hilton**—Laughlin's largest hotel— and Circus Circus Enterprises's **Edgewater** and **Colorado Belle.** ♦ From Las Vegas, take US Hwy 95 to Rte 163, a 21-mile stretch of twists and turns

16 The Grand Canyon Artists have long sought to capture the majesty of nature's crown jewel of the Southwest—one of the most famous landmarks in the US. A few skilled photographers have caught the vast perspective, but most cameras flatten it, reducing its immensity to something our senses can easily comprehend. It's one of the last awe-inspiring spectacles in this seen-everything world, whether you're a nature lover who wants to absorb its splendor or a city slicker looking to escape the urban melee. No matter how many photos of the canyon you've seen, it's only when you stand here in person that you finally face the humbling notion that there are still some things greater

than humankind and its technological achievements.

The canyon is 277 miles long, 10 miles wide, and in some places a mile deep from the rim to the Colorado River. **Grand Canyon National Park** covers 1.2 million acres, which explains why it only *looks* close to Las Vegas on a map; it's about a five-hour drive to either the North or South Rims.

Unfortunately, the canyon has become almost too popular for its own good. Park officials say the growth of Las Vegas and Phoenix has taxed the limits of their ability to accommodate tidal waves of visitors. From a practical standpoint, this means planning well ahead—particularly if you want to camp or stay overnight in the lodges within the park. And the famous rafting trips and muleback rides now accept reservations as much as *two*

years in advance. ◆ Per-vehicle entry fee. For information, contact Grand Canyon National Park (PO Box 129, Grand Canyon, AZ 86023). From Las Vegas drive about 270 miles, past Hoover Dam, via US Hwy 93. To incorporate as much casino action as possible, take the slightly longer route through Laughlin, via US Hwy 95. Both routes meet in Kingman, Arizona, where I-40 delivers you to the Grand Canyon turnoff at Williams for a 60-mile drive into the park on US Hwy 64. 602/638.7888

Within the Grand Canyon:

South Rim Most canyon visitors head to the South Rim, which is open year-round and offers greater lodging opportunities than the North Rim. How much of the canyon you ultimately see depends on how hard you want to work. Those willing to settle for a cursory visit can stick to the rim of the canyon. Those

who want to spend their time in the car rather than on the trail can take the 26-mile **East Rim Drive** (Hwy 64, open year-round), from the park's east entrance to the cluster of lodges known as **Grand Canyon Village**. A more popular route is the 8-mile **West Rim Drive**, from the village to the landmark known as **Hermits Rest**, but park officials close that road from late May through September to moderate the effects of exhaust fumes. Still you needn't miss out on the sights—during that period there's a free shuttle bus.

If you have a bit more stamina, start walking down one of the trails into the inner canyon. The **Bright Angel Trail**, near the lodge of the same name, is the most popular, a steep but gradual 4.5-mile trek to the bottom. Unlike many hikes, the trip down is a lot easier than the walk back up. A more strenuous path is

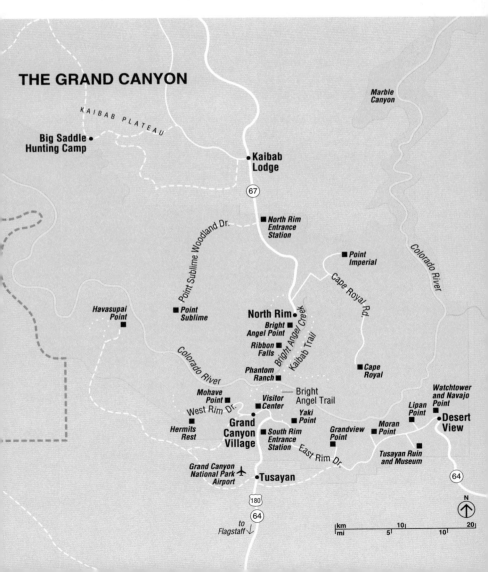

THE GRAND CANYON

KAIBAB PLATEAU

Big Saddle • Hunting Camp

Marble Canyon

• Kaibab Lodge

67

Point Sublime Woodland Dr.

■ North Rim Entrance Station

■ Point Imperial

Colorado River

Cape Royal Rd.

Havasupai Point ■

■ Point Sublime

North Rim •

Bright Angel Point ■

Bright Angel Creek

Ribbon Falls ■

Kaibab Trail

Colorado River

Phantom Ranch ■

■ Cape Royal

Mohave Point ■

Visitor Center ■

— Bright Angel Trail

Watchtower and Navajo Point

West Rim Dr.

Yaki ■ Point

Lipan Point ■

Desert View

Hermits Rest ■

Grand Canyon Village

■ South Rim Entrance Station

Grandview Point ■

Moran ■ Point

East Rim Dr.

Tusayan Ruin and Museum ■

Grand Canyon National Park Airport ✈

•Tusayan

180

64

N ↓

to Flagstaff ↓

64

|km   10| 20|
|mi   5| 10|

N

the **South Kaibab Trail,** which covers 1.5 miles each way. No permits are required for day hiking, just common sense.

The round-trip from rim to river is usually an overnight affair, so if you decide to journey to the bottom, you should arrange to stay at one of two sites below the rim: **Indian Gardens,** on Bright Angel Trail (602/638.2401), or **Phantom Ranch,** a campground along the Colorado shared by hikers, mule riders, and white-water rafters (602/638.2401). Reservations are required for both. All other campers who wish to stay either in the canyon or in undeveloped areas on the rim need a permit from the **Backcountry Reservations Office** (PO Box 129, Grand Canyon, AZ 86023). Reservations are accepted by mail only, and sometimes must be made a year in advance.

There also are established campgrounds at the top of the rim, at the **Mather Campground** (for tents and recreational vehicles without hookups) in **Grand Canyon Village,** the adjacent **Trailer Village** (hookups available), and the **Desert View Campground** (no hookups) 26 miles east of **Grand Canyon Village.** Reservations are strongly encouraged (contact MISTIX, PO Box 85705, San Diego, CA 92186-7505, 800/365.2267).

Advance reservations are mandatory for those staying at lodges inside the park. One service now books all the accommodations inside the South Rim: **Grand Canyon National Park Lodges** (PO Box 699, Grand Canyon, AZ 86023, 602/638.2401; fax 602/638.9247). There are no individual addresses or phone numbers for the lodges, and none of them has a pool. Procrastinators may have better luck checking out one of five lodges in **Tusayan,** seven miles south of the South Rim, before resigning themselves to staying in Williams or Flagstaff. Tusayan accommodations include **Grand Canyon Squire Inn** (602/638.2681); **Moqui Lodge** (602/638.2424); **Quality Inn** (602/638.2673); **Red Feather Lodge** (602/638.2414); and **Seven Mile Lodge** (602/638.2291). ♦ From Grand Canyon turnoff at Williams, take Hwy 64 for 60 miles to the South Rim

Planning the Grand Tour

Teddy Roosevelt described the **Grand Canyon** as "the one great sight which every American should see." Assuming you've taken his advice to heart, deciding which way you choose to see it is the next step. Below are some of the more imaginative ways to take in the awesome expanse that will afford a view unmatchable by foot or car.

For a bird's-eye perspective on the canyon, consider taking a flyover tour on a chartered plane or a combination air/bus tour, which run about $175 per person. Charter services advertise heavily on the Strip. Companies include:

Adventure Airlines 736.7511

Air America Tours 736.6260

Grand Canyon Specialists 383.4010

Gray Line Tours 384.1234

Guaranteed Tours 345.7177

Helicop-Tours 736.0606

Interstate Tours 293.2268

Lake Mead Air 293.1848

Las Vegas Airlines 647.3056

Scenic Airlines Inc 739.1900

Silver Air 891.0346

Western Airlines, Inc. 891.8432

Wild West Tour Co. 731.2425

While Americans may have had a harder time getting to the **Grand Canyon** in Roosevelt's day, the best way to appreciate its immensity even today is by exploring it on the back of a mule. To do so, you must plan almost a year ahead; reservations are accepted 11 months in advance and quotas fill up quickly. These rides are coordinated through **Grand Canyon National Park Lodges** (602/638.2401).

Of all the ways to see the canyon, none is more thrilling than rafting the raging Colorado. Not only is the view of the canyon towering above you magnificent, but you also experience the excitement of shooting some of the most powerful rapids in the world.

Don't plan a rafting excursion on the spur of the moment, however, since the National Park Service carefully regulates the number of permits given to commercial operators for Colorado River trips through the canyon—and the waiting lists can get very long. Private tour operators include:

Adventures West, Inc.
Phoenix, Arizona 800/828.9378

Arizona Raft Adventurers, Inc.
Flagstaff, Arizona 800/786.7238

Colorado River & Trail Expeditions, Inc.
Salt Lake City, Utah 800/253.7328

Western River Expeditions, Inc.
Salt Lake City, Utah 800/453.7450

Within the South Rim:

El Tovar Hotel $$$$ The grande dame of the **Grand Canyon** was built in 1905 and originally staffed by the famed Harvey Girls of story, song, and cinema, who were known for their starched white aprons and impeccable training. The handsome stone and Douglas fir building is famous for its 65 atmospheric period rooms, including five suites with balconies overlooking the Canyon. On the National Registry of Historic Places, the most elegant of the village's lodgings offers fine dining in its restaurant.

Bright Angel Lodge $$$ This building, designed to blend in with rather than distract from the canyon, features 50 cozy cabins, some historic, and some with fireplaces. More moderately priced than **El Tovar,** the restaurants are more basic here: There's a steak house and a dining room serving typical coffee-shop fare.

Kachina and Thunderbird Lodges $$$ These twin two-story lodges of 47 and 53 rooms respectively are newer than **El Tovar** and **Bright Angel** and offer good service and comfort. There are two double beds per room and a cafeteria in each lodge.

Yavapai Lodge $$ This 348-room motel is not in Grand Canyon Village with the above, but a few miles to the east across from the Visitors' Center. Similar in service, comfort, and style to **Kachina and Thunderbird,** this lodge also has two double beds per room and a cafeteria.

 North Rim If you're coming from Las Vegas, you should not rule out the North Rim. Visitors from the Phoenix area face an extra 200 miles of driving to get here, but those departing from Las Vegas can choose a drive comparable to the one to the South Rim, which lasts approximately five hours. However, the North Rim is a thousand feet higher in altitude—8,000 feet above sea level versus 7,000 for the South Rim—and because of the colder temperatures is only open from mid-May through late October.

A drawback: Within the park, there's only one hotel, and camping facilities aren't as abundant as at the South Rim. There are also fewer choices outside the park's boundaries, making reservations essential. Visitors from Las Vegas drive about 265 miles by heading into southern Utah on Interstate 15. The cozy town of **Hurricane** (pronounced *Hur*-kin), Utah, on Scenic Byway 9 is at the crossroads for those either planning to go on to **Zion National Park** or head south on Highway 59 to the North Rim (another option is to see Zion first, then go south on Highway 89).
♦ Fee. Daily mid-May–mid-Oct. For North Rim lodging reservations, contact TW Recreational Services (801/586.7686). For camping reservations, contact MISTIX (PO Box 85705,

San Diego, CA 92186-5705, 800/365.2267). Take I-15 north approximately 130 miles through Arizona, then through southern Utah to Scenic Byway 9 for 10 miles to State Hwy 59 south. After you've been on 59 for 22 miles, you will re-enter Arizona and the name changes to State Hwy 389; continue on 389 south through the Kaibab Indian Reservation for approximately 30 miles. At Fredonia, Hwy 389 will meet US 89. Take 89 south 30 miles to US 67, then drive south 44 miles to the North Rim.

17 **Zion National Park** Though a neighbor to **Bryce Canyon National Park,** with a common geological history, a simple rule of thumb separates these southern Utah parks: To see the splendors here you look up; at **Bryce** you look down. While the precipices of **Bryce** are more akin to those of the **Grand Canyon,** here you enter at the canyon floor, and most of the trails take you skyward.

The 229-square-mile park offers rugged and contrasting beauty, from barren sandstone cliff walls and arches to the cottonwoods and ash trees lining the cooling **Virgin River.** In warm months, visitors can wade into the latter, and will be strongly tempted to do so: The park is south of Utah's ski country and summer temperatures can reach 105 degrees.

There are 11 trails here, ranging from easy half-hour walks to taxing 16-mile treks requiring backcountry permits. Most people start at the **Emerald Pools Trail** directly across from the **Zion Lodge;** it gives you a representative taste of the park, with a trail leading to waterfalls and impressive elevations (there's an optional mile to an upper pool for the hardy). Another favorite is **Gateway to the Narrows,** a pleasant walk along a narrow trail ending at the river, which invites those who don't mind wading to keep going (bring an extra pair of old tennis shoes—it's a rocky traverse).

For those who prefer the comfort of their car, it's fun to pass through the 1.1-mile tunnel to the east entrance when the park's not too crowded (when it *is* crowded, you can find yourself stuck behind an RV waiting for clear passage through the one-way tunnel). Here you'll find plenty of rocky cliffs, and visitors tend to stick to their autos rather than exploring the often precipitous terrain by foot. Drivers will have to keep their attention on the sharp curves of the winding road; however, there are numerous turnouts for those who want to stop and take in the view.

The park itself has only one lodge, which is open year-round. For lodging information, contact the Utah Parks Division (TW Recreational Services, 451 N Main St, Cedar City, UT 84720, 801/586.7686). More abundant lodging is available outside the south entrance in **Springdale,** which is lined

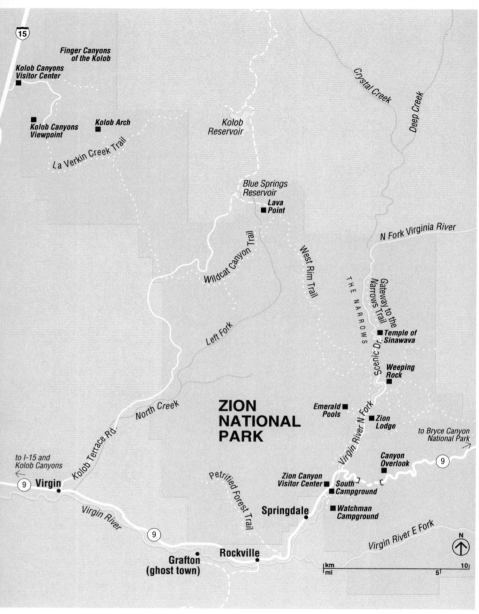

with motels and bed-and-breakfast inns. A free magazine called *Color Country,* which gives information on southern Utah's scenic routes, parks, and recreation, as well as food and lodging choices, is available from Color Country Travel Region (PO Box 1550, St. George, UT 84770-1550, 800/233.8824).
♦ Per-car entry fee. Daily 9AM-4:30PM; extended hours in the summer. From Las Vegas, take I-15 for 120 miles to St. George, Utah, then take Scenic Byway 9 for another 45 miles.

For information, contact Superintendent, Zion National Park, Springdale, UT 84767-1099. 801/772.3256

18 Bryce Canyon National Park The growth of southern Nevada has threatened the ecological harmony of both the **Grand Canyon** and **Zion National Park**, but this park is a relative oasis (nearly 250 miles from Las Vegas). While **Zion** gets hot, this northern park stays cool—perhaps too much so for those coming to Las Vegas to escape the chills of winter—thanks to elevations that range from 6,600 to 9,100 feet. And though it is a canyon, and most certainly grand, with no cliff wall on the far side, it doesn't resemble the more famous Arizona crevasse. The park is perched at the top of a precipice overlooking a vast, magnificent valley of hoodoos (eroded limestone towers) that gradually give way to the green hills and fields of southern Utah.

In fact, looking at the hoodoos here is the earthbound equivalent of finding shapes in puffy white clouds. While some view this natural amphitheater and see a collection of medieval fortresses, towers, or chess pieces on a vast playing board, others see Gothic cathedrals in multihued combinations of brown, red, orange, and gold.

Most exploration stems out from **Bryce Canyon Lodge,** which is located between the Sunrise and Sunset Point lookouts. Visitors can walk along the rim between and beyond these points, or take a more physically demanding hike to the bottom of the canyon. The **Queen's Garden Trail** takes you out and away from the rim to look back, while the steeper **Navajo Loop** leads hikers straight down into what seems like the mouth of a cavern. The short drive from the lodge to **Inspiration** and **Bryce Points** is worthwhile, since the increase in altitude renders the view even more dramatic. ♦ Entrance fee. Visitors' center daily 8AM–8PM. 210 miles northeast of Las Vegas on US 89. 801/834.5322, mule rides 800/834.5219

Within Bryce Canyon National Park:

Bryce Canyon Lodge $$ The only lodging in the park is this charming and quiet (no TVs) retreat perched just one hundred yards from the canyon rim. The original establishment, listed on the National Register of Historic Places, includes a restaurant, gift shop, and 40 rustic cabins. A pair of newer two-story buildings adds a combined 70 units near Sunrise and Sunset Points, bearing their respective names. The excellent restaurant is open for breakfast, lunch, and dinner with a basic menu of hearty fare that tastes particularly good after a day on the trail. This lodge follows the solar clock: Things get quiet soon after dark and the dining room closes by 10PM, but dawn brings a crowd to the rim to watch the sunrise. Advance reservations are recommended for a room and are encouraged for dinner. ♦ Closed November to May. For reservations, contact TW Services, 451 N Main St, Cedar City, UT 84720. 801/586.7686

Bests

Virginia Bax Valentine
General Manager, Clark County Regional Flood Control District

---

Best outdoor views: **Mount Charleston.** In the winter, indulge in a horse-drawn sleigh ride followed by Mount Charleston coffee (only if you're not driving), and in July hike to the peak through alpine meadows, ponderosa pine forests, and some of the oldest bristlecone pines in the world (it's a demanding 20-mile hike, but the spectacular view from the 12,000-foot peak all the way to beautiful **Lake Mead** is well worth the trip).

Best urban view: **The Strip** at night from almost anywhere.

Best indoor view: Seeing the basketball court from the **Sports Cafe** at the **Las Vegas Sporting House** on Thursday night when the men's leagues are playing.

Best Saturday or Sunday morning activity: Running or biking the **Red Rock Scenic Loop.** The scenery is incredibly beautiful, the air is crystal clear, and it's a great place to see native desert flora and fauna. Afterward, have breakfast with a cappuccino at the **Coffee Pub.** The service is lousy, but you're guaranteed the opportunity to read the Sunday paper cover to cover without interruption (probably before you see a menu). You may get a glimpse of Las Vegas's most famous casino executive, Steve Wynn, in Lycra.

Best shopping: After an exhausting afternoon shopping at the **Forum Shops at Caesars,** lunch at Wolfgang Puck's **Spago** or at **The Palm.** God won't speak to you from the changing heavens painted on the ceiling, but the animated statue of Bacchus will.

Best dinner: Eating with friends on the patio at **Cafe Nicolle** on a spring evening. Sample the lamb chops and indulge in the best Caesar salad in town—bar none. If you have room, and even if you don't, try the baklava cheesecake. For romance, try **Pamplemousse.**

Best place to see fossils: **McCarran International Airport** baggage-claim inspectors.

Best touristy pastimes: Drinking dollar beers at **Binion's Horseshoe** and having a picture postcard taken with a million bucks. After dark, watch the volcano erupt at the **Mirage.**

Kathy Espin
Casino Marketing, Sam's Town Gambling Hall & Casino

Four-wheeling in the desert. One of the best things about living in Las Vegas is that you are only 30 minutes away from total wilderness. Hundreds of Jeep trails lead to some of the most glorious scenery. A few of my favorite places to explore are the **Bird Spring Mountains** to the southwest, the **Meadow Valley Wash** to the north, and the **Aztec Wash** near Nelson on **Lake Mohave.**

The mission of the **Las Vegas Civic Ballet** is to give promising young dance students an opportunity to work with professionals. A small budget keeps costumes and staging simple, but if you enjoy watching beautiful, talented people dancing their hearts out, the **Civic** is for you. Concerts are held in December and in the spring.

You don't need much more than a couple of small children to have a rollicking good time at **Mount Charleston** in the winter. Sleds are nice, but cardboard boxes, plastic bags, and inner tubes work just as well for sliding down the slopes. I always take plenty of food and hot drinks, although there is a lodge and a hotel where refreshments can be purchased. When the little ones are frozen to the bone (which always takes longer than you would ever dream), put them in the car and in less than 45 minutes you'll be back in the city.

In the summer, when it's nasty hot, I head for **Lake Mead** or Lake Mohave. Give me a raft, a cooler of beer, and plenty of food that I don't have to cook, and I'm in heaven. The sun here will take the hide off you, so sunscreen is a must. My favorite places are quiet little coves and landings that most people don't know about.

Margaret Kurtz
Staff Writer/Public Relations Coordinator, Caesars Palace

The French cuisine in the **Palace Court,** especially when the chef makes his choice for the evening and Beverly is the service captain.

Dinner at the **Bacchanal** to impress out-of-town friends with a personal welcome by Caesar and Cleopatra and a flaming dessert finale.

The **Forum Shops,** where I can wander for hours finding incredible fashions and unusual gifts, have lunch at **Spago,** and watch the sun chase the stars across the Mediterranean sky every three hours—all indoors.

A motorcycle drive along the lake road in the moonlight at **Lake Mead,** marveling at the stars.

Incredible variety in the cactus garden at the **Ethel M. Chocolate Factory.** Take the factory's self-guided tour and get a free chocolate at the end. The dark chocolate macadamia nut is my favorite.

Howard Schwartz
Research Director/Director of Marketing, Gambler's Book Club

Gambler's Book Club, owned by Edna Luckman (yes, this is her real name, a fact that *Ripley's Believe It or Not* recognized in a feature once), is the world's largest and most specialized bookstore for gamblers, researchers, casino managers and dealers, writers, and law enforcement and surveillance personnel. Even the FBI occasionally shops here, as do judges and lawyers.

On weekends, there might be a book signing party (Jimmy Breslin drew a large crowd when his biography of Damon Runyon was published) or a demonstration of computer software for gamblers (there's a free catalog just for computer buffs) interested in betting on baseball, football, basketball, casino games, poker, keno, or thoroughbred racing. If Damon Runyon were alive today, this would be his Las Vegas hangout.

Carluccio's restaurant (formerly **Liberace's Tivoli Gardens** restaurant) is the city's best-kept secret for quality Italian food and service at good prices. We've been eating here for many years, every Saturday night. The spaghetti with meat sauce is excellent; order it with a cup of minestrone, a salad, and homemade bread, and it's a filling meal at a reasonable price. There's a piano bar and thousands of starlike ceiling lights, and you'll find the ambience worth the visit. Within walking distance is the spectacular **Liberace Museum.**

Chris Marcoux
Executive VP/Partner/Gourmet-in-Residence, Shonkwiler/Marcoux Advertising

Seeing the desert flowers in bloom—a palette of incredible colors.

Lunch at **Shalimar**—Indian cuisine should always be this good.

Riding a horse from **Bonnie Springs Ranch** to the base of **Red Rock Canyon**—a breathtaking visual experience.

Cirque du Soleil at **Treasure Island**—simply spectacular.

A lazy weekend brunch with friends at **Cafe Michelle**—a very Continental event.

The John Smith and Jon Ralston columns in the *Las Vegas Review-Journal* and Don Digilio's in the *Las Vegas Sun.*

Catching a performance at the **Cashman Field Theatre**—quaint and fulfilling.

The wine cellar at **Spirits Plus Liquor Store** on Flamingo Road—there *is* a heaven!

The view of Las Vegas when landing at night at **McCarran International Airport**—after all, there's no place like home.

History

Circa AD 500—The Anasazi (Navajo for "ancient ones") inhabit the area. They live in pit homes (shallow excavations with adobe floors and walls), make pottery, and are adept at weaving.

Circa AD 850—The Anasazi establish a settlement (now called **Pueblo Grande**), which by the year 1000 becomes Nevada's first ghost town. According to one of the most popular theories, the Anasazi were driven out of the area by a Southern Paiute tribe who called themselves Tudinu, or "desert people."

1776—While blazing the Old Spanish Trail, Father Francisco Garces encounters the Tudinu.

1822—Previously under Spanish jurisdiction, the territory that will be Nevada becomes part of Mexico when that country gains its independence.

1826—Fur trader and frontiersman Jedediah Smith, en route from Salt Lake City to San Diego, becomes the first American to travel through southern Nevada. He misses the Las Vegas Valley by about 40 miles.

1829—Rafael Rivera, a young scout with a Spanish trading party traveling west from Sante Fe, New Mexico, is the first white man to set foot in what will later become Las Vegas.

1840—The Old Spanish Trail, later called the Mormon Trail, becomes the primary path between Sante Fe and southern California, Mexico's two main trade centers. The trail passes through Las Vegas, then called **Big Springs**, a popular watering stop.

1844—Pathfinder John C. Frémont, leading the party exploring the route to Oregon beyond the Mississippi River, passes through Las Vegas and is the town's first famous visitor.

1848—Nevada becomes US territory after Mexico cedes what are now the western United States, following the Mexican-American War.

1855—Mormon missionaries, led by William Bringhurst, establish the first white settlement in Las Vegas. About 30 Mormons build a fort and begin teaching agriculture and religion to local Indians.

1858—Disputes between Mormon miners and farmers in the Las Vegas Mission prompt Mormon leader Brigham Young to dismantle the tiny settlement, leaving it to the Indians once again.

1861—Two days before leaving office, President James Buchanan signs the law that officially forms the Territory of Nevada.

1864—Near the end of the Civil War, President Abraham Lincoln declares Nevada the 36th state in the Union. "Battle Born" later becomes the state motto.

1865—Gold miner Octavius Decatur Gass rebuilds the former Mormon settlement and renames it the **Las Vegas Ranch,** an oasis for weary desert travelers.

1880—Gass turns his ranch over to Archibald Stewart. Four years later, Stewart is shot and killed, putting his wife, Helen, in charge of the 640-acre spread and some 400 head of cattle.

1902—Helen Stewart sells portions of her ranch to Montana senator William Clark, owner of the **San Pedro, Los Angeles, and Salt Lake Railroad,** for $55,000.

1904—A squatters' settlement springs up less than a mile west of the **Las Vegas Ranch.**

1905—The final spike in the rail route connecting Salt Lake City to Los Angeles is hammered into the ground near Jean, Nevada, about 23 miles south of Las Vegas. The railroad auctions off land near the tracks on 15 May, and Las Vegas is officially born.

The *Las Vegas Age,* a weekly newspaper, is founded by editor Charles "Pop" Squires. The new town also gets its first real hotel, a 30-room canvas-topped structure called the **Hotel Las Vegas.**

1906—**Block 16** (the parcel of land bounded by Ogden, Stewart, First, and Second Streets) is the only section of town where liquor can be sold legally. This area becomes the town's red-light district, and travelers flock to its saloons, brothels, and gambling halls.

1907—A single-cylinder engine powers the first electric lights on **Fremont Street.** Meanwhile, the Las Vegas Land and Water Company drills the town's first well and discovers that the valley rests on a ready supply of underground water.

1910—A state law prohibiting all forms of gambling takes effect on 1 October.

1911—With a population of 1,500, Las Vegas is incorporated as the first city in Nevada. Locals elect four city commissioners and a mayor, Peter Buol. William Howard Taft, the first US president to visit Las Vegas, waves from his railcar as he passes through town.

1912—**Las Vegas Ranch** owner Helen Stewart, known as the "First Lady of Las Vegas," deeds 10 acres of her property to the local Paiute.

Edward W. Griffith opens the **Majestic Theater,** featuring motion pictures and vaudeville acts.

1915—Las Vegans enjoy 24-hour electrical service for the first time.

Hollywood discovers Las Vegas when the Kalem Motion Picture Company films four episodes of *The Hazards of Helen* series in various locations around town.

1919—The Prohibition Enforcement Act (the 18th amendment to the Constitution, banning the production, distribution, and possession of alcohol) becomes law, but is ignored around Las Vegas.

1920—The first airplane lands in Las Vegas.

1925—Fremont Street is paved from Main Street to Fifth Street.

1926—**Western Airlines** provides the first commercial flight service to Las Vegas.

1928—Congress passes the Boulder Canyon Project Act and appropriates $165 million to build the world's largest arch-gravity dam in Black Canyon, about 30 miles southeast of Las Vegas along the Colorado River.

1929—The *Las Vegas Review,* which started as the *Clark County Review* in 1909, becomes the town's first daily newspaper (in 1949 it takes the name *Las Vegas Review-Journal*).

Sign maker Thomas Young, of Ogden, Utah, installs a neon sign in the window of the **Oasis Club** downtown, setting a Las Vegas trend.

1931—The Six Companies, Inc., of San Francisco begins construction on **Hoover Dam** in April.

The state government sparks an economic boom when it lowers the residency requirement for those seeking a divorce from three months to six weeks, then legalizes wide-open gambling, which, despite federal laws, had never disappeared entirely.

Mayme V. Stocker is awarded Clark County's first gaming license for her **Northern Club,** at 15 East Fremont Street.

1932—The **Apache Hotel,** boasting three floors, a hundred rooms, and the town's first elevator, opens on the northwest corner of Fremont and Second Streets. (**Binion's Horseshoe Hotel and Casino** occupies that site today.)

1935—Hoover Dam is dedicated by President Franklin D. Roosevelt. However, President Hoover is so unpopular stemming from his perceived responsibility for the Depression, that the dam is known as **Boulder Dam** for more than a decade.

The local Elks Club founds Helldorado Days, an annual event celebrating the town's heritage.

Some 5,000 Shriners meet in Las Vegas at what is the town's first full-scale convention.

1938—The construction of Hoover Dam on the Colorado River creates **Lake Mead,** the largest artificial lake in the US, stretching 110 miles upstream.

1941—Considered the first resort on the Strip, the 65-room **El Rancho Vegas** opens on 3 April at what is today the intersection of Las Vegas Boulevard South and Sahara Avenue (now a vacant lot). Meanwhile, the $250,000 **El Cortez Hotel** opens downtown at Fremont and Sixth Streets.

1942—Production begins at the Basic Magnesium Plant, about 15 miles southeast of Las Vegas. The town of **Henderson** springs up around the plant, which will eventually employ 10,000 wartime workers to produce magnesium used in bombs, airplanes, and engine parts.

The **Last Frontier** (later renamed the **New Frontier,** and then the **Frontier**) is the second resort to open on Las Vegas Boulevard South (not yet called the Strip).

Under pressure from the federal government, local authorities shut down the infamous Block 16 red-light district.

1945—**Bonanza Airlines** (later to become **Hughes Air West** after Howard Hughes purchases it in 1968) institutes flights between Reno and Las Vegas.

The Nevada legislature orders the State Tax Commission to issue licenses to casino operators and to regulate their conduct.

1946—Flashy New York mobster Benjamin "Bugsy" Siegel opens the **Flamingo Hotel** on Las Vegas Boulevard South.

1947—Singer Lena Horne debuts at the **Flamingo,** but can't stay there, because African-Americans are not allowed to eat or sleep in local hotels.

Golden Nugget founder Guy McAfee coins the term "the Strip."

1948—The **Thunderbird Hotel & Casino** (later the **Silverbird** and the **El Rancho**) is the fourth resort to open on the Strip.

McCarran Field, named after Nevada senator Pat McCarran, becomes the county airport.

1950—The 300-room **Desert Inn** goes into business on the Strip. The Committee to Investigate Organized Crime, led by Tennessee senator Estes Kefauver, comes to town and questions **Desert Inn** owners Wilbur Clark and Moe Dalitz, and Lieutenant Governor Cliff Jones, co-owner of the **Thunderbird.**

The *Las Vegas Free Press* (later the *Las Vegas Sun*) is founded under publisher Hank Greenspun.

Clark County's population is listed as 48,289.

1951—The Atomic Energy Commission detonates the first of many atom bombs above ground at the Nevada Test Site, about 100 miles from Las Vegas.

Texan Benny Binion remodels the **Eldorado Club,** turning it into the **Horseshoe Club,** the first carpeted downtown casino.

1952—The **Sands** and the **Sahara** hotels debut on the Strip.

1954—The **Desert Showboat Motor-Hotel,** later the **Showboat Hotel,** opens; it's the first big casino on the Boulder Highway.

1955—The Gaming Control Board is created to act as the enforcement and investigative arm of the State Tax Commission.

The first high-rise on the Strip, the nine-story **Riviera Hotel,** is christened, followed a month later by the **Dunes Hotel.**

1956—Guests begin staying at Nevada's tallest building, the 15-story **Fremont Hotel** in Glitter Gulch.

Elvis Presley bombs in his Las Vegas debut at the **New Frontier.**

1957—The first permanent building on the campus of the **University of Nevada, Las Vegas** (then known as **Nevada Southern**) is erected.

The **Tropicana Hotel** opens at a cost of $15 million.

1958—After four years of construction, the world's largest resort complex, the thousand-room **Stardust,** goes into business on the Strip.

1959—State lawmakers create the five-member Gaming Commission, which has the power to set policy and grant or deny licenses to casinos.

The **Las Vegas Convention Center** opens for business.

1960—**El Rancho Vegas** is destroyed in a mysterious fire, never to be rebuilt.

1964—The **Las Vegas Convention Center** hosts two concerts by the Beatles.

1965—The 26-story **Mint Hotel,** later part of **Binion's Horseshoe,** opens its doors at 100 East Fremont Street.

Heavyweight champion Muhammad Ali successfully defends his title for the first time by beating Floyd Patterson at the **Convention Center.**

1966—The opening of the **Aladdin** on the Strip ends a nine-year drought for new hotel-casinos.

Howard Hughes moves into the **Desert Inn** on Thanksgiving Day, taking over the ninth floor and embarking on a $300-million Las Vegas real estate shopping spree.

Caesars Palace opens decadently with a $1-million, three-day party.

1967—Lawmakers pass the Corporate Gaming Act, which allows publicly traded corporations to acquire gambling licenses without requiring every stockholder to be individually licensed.

Elvis Presley marries Priscilla Beaulieu at the **Aladdin.**

In March, Howard Hughes pays Moe Dalitz $13.2 million for the **Desert Inn,** in part because the reclusive millionaire doesn't want to leave the ninth floor. (Hughes eventually buys the **Sands, Castaways, Frontier, Landmark,** and **Silver Slipper** hotels.)

1968—**Circus Circus,** later to become the first family-oriented casino, opens on the Strip, across the street from the **Riviera.**

1969—Eight years after breaking ground on Paradise Road, the Hughes-owned **Landmark Hotel** is open for business. The following day financier Kirk Kerkorian opens his huge **International** (now the **Las Vegas Hilton**) next door to the **Las Vegas Convention Center.**

Elvis returns triumphantly to town, playing the **Hilton**

13 years after his disappointing debut.

1970—Four years to the day after he arrived, Howard Hughes moves out of the **Desert Inn** and leaves Las Vegas.

The Hilton Corporation buys the **Flamingo,** marking the first time a major hotel chain has bought a Las Vegas property.

1973—The now-famous "Four Corners," at the intersection of Flamingo Road and the Strip, is complete when the **MGM Grand Hotel** (now **Bally's**) opens. With 2,100 rooms, the newcomer gains the title "world's largest resort hotel," until the **Las Vegas Hilton** adds 1,500 rooms to overtake it by more than a thou.

1976—Singer Neil Diamond is the first star to perform in the $10-million **Aladdin Theater for the Performing Arts.**

1977—Clark County gaming revenues surpass $1 billion, an all-time high.

1978—The ABC TV series "Vega$," starring Robert Urich, premieres, revealing the town's touristy side.

1980—In November, a fire at the **MGM Grand Hotel** kills 84 people and injures nearly 700. That, coupled with another deadly fire at the **Las Vegas Hilton** a few months later, leads to stricter fire code regulations for Clark County's high-rise hotels.

1983—**Cashman Field,** a downtown stadium and convention facility that is the home field for the **Las Vegas Stars** minor-league baseball team, opens with an exhibition game between the **San Diego Padres** and the **Seattle Mariners.**

The city hosts its first Panasonic Las Vegas Invitational golf tournament.

1984—Las Vegas celebrates the 50th Helldorado Days and the accompanying Helldorado Rodeo.

1985—The National Finals Rodeo, which brings thousands of tourists to Las Vegas each December, is held here for the first time.

1989—**Golden Nugget** boss Steve Wynn opens **The Mirage,** a 3,049-room hotel-casino that cost an estimated $630 million to build. Its man-made volcano, which explodes on schedule throughout the evening, is instituted as one of the city's most popular photo opportunities.

1990—The owners of **Circus Circus** complete the 4,032-room **Excalibur Hotel/Casino/Las Vegas** at half the construction cost of **The Mirage.**

Local sports fans rejoice when the **University of Nevada, Las Vegas**'s **Runnin' Rebels** win their first **NCAA** college basketball title, beating **Duke University** on 2 April.

1993—Steve Wynn builds the 3,000-room **Treasure Island** resort next to the **Mirage,** while the Circus Circus corporation is creating the equally massive, pyramid-shaped **Luxor** resort. The biggest project of all takes shape on the northeast corner of Tropicana Avenue and the Strip, the new 5,009-room **MGM Grand Hotel and Theme Park.**

Index

A

Academy of International Studies and Performing Arts, Las Vegas **25**
Accessibility for the disabled **8**
Accommodations **8**
Airlines **7**
Airport **6**
Airport services **6**
Aladdin Hotel $$$ **53**
Al Dente ★★★★$$$$ **49**
Alexis Park Resort $$$$ **76**
All American Family Sports Park **32**
All that Glitters is Neon **80**
Alpine Village Inn ★★$$ **35**
Alta Villa ★★$$ **46**
Amber Unicorn **62**
American Museum of Historical Documents **39**
American Sock Company **39**
Andre's ★★★★$$$$ **25**
Antique Emporium **39**
Antonio's ★★★$$$ **70**
A Review of Revues **50**
Aristocrat ★★★$$$$ **62**
Arizona Charlie's **62**
Arizona Charlie's, Coffee Shop **62**
Armargosa Opera House (Death Valley Junction) **119**
Art Museum, Las Vegas **61**
Auto Collection **46**

B

Baccarat **90**
Bacchanal ★★★$$$$ **47**
Badwater (Death Valley National Park) **119**
Bally's Casino **49**
Bally's Las Vegas $$$$ **49**
Bamboo Garden ★★★$$ **67**
Barbary Coast $$$ **48**
Beef Barron ★★★$$$ **46**
Bella Pasta, La **86**
Benihana Village ★★★$$$ **36**
Betting Smart **89**
Bicycles **7**
Big Dog's Cafe & Casino ★★$$ **66**
Big Kitchen Buffet ★$ **49**
Bill Ladd's Silver Dollar Saloon **82**
Binion Ranch Steak House ★★$$$$ **20**
Binion's Horseshoe Casino **20**
Binion's Horseshoe Hotel and Casino $$ **19**
Binion's Horseshoe Hotel and Casino, Coffee Shop **20**
Binion's Horseshoe Hotel and Casino, Deli **20**
Binion's Horseshoe Hotel and Casino, Snack Bars **20**
Bistro ★★$$$$ **44**
Black Canyon **114**
Blackjack **92**
Bonanza Gifts **31**
Bonnie Springs Motel $$ **111**
Bonnie Springs Ranch/Old Nevada **110**
Boomtown $$ **57**
Bootlegger Ristorante ★★★$$$ **78**
Boulder Cafe ★$ **86**

Boulder City **113**
Boulder Dam Hotel $$ **113**
Boulder Station $$ **83**
Boulevard Mall, The **79**
Bourbon Street $$$ **48**
Bowling Center, Showboat Hotel **83**
Bright Angel Lodge $$$ **123**
Bright Angel Trail (Grand Canyon) **121**
Bryce Canyon Lodge $$ **125**
Bryce Canyon National Park **125**
Bryce Point (Bryce Canyon National Park) **125**
Buccaneer Bay ★★★$$$ **42**
Buffalo Bill's Resort & Casino **112**
Buffet, The **16**
Bullocks **39**
Burton, Lance **26** (bests)
Buses **7**
Buzios ★★★$$$ **70**

C

Caesars Palace $$$$ **47**
Caesars Palace Casinos **47**
Cafe Michelle ★★$$$ **78**
Cafe Michelle West ★★★$$$ **63**
Cafe Nicolle ★★★$$$ **65**
Calamity Jane's Ice Cream Shop and Coca-Cola Museum **83**
Calico Hills (Red Rock Canyon National Conservation Area) **109**
California Hotel and Casino $$$ **23**
California Pizza Kitchen ★$$ **16**
Callister, Matthew Q. **72** (bests)
Camelot ★★★$$$ **55**
Captain's Buffet $ **83**
Carluccio's ★★$$ **78**
Carnival World Buffet ★★★$ **70**
Cars, renting **7**
Cashman Field Center **25**
Casino Boardwalk, Holiday Inn $$$ **53**
Casino Royale **43**
Center Stage Restaurant ★★$$ **14**
Central Fire Restaurant ★★$$ **24**
Charlie Trotter's ★★★★$$$$ **53**
Cheng, Jim **93**
Chiasso Cafe ★★★$$ **65**
Chicago Joe's ★$ **26**
Child's Play **21**
Chinese Garden Restaurant ★$$ **66**
Chin's (The Strip) ★★★★$$$ **39**
Chin's (West Las Vegas) ★★★★$$$ **62**
Cipriani ★★★$$$ **79**
Circus Circus $ **32**
Circus Circus Casino **32**
Circusland RV Park **33**
Cirque du Soleil **42**
City Hall, Las Vegas **24**
Civil Marriage Commissioner, Office of the **17**
Clark County Courthouse **18**
Climate **8**
Coca-Cola Museum, Calamity Jane's Ice Cream Shop and **83**

Coffee Pub ★★$$ **64**
Coffee Shop, Arizona Charlie's $ **62**
Coffee Shop, Binion's Horseshoe Hotel and Casino
$ **20**
Coffee Shop, Showboat Hotel $ **83**
Coin Castle **15**
Continental Casino **77**
Continental Hotel $$ **77**
Convention Center, Las Vegas **36**
Copacabana Showroom **71**
Corner of the Strip and Sahara Avenue **32**
Cortez Casino, El **18**
Cortez Hotel, El **18**
Country Club Restaurant **79**
Courthouse, Clark County **17**
Court of Two Gators **44**
Cowboy Christmas **83**
Coyote Cafe ★★★$$$ **54**
Cranberry World West **113**
Craps **96**
Crime Story **84**
Cruises **8**
Cul-tur-ati ★★$$ **65**
Curtis, Anthony **73** (bests)

D

Daniel, Mann, Johnson & Mendenhall **24**
Death Valley Junction **119**
Death Valley National Park **118** (map)
Death Valley Ranch **119**
Debbie Reynolds Hotel/Casino, Movie Museum $$ **35**
Deli, Binion's Horseshoe Hotel and Casino ★$ **20**
Desert Inn Casino, Sheraton **38**
Desert Inn, Sheraton **38**
Desert Rose Golf Course **86**
Desert View Campground (Grand Canyon) **122**
Diamond Lil's ★★$$$ **84**
Dillards **39**
Di Napoli ★$$ **83**
Disney Store **39**
Dolphins **45**
Doña Maria's ★★$ **26**
Downtown **12** (chapter and map)
Downtown Transportation Center **23**
Dress **9**
Drinking **9**
Driving **7**

E

East Las Vegas **74** (chapter and map)
East Rim Drive (Grand Canyon) **121**
Easy Come, Easy Go: Marriage and Divorce in
Nevada **19**
El Cortez Casino **18**
El Cortez Hotel $ **18**
El Gaucho ★★$$$ **56**
El Paso Kitchens ★★$ **71**
El Sombrero ★$ **25**
El Tovar Hotel $$$$ **123**
Embers ★★$$$ **45**
Emerald Pools Trail (Zion National Park) **123**

Emergencies **10**
Enter the Night **35**
Espin, Kathy **126** (bests)
Ethel M. Chocolate Factory **112**
Excalibur Casino **55**
Excalibur Hotel/Casino/Las Vegas $$ **55**
Excursions **108** (chapter and map)

F

Fashion Show Mall **39**
Feast Buffet ★$ **63**
Ferraro's Cafe ★★★$$$ **66**
Ferris & Sons **25**
Fiore ★★★★$$$$ **70**
Fisherman's Broiler ★★$$$ **63**
Fitzgeralds Casino **17**
Fitzgeralds Casino/Hotel $$ **17**
Flame, The **30**
Flamingo Casino **46**
Flamingo Hilton (Las Vegas) $$$ **46**
Flamingo Hilton (Laughlin) **120**
Floyd Lamb State Park **111**
Folies Bergere **56**
Forum Shops **48**
Foster, Lynne **87** (bests)
Four Queens Casino **17**
Four Queens Hotel $$ **16**
Fox Tail Snow Play Area (Lee Canyon) **111**
French Quarter **18**
Frome, Lenny **73** (bests)
Frontier Gambling Hall **39**
Frontier Hotel & Gambling Hall $$ **38**
Furnace Creek Inn $$ **119**
Furnace Creek Ranch $$ **119**

G

Galerie Lassen **55**
Gambler's Book Club **26**
Gambler's General Store **25**
Gambling **9, 88** (chapter)
Garlic Cafe ★★$$ **67**
Gates & Sons Bar-B-Q ★★$ **79**
Gateway to the Narrows (Zion National Park) **123**
Gaucho, El **56**
George Tate & Associates **25**
Getting Around Las Vegas **7**
Getting to Las Vegas **6**
Girls of Glitter Gulch **20**
Gold Coast Casino **70**
Gold Coast Hotel $$ **67**
Golden Canyon (Death Valley National Park) **119**
Golden Gate $ **15**
Golden Nugget Casino **16**
Golden Nugget Hotel $$$$ **16**
Golden Nugget (Laughlin) **120**
Golden Steer ★$$$ **31**
Gold River **120**
Gold Spike Casino **18**
Gold Spike Hotel & Casino, Jackie Gaughan's **18**
Gold Strike Inn & Casino $ **113**
Grand Canyon National Park **120**

Index

Grand Canyon, The **120**
Grand Garden **54**
Grand Slam Canyon **33**
Great Radio City Music Hall Spectacular, The **46**
Green Shack, The **82**
Grossman, Larry **72** (bests)
Guadalajara Bar and Grill ★$ **63**
Guinness World of Records Museum **32**

H

Hacienda Hotel & Casino $$ **57**
Hard Rock Cafe ★$ **76**
Hard Rock Hotel $$$ **76**
Harmony Borax Works (Death Valley National Park) **119**
Harrah's Casino **43**
Harrah's Hotel $$$ **43**
Harrah's (Laughlin) **120**
Harris, Claire **27** (bests)
Harris Sharp Associates **24**
Henderson **112**
Hermits Rest (Grand Canyon) **121**
High Flying Theater **62**
Hilton Country Club, Las Vegas **79**
Hilton, Las Vegas **38**
Holiday Inn Casino Boardwalk **53**
Holy Cow! Casino **30**
Hometown News **67**
Hoover Dam **114**
Hotel San Remo **56**
House of Lords ★★$$$$ **31**
Hugo's Cellar ★★$$$$ **17**
Huntridge Performing Arts Theater **82**
Hurricane **123**

I

Imperial Palace $$$ **45**
Imperial Palace Casino **45**
Indian Gardens (Grand Canyon) **122**
In-N-Out Burger ★$ **64**
Inspiration Point (Bryce Canyon National Park) **125**
In the Casino **89**
Isis ★★★$$$ **57**
Italiano, Ristorante **33**

J

Jackie Gaughan's Gold Spike Hotel & Casino $ **18**
Jackie Gaughan's Plaza Hotel-Casino $$ **14**
Joe's Bayou ★$$ **43**
Joseph, Erik **72** (bests)
Jubilee! **53**

K

Kachina and Thunderbird Lodges $$$ **123**
Kane, Ed **73** (bests)
Keno **99**
King 8 Hotel & Gambling Hall $$ **71**
Kodiak Lodge ★★★$$ **60**
Kokomo's ★★★$$$ **44**
Kunitz, Craig **73** (bests)
Kurtz, Margaret **126** (bests)

L

La Bella Pasta ★$$ **86**
Lake Mead **114**
Lake Mead National Recreation Area **115** (map)
Lake Mohave **120**
Lance-alotta-Pasta ★$ **55**
La Piazza $ **7**
Las Olas ★★$$$ **49**
Lassen, Galerie **55**
La Strada ★★★$$$ **77**
Las Vegas **2** (map)
Las Vegas Academy of International Studies and Performing Arts **25**
Las Vegas Art Museum **61**
Las Vegas City Hall **24**
Las Vegas Club Casino **20**
Las Vegas Club Hotel and Casino $$ **20**
Las Vegas Convention Center **36**
Las Vegas Hilton $$$ **35**
Las Vegas Hilton Casino **36**
Las Vegas Hilton Country Club **79**
Las Vegas Mormon Temple **86**
Las Vegas Natural History Museum **24**
Las Vegas Public Library **24**
Las Vegas Sporting House **38**
Las Vegas Super 8 Motel $$ **86**
Las Vegas Western Village **17**
Laughlin **119**
Lee Canyon Ski Area **112**
Legends in Concert **46**
Le Montrachet ★★★★$$$$ **36**
Leonardo's ★★★$$ **54**
Leon, Riqui **27** (bests)
Liberace Museum, The **78**
Liberace Plaza **78**
Library, Las Vegas Public **24**
Library, West Charleston **62**
Lied Discovery Children's Museum **24**
Lillie Langtry's ★★$$$ **16**
Limousines **7**
Lorenzi Park **61**
Lost City Museum **117**
Lost City (Valley of Fire State Park) **116**
Luxor Hotel & Casino $$$$ **56**

M

Mad Dogs and Englishmen ★$ **25**
Main Events, The **5**
Mamounia ★★★$$$ **77**
Marcoux, Chris **126** (bests)
Mardi Gras Food Court $ **33**
Margarita's ★$$ **39**
Marino, Frank **73** (bests)
Marjorie Barrick Museum of Natural History (University of Nevada, Las Vegas) **77**
Marriage License Bureau **17**
Mary Jane Falls Trail (Mount Charleston) **111**
Mary's Diner ★$ **84**
Mastering the Basics **89**
Mather Campground (Grand Canyon) **122**
Maxim $$ **48**

May Company **39**
Mayflower Cuisinier ★★★$$$ **65**
McBride, D.R. **27** (bests)
McCarran International Airport, ground
    transportation **7**
McCarran International Airport (LAS) **6** (map)
Meadows Mall **61**
Mesquite **117**
Metz, The **53**
MGM Grand Hotel and Theme Park $$$ **53**
Michael's ★★★$$$$ **48**
Michelle, Cafe **78**
Michelle West, Cafe **63**
Mikado ★★$$$$ **44**
Miner Restaurant **110**
Ming, Marilyn **57** (bests)
Mirage Casino, The **44**
Mirage, The **44**
Mr. Boxer **39**
Mr. Hat **39**
Money **9**
Money Wheel, The **101**
Monte Carlo ★★★$$$$ **38**
Montrachet, Le **36**
Moongate ★$$$$ **44**
Mormon Temple, Las Vegas **86**
Morton's ★★★$$$ **39**
Mount Charleston **111**
Mount Charleston Hotel $$$ **111**
Mount Charleston Restaurant and Lodge
    ★★★$$ **111**
Mouse's Tank (Valley of Fire State Park) **116**
Movie Museum, Debbie Reynolds Hotel/Casino **35**

N

Natural History Museum, Las Vegas **24**
Nature Company **79**
Navajo Loop (Bryce Canyon National Park) **125**
Neiman Marcus **39**
Nellis Air Force Base **87**
Nellis Visitors' Center **87**
Nevada Palace Casino **86**
Nevada Palace Hotel-Casino $$ **86**
Nevada State Museum and Historical Society **61**
Nicolle, Cafe **65**
Nippon ★★$$ **35**
North Beach Cafe ★★★$$ **65**
North Rim **123**

O

Oak Creek (Red Rock Canyon National Conservation
    Area) **109**
Office of the Civil Marriage Commissioner **17**
Oklahoma Kitchen, The **82**
Olas, Las **57**
Old Mormon Fort **24**
Old Nevada **110**
Olympic Gardens **30**
Omaha Lounge **15**
Orientation **2**
O'Sheas Casino **46**

Overton Beach **116**

P

Palace Court ★★★★$$$$ **47**
Palace Station Casino **63**
Palace Station Hotel $$ **63**
Palatium, The **47**
Pamplemousse ★★★$$$ **30**
Paradise Buffet & Grill, The **117**
Parking **8**
Paso Kitchens, El **71**
Pasta Mia ★★★$$ **79**
Pasta Pirate ★★★$$ **23**
Pawn Shop Plaza **16**
Pegasus Gourmet Room ★★★$$$$ **76**
Peppermill Cafe and Lounge ★$$ **34**
Performing Arts Center (Univeristy of Nevada, Las
    Vegas) **77**
Personal Safety **9**
Petroglyph Canyon Trail (Valley of Fire State Park) **116**
Phantom Ranch (Grand Canyon) **122**
Philip's Supper House ★★$$$$ **64**
Piazza, La **55**
Piero's ★★★$$$$ **35**
Pioneer Club **15**
Planning the Grand Tour **122**
Plantation ★$$ **83**
Play & Eat ★★$$ **56**
Plaza Casino **14**
Plaza Coffee Shop ★$ **15**
Poppa Gar's ★$$ **63**
Portofino ★★$$$ **38**
Port Tack ★$$$ **64**
Postal service **9**
Predock, Antoine **24**
Primadonna Resort & Casino **112**
Primadonna Resorts $$ **112**
Prostitution **9**
Publications **9**

Q

Queen's Garden Trail (Bryce Canyon National
    Park) **125**

R

Radio stations **9**
Railroad Pass Hotel & Casino $ **113**
Ralph's Diner $ **34**
Ramada Express **120**
Redd Room Steak House, The **117**
Red Rock Canyon **110** (map)
Red Rock Canyon National Conservation Area **109**
Reels of Fortune: Vegas Goes to Hollywood **68**
Regency Ristorante ★★★$$$ **43**
Renata's ★★★$$$ **112**
Rental cars **7**
Restaurants **9**
Review of Revues, A **50**
Rio Suite Casino **70**
Rio Suite Hotel $$$ **70**
Ristorante Italiano ★★$$$ **33**

Riverside Resort, The **120**
Riviera Casino **33**
Riviera Comedy Club **34**
Riviera Hotel $$$ **33**
Riviera's Shows, The **33**
Roberta's ★$$ **18**
Rotisserie Buffet ★$ **33**
Roulette **102**
Rubin, Max **11** (bests)

S

Sahara Casino **31**
Sahara Hotel & Casino $$ **31**
Saigon Restaurant ★★$ **64**
St. Thomas Seafood Grotto ★$$$ **39**
Saks Fifth Avenue **39**
Sam Boyd's Fremont Hotel and Casino $ **18**
Sam's Town Casino **84**
Sam's Town Hotel & Gambling Hall $$ **83**
Sands Casino **42**
Sands Hotel $$$ **42**
San Francisco Bar $ **15**
San Remo, Hotel **56**
Santa Fe Hotel and Casino $$ **60**
Sassy Sally's **20**
Schwartz, Howard **126** (bests)
Scotty's Castle **119**
Seasons ★★★$$$$ **57**
Second Street Grill ★★★$$$ **19**
Sesame Street General Store **79**
Shalimar Fine Indian Cuisine ★★$$ **66**
Sheraton Desert Inn $$$$ **38**
Sheraton Desert Inn Casino **38**
Shopping **10**
Shore, Louis A. **73** (bests)
Showboat Casino **82**
Showboat Hotel $$ **82**
Siegfried & Roy **45**
Siegfried & Roy House **61**
Silverado Saloon & Dance Hall **86**
Silver City **34**
Si Redd's Oasis $$$ **117**
Si Redd's Oasis, The Coffee Shop **117**
Sir Galahad's Prime Rib House ★★$$ **55**
Sir Reginald's ★★★$$$ **54**
Slots **105**
Slots A Fun **34**
Slugger Stadium **32**
Smokey Joe's Cafe & Market $ **84**
Smoking **10**
Snack Bars $ **20**
Snyder, Arnold **87** (bests)
Sombrero, El **25**
Southern Nevada Zoological Park **60**
South Kaibab Trail (Grand Canyon) **122**
South Rim **121**
Sporting House, Las Vegas **38**
Sports betting **106**
Springdale **123**
Spring Mountain Ranch State Park **110**
Stardust Resort & Casino $$$ **36**

Steak House ★★$$$ **32**
Stefano's ★★★★$$$ **16**
Sterling Brunch ★★★★$$$$ **49**
Stoney's Loan and Jewelry **16**
Stovepipe Wells Village $$ **119**
Strada, La **77**
Street plan **10**
Strip, The **28**
Summerlin **61**
Sun Harbor Budget Suites $ **36**
Super 8 Motel, Las Vegas **89**
Suzette's ★★★★$$$$ **60**
Swiss Cafe ★★★$$$ **26**

T

Taxes **10**
Taxis **7, 8**
Terrible Herbst's Detail Plus **67**
The Boulevard Mall **79**
The Buffet ★★$$ **16**
The Coffee Shop, Si Redd's Oasis **117**
The Flame ★★$$$ **30**
The Grand Canyon **120** (map)
The Great Radio City Music Hall Spectacular **46**
The Green Shack ★$$ **82**
The Liberace Museum **78**
The Main Events **5**
The Metz **53**
The Mirage $$$$ **44**
The Mirage Casino **44**
The Money Wheel **101**
The Oklahoma Kitchen ★$ **82**
The Palatium ★★$$ **47**
The Paradise Buffet & Grill ★★$$ **117**
The Redd Room Steak House ★★$$$ **117**
The Riverside Resort **120**
The Riviera's Shows **33**
The Strip **28** (chapter and map)
The Venetian Ristorante ★★★$$$ **64**
Thomas & Mack Center (University of Nevada, Las Vegas) **77**
Thomas Charles Gallery **55**
Thunderbird and Kachina Lodges **123**
Thunderbird Museum **87**
Ti Amo ★★★$$ **60**
Tickets **10**
Tigers **45**
Time Zones **10**
Tipping **10**
Toiyabe National Forest **111**
Tony's Greco-Roman Restaurant ★$$$ **31**
Tours **8**
Tovar Hotel, El **123**
Trailer Village (Grand Canyon) **122**
Trains **7, 8**
Traveling Books & Maps **66**
Treasure Island $$$ **42**
Tricks of the Trade: Nevada's Adult Entertainment Industry **37**
Tropicana Casino **56**
Tropicana Hotel $$$$ **56**

Turf Club Deli ★$ **31**
Tusayan **122**

U

University of Nevada, Las Vegas (UNLV) **77**
Uptown Buffet $ **84**
US Bureau of Land Management Visitors' Center (Red Rock Canyon National Conservation Area) **109**

V

Valentine, Virginia Bax **125** (bests)
Valley of Fire State Park **116** (map)
Velvet Canyon (Red Rock Canyon National Conservation Area) **109**
Venetian Ristorante, The **64**
Vicious Rumors ★★★$$$ **57**
Victory Hotel $ **15**
Video Poker **106**
Virgin River **123**
Virgin River Hotel/Casino/Bingo $ **117**
Visitors' information **10**
Volumes on Vegas **95**

W

Walker, Steve "Biscuit" **72** (bests)
Walking **8**
Welles-Pugsley **62**
West Charleston Library **62**
Western Emporium **83**
West Las Vegas **58** (chapter and map)
West of Dallas **39**
West Rim Drive (Grand Canyon) **121**
Westward Ho Hotel & Casino $$ **34**
Wet 'n Wild **32**
Whiskey Pete's Hotel–Casino **112**
Williams, John Earl **73** (bests)
Willy & Jose's Mexican Cantina ★★$$ **86**
Wolfgang Puck Cafe ★★★$$ **54**
Wong, Stanford **11** (bests)
Working the Main Room **40**

X

Xanadu ★★★$$$ **42**

Y

Yavapai Lodge $$ **123**
Young Electric Sign Company (YESCO) **71**
Young People's Library (Las Vegas Public Library) **24**

Z

Zabriskie Point (Death Valley National Park) **119**
Zion Lodge **123**
Zion National Park **123**, **124** (map)

Restaurants

Only restaurants with star ratings are listed below. All restaurants are listed alphabetically in the main (preceding) index. Always call in advance to ensure a restaurant has not closed, changed its hours, or booked its tables for a private party. The restaurant price ratings are based on the average cost of an entrée for one person, excluding tax and tip.

★★★★ An Extraordinary Experience
★★★ Excellent
★★ Very Good
★ Good

$$$$ Big Bucks ($25 and up)
$$$ Expensive ($20-$25)
$$ Reasonable ($13-$20)
$ The Price Is Right (less than $13)

★★★★

Andre's $$$$ **25**
Buccaneer Bay $$$ **42**
Charlie Trotter's $$$$ **53**
Chin's (The Strip) $$$ **39**
Chin's (West Las Vegas) $$$ **62**
Cipriani $$$ **79**
Coyote Cafe $$$ **54**
Fiore $$$$ **70**
Isis $$$ **57**
Le Montrachet $$$$ **36**
Michael's $$$$ **48**
Monte Carlo $$$$ **38**
Morton's $$$ **39**
Palace Court $$$$ **47**
Pamplemousse $$$ **30**
Seasons $$$$ **57**
Stefano's $$$ **16**
Sterling Brunch $$$$ **49**
Suzette's $$$$ **60**

★★★

Antonio's $$$ **70**
Aristocrat $$$$ **62**
Bacchanal $$$$ **47**
Bamboo Garden $$ **67**
Beef Barron $$$ **46**
Benihana Village $$$ **36**
Bootlegger Ristorante $$$ **78**
Buzios $$$ **70**
Cafe Michelle West $$$ **63**
Cafe Nicolle $$$ **65**
Camelot $$$ **55**
Carnival World Buffet $ **70**
Chiasso Cafe $$ **65**
El Gaucho $$$ **56**
Ferraro's Cafe $$$ **66**
House of Lords $$$$ **31**
Hugo's Cellar $$$$ **17**
Kodiak Lodge $$ **60**
Kokomo's $$$ **44**
La Strada $$$ **77**
Leonardo's $$ **54**
Mamounia $$$ **77**
Mayflower Cuisinier $$$ **65**
Mount Charleston Restaurant and Lodge $$ **111**
North Beach Cafe $$ **65**
Pasta Mia $$ **79**
Pasta Pirate $$ **23**
Pegasus Gourmet Room $$$$ **76**
Piero's $$$$ **35**

Regency Ristorante $$$ **43**
Renata's $$$ **112**
Sir Reginald's $$$ **54**
Swiss Cafe $$$ **26**
The Venetian Ristorante $$$ **64**
Ti Amo $$ **60**
Vicious Rumors $$$ **57**
Wolfgang Puck Cafe $$ **54**
Xanadu $$$ **42**

★★

Alpine Village Inn $$ **35**
Alta Villa $$ **46**
Big Dog's Cafe & Casino $$ **66**
Binion Ranch Steak House $$$$ **20**
Bistro $$$$ **44**
Cafe Michelle $$$ **78**
Carluccio's $$ **78**
Center Stage Restaurant $$ **14**
Central Fire Restaurant $$ **24**
Coffee Pub $$ **64**
Cul-tur-ati $$ **65**
Diamond Lil's $$$ **84**
Doña Maria's $ **26**
El Paso Kitchens $ **71**
Embers $$$ **45**
Fisherman's Broiler $$$ **63**
Garlic Cafe $$ **67**
Gates & Sons Bar-B-Q $ **79**
Las Olas $$$ **49**
Lillie Langtry's $$$ **16**
Mikado $$$$ **44**
Nippon $$ **35**
Philip's Supper House $$$$ **64**
Play & Eat $$ **56**
Portofino $$$ **38**
Ristorante Italiano $$$ **33**
Saigon Restaurant $ **64**
Shalimar Fine Indian Cuisine $$ **66**
Sir Galahad's Prime Rib House $$ **55**
Steak House $$$ **32**
The Buffet $$ **16**
The Flame $$$ **30**
The Palatium $$ **47**
The Paradise Buffet & Grill $$ **117**
The Redd Room Steak House $$$ **117**
Willy & Jose's Mexican Cantina $$ **86**

★

Big Kitchen Buffet $ **49**
Boulder Cafe $ **86**
California Pizza Kitchen $$ **16**
Chicago Joe's $ **26**
Chinese Garden Restaurant $$ **66**
Deli, Binion's Horseshoe Hotel and Casino $ **20**
Di Napoli $$ **83**
Feast Buffet $ **63**
Golden Steer $$$ **31**
Guadalajara Bar and Grill $ **63**
Hard Rock Cafe $ **76**
In-N-Out Burger $ **64**
Joe's Bayou $$ **43**
La Bella Pasta $$ **86**

Lance-alotta-Pasta $ **55**
Mad Dogs and Englishmen $ **25**
Margarita's $$ **39**
Mary's Diner $ **84**
Moongate $$$$ **44**
Peppermill Cafe and Lounge $$ **34**
Plantation $$ **83**
Poppa Gar's $$ **63**
Port Tack $$$ **64**
Roberta's $$ **18**
Rotisserie Buffet $ **33**
St. Thomas Seafood Grotto $$$ **39**
The Green Shack $$ **82**
The Oklahoma Kitchen $ **82**
Tony's Greco-Roman Restaurant $$$ **31**
Turf Club Deli $ **31**

Hotels

The hotels listed below are grouped according to their price ratings; they are also listed in the main index. The hotel price ratings reflect the base price of a standard room for two people for one night during the peak season.

$$$$ Big Bucks ($80 and up)
$$$ Expensive ($50-$80)
$$ Reasonable ($30-$50)
$ The Price Is Right (less than $30)

$$$$

Alexis Park Resort **76**
Bally's Las Vegas **49**
Caesars Palace **47**
El Tovar Hotel **123**
Golden Nugget Hotel **16**
Luxor Hotel & Casino **56**
Sheraton Desert Inn **38**
The Mirage **44**
Tropicana Hotel **56**

$$$

Aladdin Hotel **53**
Barbary Coast **48**
Bourbon Street **48**
Bright Angel Lodge **123**
California Hotel and Casino **23**
Flamingo Hilton **46**
Hard Rock Hotel **76**
Harrah's Hotel **43**
Holiday Inn Casino Boardwalk **53**
Imperial Palace **45**
Kachina and Thunderbird Lodges **123**
Las Vegas Hilton **35**
MGM Grand Hotel and Theme Park **53**
Mount Charleston Hotel **111**
Rio Suite Hotel **70**
Riviera Hotel **33**
Sands Hotel **42**
Si Redd's Oasis **117**
Stardust Resort & Casino **36**
Treasure Island **42**

$$

Binion's Horseshoe Hotel and Casino **19**
Bonnie Springs Motel **111**
Boomtown **57**
Boulder Dam Hotel **113**
Boulder Station **83**
Bryce Canyon Lodge **125**
Continental Hotel **77**
Debbie Reynolds Hotel/Casino, Movie Museum **35**
Excalibur Hotel/Casino/Las Vegas **55**
Fitzgeralds Casino/Hotel **17**
Four Queens Hotel **16**
Frontier Hotel & Gambling Hall **38**
Furnace Creek Inn **119**
Furnace Creek Ranch **119**
Gold Coast Hotel **67**
Hacienda Hotel & Casino **57**
Jackie Gaughan's Plaza Hotel-Casino **14**
King 8 Hotel & Gambling Hall **71**
Las Vegas Club Hotel and Casino **20**
Las Vegas Super 8 Motel **86**
Maxim **48**
Nevada Palace Hotel-Casino **86**
Palace Station Hotel **63**
Primadonna Resorts **112**
Sahara Hotel & Casino **31**
Sam's Town Hotel & Gambling Hall **83**
Santa Fe Hotel and Casino **60**
Showboat Hotel **82**
Stovepipe Wells Village **119**
Westward Ho Hotel & Casino **34**
Yavapai Lodge **123**

$

Circus Circus **32**
El Cortez Hotel **18**
Golden Gate **15**
Gold Strike Inn & Casino **113**
Jackie Gaughan's Gold Spike Hotel & Casino **18**
Railroad Pass Hotel & Casino **113**
Sam Boyd's Fremont Hotel and Casino **18**
Sun Harbor Budget Suites **36**
Victory Hotel **15**
Virgin River Hotel/Casino/Bingo **117**

Features

A Review of Revues **50**
All that Glitters is Neon **80**
Betting Smart **89**
Child's Play **21**
Crime Story **84**
Easy Come, Easy Go: Marriage and Divorce in Nevada **19**
In the Casino **89**
Mastering the Basics **89**
Planning the Grand Tour **122**
Reels of Fortune: Vegas Goes to Hollywood **68**
The Main Events **5**
Tricks of the Trade: Nevada's Adult Entertainment Industry **37**
Volumes on Vegas **95**
Working the Main Room **40**

Bests

Burton, Lance (World Champion Magician/Headliner, Hacienda) **26**
Callister, Matthew Q. (Nevada State Senator) **72**
Curtis, Anthony (Publisher, *Las Vegas Advisor*) **73**
Espin, Kathy (Casino Marketing, Sam's Town Gambling Hall & Casino) **126**
Foster, Lynne (Stage Producer, Dick Foster Productions, Inc.) **87**
Frome, Lenny (Author of Video-Poker Books) **73**
Grossman, Larry (Columnist/Photojournalist/National Radio Talk Show Host, American Sports Network) **72**
Harris, Claire (Las Vegas Resident) **27**
Joseph, Erik (Associate Director, Motion Picture Division of the State of Nevada Commission on Economic Development) **72**
Kane, Ed (Chef) **73**
Kunitz, Craig (Promotions Supervisor, Fitzgeralds Casino/Hotel) **73**
Kurtz, Margaret (Staff Writer/Public Relations Coordinator, Caesars Palace) **73**
Leon, Riqui (Freelance Publicist) **27**
Marcoux, Chris (Executive VP/Partner/Gourmet-in-Residence, Shonkwiler/Marcoux Advertising) **126**
Marino, Frank (Female Impersonator/Star of *An Evening at La Cage*) **73**
McBride, D.R. (Horror Novelist/ Las Vegas Native) **27**
Ming, Marilyn (Publicity Manager, Four Queens Hotel & Casino) **57**
Rubin, Max (Professional Gambler/Author of *Comp City*) **11**
Schwartz, Howard (Research Director/Director of Marketing, Gambler's Book Club) **126**
Shore, Louis A. (Longtime Las Vegas Resident) **73**
Snyder, Arnold (Author/Editor/Publisher, *Blackjack Forum* magazine) **87**
Valentine, Virginia Bax (General Manager, Clark County Regional Flood Control District) **125**
Walker, Steve "Biscuit" (Rapper/Actor) **72**
Williams, John Earl (Host of "Cruisin' for a Bluesin' "/DJ, KKLZ 96.3FM) **73**
Wong, Stanford (Writer/Publisher, Pi Yee Press) **11**

Maps

Death Valley National Park **118**
Downtown **12**
East Las Vegas **74**
Excursions **108**
Lake Mead National Recreation Area **115**
Las Vegas *see inside front cover*
Las Vegas area **2**
Map Key **4**
McCarran International Airport **6**
Red Rock Canyon **110**
Southern Nevada and Environs *see inside front cover*
The Grand Canyon **120**
The Strip **28**
Valley of Fire State Park **116**
West Las Vegas **58**
Zion National Park **124**

ACCESS® Notes

Page	Entry #	Notes

Page	Entry #	Notes

Page	Entry #	Notes

Page   **Entry #**   **Notes**

Page	Entry #	Notes